GLORY ☆ GLORY
GLORIETA
THE GETTYSBURG OF THE WEST

BY ROBERT SCOTT

Johnson Books : Boulder

*The author gratefully acknowledges
the enormous and generous assistance of the
staff of the Fort Collins, Colorado, Public Library
and Mr. Brad Lapsley, Dallas, Texas
(Civil War Round Table)*

Library of Congress Cataloging-in-Publication Data

Scott, Robert, 1938–
   Glory, glory, Glorieta : the Gettysburg of the West / by Robert
Scott.
      p.   cm.
   Includes bibliographical references and index.
   ISBN 1-55566-098-3
   1. Glorieta Pass (N.M.), Battle of, 1862.   I. Title.
E473.4.S36   1992
973.7'31—dc20   92-25235
                                                              CIP

Printed in the United States of America by
Johnson Printing Company
1880 South 57th Court
Boulder, Colorado 80301

CONTENTS

FOREWORD

The time will surely come when some worthy memorial, either a towering shaft or a public edifice, will be raised and dedicated by the people of Colorado, in their capital city, to their hardy and intrepid volunteers who fought for the preservation of the Union; and especially to those who constituted their First regiment, whose staunch patriotism and willing sacrifices were exhibited, without any reserve, in aiding so effectively to preserve a vast territory in the West and in the Southwest to the Union, and whose riddled and torn battle flag is still cherished as a sacred emblem.

William C. Whitford, D.D.
President of Milton College
Author of *The Battle of Glorieta Pass*

Were I to claim that the outcome of the American Civil War was ultimately decided on an unknown battlefield in the mountains of New Mexico, I would no doubt be met with skepticism or accusations of "non compos mentis." In truth, even many historians who are familiar with the grand scheme of the Confederacy to capture everything west of Kansas are inclined to discount the importance of the plan or the campaign in relation to the eventual outcome of the war.

Yet there is compelling evidence that the most brilliant military strategists and civilian planners of the Confederacy were convinced that capturing the West would mean ultimate Southern victory in the war, and to that end they devoted considerable of their limited resources and manpower. Jefferson Davis certainly believed it; he assigned great importance to the cam-

paign as evidenced by the man he appointed to carry it out—
Henry Hopkins Sibley, one of the most competent officers in
the Southern military. And other Southern leaders were convinced that victory in the West would solve two of the most
pressing problems of the Confederacy: a lack of ready cash and
a crippling shortage of good, deep-water seaports from which to
carry out essential commerce with other nations. They believed
that successfully conquering the West would make it possible for
the South to ultimately defeat the Union.

How good was the Southern plan? Historian LeRoy Boyd,
writing in 1947, said that "had Sibley been successful, it could
have won the war for the South." But Sibley did not win, and
that is what this story is all about.

Later, after Sibley's effort failed, the South made a deliberate
effort to conceal the value they had placed on the campaign,
hoping thereby to gain another opportunity to make it succeed
sometime in the future. They hid their grand scheme and their
hopes in a cloak of official censorship and sworn secrecy. They
even went so far as to deliberately discredit the brilliant general
who conceived the original plan and who personally led the
troops, relegating him to the position of buffoon and town
drunk. And they were largely successful in both hiding their
intent and discrediting General Henry Sibley—and aided by the
attention-getting distractions of bloody campaigns being waged
in the East, the plan for a Western Confederacy has been largely
lost to history.

Even some of the handful who have published accounts of the
campaign have been victimized by the subsequent Confederate
campaign of disinformation and have come to question its significance. In the "Publisher's Preface" to the book, *Colorado Volunteers in New Mexico, 1862*, the editors comment that a "victory
that might have given the South control of the Southwest and of
California could hardly have played a decisive part in the outcome of the war."

There are, of course, other reasons some have questioned the
importance of the New Mexico campaign. For one thing, only
about 7500 or 8000 soldiers were involved in the fighting—
a minuscule number when compared to the approximately
163,000 who battled at Gettysburg, the 194,000 at Chancel-
lorsville, and similar huge numbers engaged elsewhere on the

Civil War battlefields. [Source: Mark M. Boatner III, *The Civil War Dictionary*. New York: David McKay Company, 1959.]

As recently as the fall of 1990, *Rocky Mountain News* (Denver) columnist Gene Amole wrote, "Some historians like to believe that the Battle of Glorieta Pass was the turning point of the Civil War because it ended Confederate dreams of establishing a new nation that would extend all the way to the Pacific Ocean and even into Mexico. But a more realistic evaluation was that it was no more than a footnote to the Civil War, a savage little firefight in the backwaters of the frontier." Yet in the same column, Amole suggests what may well be the real reason the significance of the fighting, and the battle itself, has been lost to history: "President Lincoln didn't come out here to make a speech. Mathew Brady didn't photograph the battle. Walt Whitman didn't write about it. We [Colorado] didn't even have a state so that we could either secede from or remain with the Union; we were just an outpost in the vast Kansas Territory." He might well have added that those who stood to gain by concealing the intent and value of the Confederate campaign were also successful in minimizing the importance of the plan to seize and control the West.

In fact, one of the saddest elements of the story is that the world seems to have forgotten the men who fought and died in the New Mexico campaign. Most people have no knowledge of the battles, and those who do generally have incorrect or incomplete information. In his book, *The Mines Of Colorado*, published five years after the battle, journalist Ovando J. Hollister wrote:

It is perhaps doubtful as to whether or not [the First Colorado Volunteers] would have even been recognized had they not marched nearly a thousand miles, and in one hard fought battle and two brisk skirmishes, broken and driven from New Mexico all those lean and hungry Texans. . . . "Baylor's babes" left San Antonio for the Pikes Peak gold region about three thousand strong, swallowed Fort Fillmore without winking, rather beat [General Edward] Canby at Valverde, and had since that event been coming northward, covering the country as the frogs did Egypt, and wearing it out. They had got 25 miles north of Santa Fe when they were met by the 'Pet Lambs.' The Babes and the Lambs each rebounded some five miles from the first shock, which was more like the shock of lightning than of battalions. The reserves of both sides having come up the next day, the Babes and the Lambs each went forth to mortal combat again. The ground was not unlike the roof of a house; the Babes reached the ridge-pole first and by the weight of numbers and the advantage in position, during a seven hours' fight, forced the Lambs back off the roof. Night fell upon the scene and the Babes and the Lambs each sought their own corner. The Lambs found theirs all right, but the Babes did not. It appeared that a part of the Lambs had been there during the fight and destroyed their commissary and transportation, totally. There being no grub in New Mexico in a general way, there certainly was none now since armies had been sustained by her during the winter, so that the Babes had to go home to get something to eat. The Lambs accompanied them to the door and wished them a safe journey. And so ended the war of the Babes and the Lambs in the Rocky Mountains!

In his marvelous book *The Civil War in the American West,* historian Alvin M. Josephy, Jr., laments the fact that history has ignored this Western war but says it is easy to understand why this was the case:

It was understandable that the Federal government was less concerned with the sparsely populated Trans-Mississippi West than with the eastern theaters, where the great armies were being assembled, where the great battles would be fought, and, indeed, where the war would be won or lost. But especially during the first year of the war, the western territories—and particularly New Mexico—were treated at times as if they were a nuisance. Few officials in Washington seemed to know where New Mexico was, much less care what happened to its people, most of whom were dismissed as troublesome Mexicans who contributed nothing to the country and whose constant need for protection from the Indians was a costly bother and burden. A typical attitude about the Territory was expressed by Secretary of War Simon Cameron on May 11, 1861. In replying to a waring from Secretary of the Interior Caleb Smith that the southern counties of New Mexico were in "imminent danger" of invasion from Texas and that Loring was disloyal and should be replaced, Cameron answered casually that "measures have been or will be taken commensurate with (New Mexico's) importance." Six days later, the measures were taken: many of the Regulars in New Mexico were ordered withdrawn to the East. So much for the Territory's importance, a perception in sharp contrast to that of the Confederacy.

Was the campaign really a key, perhaps *the* key, to the Civil War as some suggest? Or was it, as Amole wrote, nothing more than a "savage little firefight in the backwaters of the frontier"? That conclusion must be drawn by the reader after digesting the facts that follow.

NOTE

Throughout this tome you will find comments made by Ovando J. Hollister who was first a private and later a sergeant in Company F, First Colorado Volunteers. All of these remarks unless otherwise noted are taken from Hollister's personal diary, which has been published on several occasions since the Civil War. The most recent such publication is under the title, *Colorado Volunteers in New Mexico, 1862*, edited by Richard Harwell, and published by The Lakeside Press, R. R. Donnelley & Sons Company, Chicago, 1962.

PART ONE

Political, Strategic, and Military Considerations

CHAPTER ONE

PREVIEW OF THINGS TO COME

It seems strange that man will organize war. He never would, did he realize its horrors which only come home to the soldier, and to him but on the field of carnage. Pride and ignorance buoy him up at first, a few battle-fields brutalize him, and he is moved as any other machine. Why should man, endowed with reason, thus resign his free agency? Why should he not? What boots this much vaunted free will? Can he choose but life, or can he choose his time to die? And even could he, who creates the causes of his choice? He is the creature of chance if not of fate. Then why borrow trouble? Let us enjoy, if possible, this idleness, and contentedly allow them to do our thinking who are paid for it, since thinking cannot alter the case!

Ovando J. Hollister, Company F
First Colorado Volunteers

A cannon ball smashed into the line of Union soldiers, cutting a swath of death through their ranks. Colonel Christopher "Kit" Carson glanced up from the sights of his rifle and watched the volunteers—confused, scattered and broken. The shot had been a lucky one for the Confederates; it had struck the cannon that the New Mexico militiamen had hidden in a grove of trees and had not yet fired. Now the weapon, and the soldiers assigned to man it, would never be involved in the war.

Carson thought about running over to see whether he could help restore the Union line and calm the volunteers, but he knew it was useless. The soldiers had been showing signs of panic for the past half hour, and Carson knew the end was now very near.

Turning back toward the enemy, Carson again calmly sighted down the long barrel of his rifle. He held steady on the chest of a Confederate soldier who was running directly toward his position. Gently he squeezed the trigger, being careful not to jerk the barrel off target. The minié ball found its mark, and the Rebel soldier tumbled to the ground, rolled twice down the hill and came to stop against a rock. By the time he had stopped rolling, Carson had already reloaded. He laid the rifle barrel across the fallen tree and took aim at another enemy soldier.

All around him, the tempo of battle had quickened now. The Confederate cannons were finally in place, lined up across the top of a ridge five hundred yards east of Carson's position. In a few seconds they would be hurling deadly grape shot and canister into the heart of the Yankee positions. Rebel infantry was spread out all along the central and right side of the hill, and it looked as if cavalry had begun moving forward through the trees on the left.

Carson wondered how much longer the raw Union volunteers would be able to hold out against this all-out Confederate attack. He glanced to his right and saw a frightened soldier—a boy, really—kneeling behind a tree stump, watching wide eyed as the enemy attacked. Most of the soldiers on this side of the river were nothing more than local farmers and fur trappers. They were ill prepared for this sort of battle against a well-armed and well-trained enemy. The Union volunteers had been pressed into service at the last moment. They had almost no training and were armed with a motley collection of rusty old rifles and shotguns. And now this pitiful army was locked in deadly combat with disciplined troops armed with the latest in weaponry. And as if that was not problem enough, the Rebels also outnumbered the Yankees by a huge margin, perhaps three and a half or four to one.

The militiamen commanded by Colonel Carson were supposed to be the best of the New Mexican volunteers. Unlike most of the others, these men had not run away when news of the Confederate invasion first swept the countryside several weeks earlier. But these volunteers were in a real battle for the first time, and it was clear that they were already physically exhausted and emotionally overwhelmed. Carson knew that panic and a full-scale rout were only moments away; he had seen the symptoms developing steadily over the past hour.

He wondered how General Canby and the handful of soldiers from the Second Colorado were doing, off to his right. He feared that the Coloradans might have been overwhelmed in the last Confederate charge. He knew that bitter hand-to-hand fighting was underway at about the spot where the Colorado artillery had been situated. It would be a miracle if the thin line of Union soldiers lasted another hour.

This was not the first time Kit Carson had been in a potentially fatal bind. In fact, while scouting for the U.S. Army over a period of several years he had frequently been with small groups of soldiers fighting a far larger force of Indians. But of course, this was different. Indians were usually armed with only a few rifles, and most of them not of the latest design. A majority of the New Mexico Indians still fought with bow and arrow or with spears. The soldiers were always better equipped and better disciplined. They usually had little trouble defeating the Indians in battle, even when out-numbered.

Here, it was the enemy with the better training, the superior firepower, and the overwhelming edge in manpower. Carson was grateful that over the past few weeks he had been able to map out several possible escape routes just in case they were needed. He was virtually certain they would be needed in the next few minutes.

Over on the far right side of the hill, just above the Colorado lines, Carson saw a new Confederate charge begin. Hundreds of the men in grey were running down the hill, screaming that awful "Rebel yell" as they ran. They were well out of Carson's rifle range, and for the moment he could do nothing but watch in a sort of detached fascination. Clearly, they were about to overrun the two remaining Union guns that had been anchoring the right and center of the Union line.

Actually, Carson was mildly surprised that the Yankees had lasted even this long. They had been locked in combat since early morning, and the battlefield was now littered with the dead and dying. Moans and occasional screams of the wounded could be heard during momentary lulls in the firing. On the battlefield directly across the river, where vicious hand-to-hand combat had taken place that morning, dozens of victims of both sides lay sprawled silently, grotesquely, in the grass.

The fighting had raged back and forth during the day. At one point shortly after noon, the Union actually drove the larger enemy army back up the hill, and there was a moment when it appeared the Union might win the battle. But it didn't last. The Texans counterattacked, and the Union line crumbled. Now it appeared that the tide had turned for one last time, and Carson figured it was only a matter of minutes, or seconds, until the Union line fully collapsed and the rout began.

Up the slope on the opposite side of the Rio Grande, the Confederates suddenly rose in unison and formed a line stretching from one side of the valley to the other. Then on they came, a solid line of death trotting resolutely forward. Already the leading elements of the Rebel army were splashing into the water just below Carson's position. As they came closer, Carson again sensed the growing panic among the volunteer soldiers off to his right. A split second later, the volunteers began hurling their rifles to the ground. Turning away from the river, they ran as fast as they could, away from the grove of trees, away from the battle, shedding their backpacks, canteens, and anything else that would make them lighter and able to run faster. Back through the bushes they fled, on up into the rolling hills beyond.

Turning back toward the charging Texans, Carson calmly took aim one final time. He squeezed the trigger and watched unemotionally as another Rebel went down, this one falling heavily into the water a mere twenty-five yards in front of his position. Then Carson was on his feet, running half-crouched after the Union soldiers who were disappearing into the trees to the west of the river.

Carson knew this was a total disaster for the Federal troops. The Union had lost not only the battle, but also its entire fighting force in the West. The battered remnants now retreating from the Confederates would be lucky to survive as any kind of an army whatsoever. In a matter of seconds, the Texans would completely overwhelm any volunteers who had not already run away. Those who survived the final Rebel charge might be ultimately worse off than if they had died on the battlefield.

As Carson ran, he thought about the implications of the Yankee rout. February 21, 1862, would go into the records as the day the Union lost the West!

Carson and General Canby had been aware well before the battle began that it was likely to end this way, in total defeat for the Union. They had made plans for this contingency. In keeping with that plan, Carson now began leading a handful of his better soldiers, who had not panicked and fled, out of the area. Their object was to move quickly enough to prevent capture—or massacre. He wondered whether Canby himself would survive and whether they would meet again, as planned, at Fort Craig.

What a strange war! Here was Kit Carson, a frontier scout and Indian fighter, leading a handful of farmers in a battle against well-trained Confederate troops. Most of the world thought all of the fighting was being done 1500 miles east of the bloody little valley in the heart of New Mexico. Why was the Civil War being fought in this desolate western frontier location anyway? And why was Washington unable or unwilling to send help?

In the final scheme of things, did it matter? Was New Mexico even worth defending by the Union, or attacking by the Rebels? Carson wondered whether anyone outside this little valley would ever know of the fierce, bloody struggle that had occurred that day at the North Ford of the Rio Grande.

WESTERN UNITED STATES
1861 - 1862

Oregon

Utah Territory

California

Colorado
Territory

• Denver
City

New Mexico
Territory

• Glorieta
Pass

• El Paso

Texas

CHAPTER TWO

PREAMBLE TO WAR

The noble men in our Volunteer Army will die in harness, and their mantles will be caught by myriads rushing to fill their places. They may be thwarted for a time, discouraged by treachery and incompetence in high places; but their Sun will rise, the gloom of doubt and despair will be dissipated and they will sweep from the soil the last vestige of bondage and treason.

Ovando J. Hollister, Company F
First Colorado Volunteers

*W*hy, indeed, had the Confederates chosen to launch a major campaign in the sparsely settled West? And why would the battle for the West become the deciding factor in which side won the Civil War?

To understand how critical the Confederate campaign to capture the West really was it is necessary to first understand what was required before the Confederate States of America could survive as an independent nation. Separating from the North had serious economic ramifications for the South; secession divorced the Confederacy from its normal supply of clothing, machinery and other essentials of life. Before the war, all of those came to the South from the North. Now it would be necessary to find another source for these items critical to survival.

But the Confederacy was not worried. In the words of South Carolina's James H. Hammond, speaking before the U.S. Senate eighteen months before the Civil War began, "without firing a gun, without drawing a sword, should they make war on us we could bring the whole world to our feet. You dare not make war on cotton. No power on earth dares to make war upon it. Cotton is king!"

Hammond's complete confidence in King Cotton was shared by most Southerners; the world must have cotton, and the Confederate states provided a lion's share of the crop. All the South had to do in order to blossom as an independent nation was to continue or expand its already well-established trade with England, France, and Germany. In exchange for the cotton they must have, those countries would give the South virtually everything it needed to remain independent: clothing, guns, and other manufactured necessities. So long as the Confederate States energetically pursued international trade, it would be on a solid financial foundation.

That is why Abraham Lincoln, as one of the first Union reactions to Fort Sumter, proclaimed a naval blockade of all Southern ports. The strategy was to cut off the Confederacy's access to foreign markets and strangle the new nation.

The Union navy quickly organized a fleet of ships; it commandeered virtually anything that floated and equipped the vessels with the armor and armament of war. The navy started by quickly modifying five powerful steam frigates, the best vessels afloat. The ships were all in dry dock when the first shots of the war were fired, but that simply made it easier and quicker to modify the vessels for blockade duty. The frigates were heavily armed with large caliber smooth-bore and rifled guns.

In addition, the navy had five "first-class screw sloops," only slightly smaller and less well armed than the frigates, plus fourteen smaller screw sloops, four paddle-wheelers, and assorted tug boats and other smaller vessels.

With these approximately forty vessels, the Union navy undertook to shut down 3500 hundred miles of Confederate coast, including 189 harbors. It was, of course, an impossible task and might never have worked were it not for the South's stubborn belief that the rest of the world would do anything to gain access to the Confederate's cotton.

When Lincoln announced the blockade, Jefferson Davis was faced with a problem. He could either quickly ship out all available cotton and begin buying up the arms and ammunition he needed for the war, or he could immediately stop shipping cotton and hope to create an artificial world shortage. The latter strategy assumed that Europe needed cotton so badly it would not only agree to pay greatly inflated prices, but it would help the South break the Union blockade in order to have access to cotton. Adhering to the King Cotton mentality, many Southerners believed it likely that England, France, and Germany would immediately grant recognition to the Confederate government and even help the South win the war in order to get cotton. Davis and his advisors chose to pursue the latter course.

Unfortunately for the South, the Confederate reasoning was basically flawed from the beginning. It doomed the South to failure.

In the first place, when the war began the world was suffering from a huge oversupply of cotton. Banner crops the previous two seasons, accompanied by unrestricted shipping to foreign markets, had left warehouses throughout Europe stuffed with cotton for which there was no use. As a result, there was no great demand that might force the rest of the world to side with the Confederacy. (In fact, when the blockade really became effective later in the war and Southern farmers had switched from growing cotton to growing food crops, Europe actually would sell cotton back to the Confederates!)

In effect, the Confederate decision to withhold cotton from the market during the first year of hostilities did what the Union navy could not do; it made the blockade effective. The lack of access to international trade cut off Southern commerce and left the Confederates desperate for basic necessities.

As the war progressed, the Union blockade did become effective as more and more ships were constructed, purchased, or leased and sent to the picket lines. It is true that scores of "blockade runners"—sleek, fast vessels built especially for the purpose—managed to slip through the blockade throughout the war. But they were not nearly enough to bring the supplies required by the increasingly hungry South.

Jefferson Davis eventually appealed to plantation owners to stop growing cotton and concentrate, instead, on growing corn, wheat and other crops to feed the nation. Southern farmers responded by the thousands, but even that turned out to be a two-edged sword. Cotton production fell from 1.5 million bales in 1862 to fewer than 300,000 bales in 1864. In 1863, Jefferson

Davis proudly told his congress that "Southern fields are no longer whitened by cotton; they are devoted to the production of cereals and the growth of stock formerly purchased with the proceeds from cotton."

But when the fortunes of war began to turn for the Confederates and the Rebel army was in retreat, those crops were used to feed invading Union soldiers who otherwise might have been unable to continue to pursue the war because of overextended supply lines. General William Tecumseh Sherman said of the South's switch to food crops, "Convey to Jeff Davis my personal and official thanks for abolishing cotton and substituting corn and sweet potatoes in the South. These facilitate our military plans much, for food and forage are abundant."

The effectiveness of the Union blockade played a key role in the eventual defeat of the South. The Confederacy increasingly struggled against severe shortages as the war progressed. The habit of Rebel soldiers of stripping the bodies of the Union dead following each battle did not come from spite; it was the only way most of the Southern soldiers could get a pair of boots or a change of clothes. Some Rebel soldiers joked that if they were taken prisoner by the Yankees, at least they would get a good meal, a warm coat, and a place to sleep!

As the months turned to years, Southerners found themselves doing without more and more items or paying outrageous prices for the things they bought. The shortages imposed on the South by the Union blockade were staggering; by 1864, a woman's bonnet cost $250, and genteel Southern belles began wearing cornhusks and palmetto leaves to cover their heads. A cup of coffee in Richmond, Virginia, cost five dollars in 1864, and loaves of bread sold for up to three dollars each.

But although the Union blockade ultimately did just what it was intended to do, it never caught the Confederates by surprise. There was no secret that the key to winning the war for the South lay in its ability to trade with the rest of the world. It was common knowledge that the Union's first priority, articulated over and over again by Northern politicians and military leaders, was to starve the Confederacy by blockading her harbors.

It also was no surprise that the Union would have the ability, sooner or later, to make a naval blockade really effective. Unless European nations could be convinced to recognize the South and help break the blockade militarily, the Confederacy was doomed to failure.

But there was one other possibility, one other way the South could continue trade with Europe, unhindered by the Yankee blockade. If the South could somehow find new harbors that could not be shut down by the North, it would render the Union blockade strategy useless.

And those harbors already existed; harbors that were absolutely safe from the Union navy. To trade unhindered with the rest of the world, all the Confederates had to do was capture those harbors; victory would then be within their grasp.

Those safe harbors were in California and Oregon, the two newest North American states. There were scores of excellent, deep-sea ports from San Diego to Portland. And there was no way the Union could blockade them. If the Confederates controlled California and Oregon, Union ships would have to travel many thousands of miles from New York, around the tip of South America and back up the Pacific Coast to even reach these new Confederate harbors. By the time they took up station to blockade the Pacific ports, they would already be desperately short of supplies. And with no friendly base anywhere on the Pacific Coast, they would have to turn around at once in order to reach New York before the crew starved to death!

There were other, equally compelling reasons that the South coveted the West. Historian Alvin Josephy says that Jefferson Davis believed that Utah would be a perfect place to establish huge new plantations and grow cotton, and that Texans desperately wanted control of mail routes and natural resources in the West. Josephy reports:

By [the outbreak of the Civil War] other Southern leaders had come to share Jefferson Davis's recognition of the importance of New Mexico, perceiving that its possession by the Confederacy could open the way for the seizure of much of the rest of the western country. Such a conquest, observed one Southern officer, would provide "plenty of room for the extension of slavery which would greatly strengthen the Confederate States." There would be other dividends, too—most notably the securing of the western gold and silver regions, whose wealth could finance the Confederacy. . . . California—or at least its southern half—would give the South a coastline and ports too distant for the North to blockade effectively.

The question was what might be involved in capturing the far West. To the Confederates the answer seemed surprisingly simple; a token military force could probably sweep westward and conquer everything from Kansas City, the edge of civilization, to Los Angeles. After all, the Confederates reasoned, there was not much between Texas and California to slow down the invaders. The New Mexico territory was sparsely populated by farmers of Mexican descent. Most of the farmers harbored strong hatred of the United States which had wrested the land from Mexico in the Mexican-American War of 1848–49.

The Colorado Territory was scarcely settled at all. The Utah Territory was settled by Mormons who hated the U.S. Government. Oregon had only a few settlers, and California was filled with gold miners from both North and South; there were an estimated one hundred thousand Southerners in California and they would not likely resist a Confederate invasion.

Actually, this line of reasoning was fundamentally flawed. New Mexicans may not have been thrilled with the United States, but they had an even deeper hatred for Texas. Since as early as 1841, Texans had been claiming great chunks of the New Mexico territory and had even actually sent raiding parties into the area on at least three occasions. In 1850, Congress paid Texas ten million dollars in an effort to settle the Texas claim to a strip of land stretching from the western border of that state to the Rio Grande and northward to Nebraska. But even then, the Texans wouldn't quit coming.

The government of Texas sent a state judge to Mesilla, claiming he had legal authority over the entire New Mexico Territory. The judge, Spruce M. Baird, appeared genuinely surprised at the hostility he encountered, and soon resigned. The Santa Fe "Republican" commented in a front page editorial, "We would now inform our Texas friends that it is not necessary to send us a judge . . . for there is not a citizen, either American or Mexican, who will ever acknowledge themselves as citizens of Texas!"

An angry Judge Baird wrote back that "The people of New Mexico are one-fourth Pueblo Indians. Of the rest, three-quarters are peons without shirts, shoes or hats, and not worthy to be trusted in any way. The remainder, to say the least of them, are Mexicans."

And the hostilities between Texans and New Mexicans continued to fester. After the Mexican-American War, Texas began to award great chunks of New Mexico land to Texas veterans, saying "it is the least they deserve." The land grants were not only illegal, they were unspecific—so that Texas soldiers began arriving in southeastern New Mexico and laying claim to land which was already owned and being farmed by New Mexico residents. The Texans and their long rifles soon drove the New Mexicans off the land, and the hatred for Texans grew even stronger.

But all of this history was ignored by Texans and the Confederacy, and they were absolutely convinced that most New Mexico residents would welcome an invasion by a Rebel army. Perhaps the South in this instance was blinded by its own greed—lulled into a false security by its own hatred of the North and its desire to own the West. As one historian noted, "The West might be largely empty and unexplored—only about five million Americans, or 14 percent of the population, lived beyond the Mississippi in 1861—but it was nevertheless an enormous prize which offered 'plenty of room,' as one Southern officer noted, 'for the extension of slavery which would greatly strengthen the Confederate States.'"

Also Confederate strategists saw additional advantages for the South in a conquest of the West. One historian noted that the capture of the gold in Colorado and California would have made it possible for the Confederate to purchase all their needed supplies abroad, but it had even more important political implications. "The vast seacoast of California and parts of Mexico would have been at the disposal of the Confederate commerce destroyers, and would also have provided a place of entry for supplies from Europe. Most important of all, the easy conquest of such a vast territory was expected to enhance the prestige of the Confederates in Europe to a point where recognition for the government in Richmond would be forthcoming. As such recognition could have undoubtedly brought England and France into the war against the North, the Confederates assumed that it would win the struggle for them. Such was the grandiose scheme of the Confederacy."

Thus the possibility of gold and access to good harbors (and diplomatic recognition from European nations) made the early conquest of the western United States of prime importance to Jefferson Davis and the Confederacy almost as soon as the first shots of war were fired. If the South succeeded in capturing the

Pacific Ocean seaports, there would be no way the rest of the world could avoid recognizing the Confederacy. The South would be able to trade for anything it needed, the European nations would help militarily, and the North would soon be crushed.

Ironically, Jefferson Davis had been one of the first in the United States to recognize the great potential of the western frontier. He began thinking about it long before there was talk of a Civil War; he even discussed it while serving as a colonel in the Mexican War. He is said to have broached the subject with his former father-in-law, ex-President Zachary Taylor, under whom Davis served in the Mexican War. At first, Davis was merely fascinated by the untamed wilderness and the rich fur trade, but as time passed he began to recognize more and more the promises of this vast, unsettled land, especially after gold was discovered in California in 1849.

When Davis was sent home from the Mexican-American War, a hero hobbling on crutches because of wounds suffered in the battles of Monterrey and Buena Vista, he spent much of his time learning about, talking about, and promoting the West. He continued his enthusiastic support after being appointed to the U.S. Senate from Mississippi, and continued to do so after being appointed secretary of war under President Franklin Pierce in 1853.

The secretarial appointment put Davis into possibly the second most powerful post in the United States government; it certainly was the most important in the cabinet. Davis quickly became the dominating figure in the Pierce administration.

He was a good secretary of war, and worked toward improving and strengthening the army. Soldiers were given better training, better equipment and better organization. He also increased the strength of the standing army from eleven thousand to sixteen thousand men. Davis sent a majority of the soldiers to the West with which he was so enamored, and in the process, he became even more thoroughly knowledgeable about the region.

Using his enormous power and influence in the cabinet, Davis began pressing for the government to fund the construction of a transcontinental railroad. Under his plan, the eastern terminus of the railroad would be in Memphis. From there the tracks would head west, eventually moving through Texas, across the

New Mexico Territory, and terminate at Los Angeles. The plan ran into immediate opposition from Illinois Senator Stephen Douglas, who believed the railroad should run from the heavily populated and industrialized northern part of the country—like Chicago, for instance—and take a northerly route to the west coast, possibly by following the Oregon Trail.

The debate involving the routing of the proposed railroad plunged Jefferson Davis into his first real public controversy and first public criticism, especially from those who believed Davis had something to gain personally by a southern routing. The railroad became a political hot potato, linked to the rising debate between North and South.

General Winfield Scott, with whom Davis had exchanged harsh words during the Mexican War, strongly criticized Davis. Said General Scott, "He is not a cheap Judas. I do not think he would have sold the Savior for thirty shillings—but for the successorship to Pontius Pilate, he would have betrayed Christ and the Apostles and the whole Christian Church!"

A close friend and admirer of Davis was Sam Houston of Texas, who nonetheless said that Davis was "as ambitious as Lucifer and as cold as a lizard."

Davis's own wife said of him, "If anyone differs with Mr. Davis, he resents it and ascribes the difference to the perversity of his opponent." To which Davis responded, "I have an infirmity of which I am heartily ashamed; when I am aroused in a matter, I lose control of my feelings and become personal."

By the time Pierce's term of office had expired in 1856, Jefferson Davis had grown extremely personal about state's rights and the new Southern cause. He had become a leading spokesman for the South, and an outspoken enemy of Stephen Douglas and Abraham Lincoln. And through it all, Davis maintained his passion for the West.

In fact, as the possibility of a North-South war grew ever more likely, the relative importance of the transcontinental railroad grew by leaps and bounds. Davis knew that the railroad would provide any new Confederacy with a rail link to the rich gold fields and spectacular deep-sea ports of California.

As the 1850s drew to a close, Davis was among those who recogized that Southern secession was likely and war a growing possibility. More and more, he became the most visible and outspoken defender of the emerging South. When in 1860 his fellow Mississippian Andrew Johnson warned against secession and said that anyone who fired on the Union flag should meet a traitor's death, Davis was outraged. He thundered that Johnson was "a degenerate son of the South, unworthy to sit in the Senate. . . ."

Personally Davis opposed secession, and privately he argued against it. But as the rift deepened, Davis, like others, was forced to publically choose sides, and he opted to remain with the South he loved so much.

In December, 1860, South Carolina seceded from the Union by a vote of 169 to 0. A few days later on January 9, 1861, Mississippi followed suit. Davis formally notified the U.S. Senate on January 20 that he was resigning from that body, since the state he represented was no longer a part of the Union. It pained Davis to witness this breakup of the Union which he had served as a military officer and a high-ranking government official.

In his farewell address to the senate, Davis assured fellow lawmakers that his resignation was not personal; "I am sure I feel no hostility to you, senators from the North. I am sure there is not one of you, whatever sharp discussion there may have been between us, to whom I cannot now say, in the presence of my God, I wish you well. Mississippi parts from the Union not in hostility to others, not to injure any section of the country, not even for our own pecuniary benefit, but from high and solemn motive of defending and protecting the rights we inherited and which it is our duty to transmit unshort to our children. . . . It only remains for me to bid you a final adieu."

Close friends said that Davis was emotionally shattered by the secession of Mississippi and the inevitability of the war that was sure now to follow. After resigning from the senate he lingered in Washington for more than a week, sending telegrams to Southern leaders urging against further secession. His wife said that Davis hoped to be arrested by the North, although there is no independent evidence that was the case. When he was not arrested, he bid personal farewells and headed for Memphis.

At the time of Mississippi's secession and his resignation from the senate, Davis was physically quite ill. He had lost considerable weight in recent weeks and was suffering from what his doctors called neuralgia. During his final days in Washington, Davis spent considerable time bedridden. He lost sight in his left eye and began to walk in a stooped manner. He was never to fully regain his health.

When he arrived back home in Mississippi, Davis assumed he would simply be given a military assignment by the leaders of the emerging nation. He appeared genuinely surprised when he was drafted for the job of President of the Confederacy. (He was the compromise choice, chosen after considerable wrangling by other Southern leaders.)

Even in accepting the leadership of the Confederate government, however, Davis worried privately that the South could not win any war with the North. A friend of Davis said that he "laughed at our faith in our own powers. He says we are like the British in that we think every Southerner equal to three Yankees at least. We shall have to be the equivalent to a dozen now. Only fools doubt the courage of the Yankees or their willingness to fight when they see fit. And now that we have stung their pride, we have roused them till they will fight like devils!"

During the final years of the decade, President Buchanan had appointed as his secretary of war, one John B. Floyd who was from Virginia and who harbored strong Southern sympathies. Occupying one of the most powerful positions in Washington, Floyd helped to set the stage for the war by either accidentally or purposefully flooding those frontier army forts—established by Davis—with all the modern weapons of war. Josephy says of the government's sudden generosity in stocking Western forts, "Northerners suspected that [President] Buchanan's Secretary of War, the Virginian John B. Floyd, had deliberately sent huge stockpiles of military equipment to the West, where Southern officers could seize them when hostilities began."

Noted historian Bruce Catton said that Floyd was ". . . a bumbling incompetent who had permitted much corruption without (as would finally appear) being personally touched by very much of it. . . ." Catton believes that Floyd's inabilities permitted others to make certain that a considerable amount of Union military supplies would wind up in the hands of Confederates.

Other historians disagree with Catton's assessment of Floyd, whom they portray as a brilliant, conniving Southern sympathizer. Their version of "factual" history says that Floyd knew full well that war was coming, so he deliberately began flooding those forts in the West with arms, ammunition, and all sorts of other military supplies. He knew that troops who quit the Union army for the Confederate army would take the supplies along with them. Thus he was able to go a long way toward equipping the Rebels with the most modern available U.S. Army materials.

One who held the latter view was Dr. William C. Whitford. He writes:

> For a year or so before South Carolina seceded, Mr. John B. Floyd, secretary of war in President Buchanan's cabinet, caused to be sent to various army posts in the South and Southwest vast quantities of military supplies in great variety, of which this preparatory distribution of the materials of war New Mexico received a large share, designed chiefly for the use of soldiers of the South when the contemplated Confederacy should attempt to establish its authority over the Southwest and into the country that soon afterward became the Territory of Colorado. He also caused to be moved into New Mexico an unusually large number of soldiers of the regular army, under the command, to a great extent, of officers from the Southern states. It was expected that these officers would influence the people of that territory to favor and aid materially the secession movement, and that when the proper time had arrived they would resign their positions and accept commissions in the Southern army. It was also the intention that they should persuade the soldiers of their commands to abandon their flag and enlist under that of the new government.

Whether Floyd was really bumbling or a conniving genius is not materially important. The fact remains that during his term of office, western forts were flooded with arms, ammunition and supplies. A huge majority of that war matériel would ultimately wind up in the service of the Confederacy.

CHAPTER THREE

THE CONFEDERATE GRAND SCHEME

Some thought that if a few of the leading Secessionists and Abolitionists could be hung together, the country would get on better.

Ovando J. Hollister, Company F
First Colorado Volunteers

Now the Southern states began seceding in rapid order: Florida, Alabama, Georgia, Louisiana, and Texas. Early in 1861, the first group of states was followed by Virginia, North Carolina, Tennessee, and Arkansas.

The many secessions caused some immediate and dramatic changes in the United States Army. From one end of the country to the other, scores of soldiers, many of them in high, sensitive assignments, resigned their position (or simply deserted) and headed for the South to join the new army of the Confederacy.

Among those who left the western frontier for the South were Richard Ewell, Albert Johnston, Joe Wheeler, James Longstreet and J.E.B. Stuart (who had been fighting Indians in Colorado). Stuart was still recovering from a gunshot wound suffered in a battle with the Southern Cheyenne Indians near modern-day Limon, Colorado, when he handed in his resignation as a U.S. Army Lieutenant and headed for the South.

Although most of the rank and file soldiers in the U.S. Army were from the more heavily populated North and remained loyal to the Union, many of the officers were from the South. As noted, a substantial number of the officers now joined the Confederate army. Altogether, at least five hundred officers left the Union army to serve in the Confederacy. Of these, nearly three hundred were from western bases alone! One Union soldier stationed in New Mexico later complained that it was practically an army without officers. The departing officers were accompanied by up to four thousand soldiers and non-commissioned officers who joined the exodus to Dixie. One reason for the disproportionate number of officers who left the Union may have been because the Confederacy promised all officers an immediate promotion if they would serve the South.

A great many of the officers who left their posts to join the Confederacy had seen prior military action in the Mexican-American War or recent Indian wars. The disappearance of so many fine and experienced officers from the Union Army left the North in dire straits and at a distinct disadvantage in the conflict that was soon to follow.

And the vanishing of so many officers and men from military bases had its greatest impact on the frontier West. The frontier region was where a majority of the U.S. Army was then concentrated. In 1860, perhaps 70 percent of the United States Army was stationed in forts situated between Kansas City and Los Angeles. The men in uniform were being used primarily to prevent or stop trouble on the frontier; soldiers who had been stationed in the West were there to protect settlers from hostile Indians. These were the same troops who now began to leave in huge numbers.

The biggest single concentration of these Indian fighting soldiers was in the New Mexico Territory. New Mexico got more than its share of pre-war soldiers for two reasons. Most importantly, the territory had an abundance of Apache and other hostile Indians who frequently tangled with the white settlers; clashes further north with the Cheyennes, Arapahos, and Sioux had not yet reached the crescendo that marked the Great Plains Indian Wars which started a few months later. Of lesser significance, the territory until only a decade earlier had been a possession of Mexico, and some of the residents still were not pleased to have seen their land change from Mexican to United States control. In parts of New Mexico there was still open hostility toward the U.S., although both the Union and the Confederacy appeared to overestimate the amount of anti-Union sentiment.

By mid-summer of 1861, so many of these western soldiers had left for Dixie that some forts in Colorado, New Mexico, and Utah Territories had to be abandoned altogether. Many other forts were being staffed by skeleton forces which could not possibly have fought a major battle.

When the war finally erupted, soldiers in New Mexico were stationed at Forts McLane, Thorn, Craig, Fillmore, and Bliss on the Rio Grande; Forts Union near Las Vegas; Marcy at Santa Fe; Stanton in the Lincoln Mountains; and Defiance (in the center of the territory, near the current Arizona state line). Further west were Forts Breckenridge and Buchanan, both near the city of Tucson in Arizona. Within three months, the Confederates had seized Bliss, Breckenridge and Buchanan, and within six months they also occupied Fillmore. Forts Marcy, Stanton, and Defiance were abandoned for lack of manpower. By early 1862 the Yankees held only Fort Craig and Fort Union.

As already noted, conflict with hostile western Indians had not yet reached the crescendo to which it would rise just three or four years later; serious clashes were still relatively rare in New Mexico. Even if the Indian threat had been greater, there wasn't a great deal the United States War Department could have done about it. The simple fact was that there was no manpower to send to the forts, especially now that whatever troops remained were desperately needed to defend the industrialized and populated North.

But the loss of thousands of troops from these southwestern forts was not the only blow to the U.S. Army; most of those soldiers leaving western forts for the South took with them their weapons and their horses—and frequently anything else they could get away with. (This was the material so generously supplied to the forts at the direction of War Secretary Floyd over the past several years.) Wagonloads of cannons, gunpowder, ammunition, spare parts, food, clothing, blankets, and tents were carted away from these frontier outposts. And what items were not taken to the South by future Confederate soldiers were "recalled" to Washington, along with virtually all of the remaining soldiers. That left the forts, like Old Mother Hubbard's Cupboard, completely bare!

On March 18, loyalist Union Lieutenant Colonel Benjamin S. Roberts learned that his commanding officer, Colonel George

B. Crittenden, a Kentuckian, was about to take his infantry troops from New Mexico and march them into Texas, there to hand them over to the Confederacy, as soldiers if they would enlist, as prisoners if they refused to do so.

Colonel Roberts went immediately to the overall military commander of the New Mexico Territory, Colonel William W. Loring and reported this treasonous plan. To Roberts's amazement, Colonel Loring ordered nearby guards to seize and place him in the fort's brig "for investigation of treason." Then, with Roberts safely out of the way, Loring, a strong Confederate sympathizer, joined Colonel Crittenden in leaving for Texas!

On March 22, 1861, Loring's letter of resignation reached Washington. The War Department immediately promoted Loring's top assistant, Colonel Henry Hopkins Sibley, as the new commander of U.S. troops in the territory of New Mexico. Unfortunately for the Union, Sibley was also a Southerner who had already decided that he, too, would join the Confederacy. He delayed his New Mexico departure only long enough for his troops to seize all of the arms, ammunition and other supplies from several Union forts that were in the process of being vacated. According to rumors, he also spent the time swapping sick, aged or otherwise undesirable mules and horses for the fine animals of the Union army. Whether he eventually kept the healthy animals for himself or took them with him to Texas is unclear.

At the time, Sibley complained to a friend because there was stronger pro-Union sentiment among the remaining Federal troops than he had anticipated. Sibley said, "I sincerely regret the sickly sentimentality which prevents me from taking every last man with me to the Lone Star state!"

Colonel Sibley, born and raised in Lousiana, was a brilliant and seasoned army officer and as Southern as they came. Although the Confederacy would later try to discredit Sibley, the efforts appeared to be more designed to save face, or to protect the South's hope of invading the West for a second time, rather than as a result of anything Sibley did. Certainly up until the western invasion, Sibley's career was clearly on the fast track. He was considered one of the army's best strategists, and had solved numerous problems through his creative genius. Sibley's only known shortcoming, and it would prove his ultimate undoing, was that he was less than great as a tactician. Later, there would be rumors of another short-coming; some modern historians suggest that Sibley was a heavy drinker and that his battlefield performance was often hampered because he was too drunk to know what was going on.

Regardless of his later reputation, however, Henry Sibley was a born leader and an excellent soldier. He was described by historian LeRoy Boyd as "perhaps the most brilliant general officer in the Southern ranks, the only one of the glittery galaxy of Confederate warriors whose mind grasped the grand strategy necessary to win the war" [LeRoy Boyd, "Thunder on the Rio Grande," *Colorado Magazine* (July 1947)].

But Sibley was more than an outstanding strategist. It seems that this veteran field officer was also a military inventor of uncommon ability. In this arena alone he left an indelible mark on soldiering throughout the world for decades to come. As his first such contribution, the colonel (and later general) invented the "Sibley tent" which was used by the U.S. Army for more than a hundred years. Then he invented the "Sibley stove" to heat the tents and keep the soldiers warm and comfortable in almost any weather conditions. The stove, too, was used by armies all over the world well into the twentieth century. He also invented the "Sibley saddle," which he designed specially for his cavalry troops. The saddle made it considerably easier for the men to ride in comfort and still have immediate access to their weapons. (A Northern General, George McClellan, would make one minor change in the saddle and it thereafter was called the McClellan, rather than the Sibley, to whom credit was really due.)

But Sibley was not through. He next invented small, portable bronze howitzers which could easily be carried on the backs of mules. That made it possible for the first time to carry heavy weapons into battle against Indians in the rugged mountain country of the West and Southwest. These specially designed howitzers were known as "Sibley guns," and they continued in use until near the turn of the century. Sibley brought eight of these weapons with him into the New Mexico campaign and they figured prominently in the subsequent Battle of the North Ford or Valverde.

A career soldier, Sibley graduated from the United States Military Academy at West Point on July 1, 1838, and was commissioned a second lieutenant. Two years later he was promoted to the rank of first lieutenant, a rapid promotion for the small peace-time army of that day.

In 1847, while fighting in the Mexican-American War, Sibley was promoted to captain in recognition of his demonstrated battlefield abilities and leadership. After his capabilities were repeatedly demonstrated under enemy fire, he was briefly breveted to the rank of major, although when the war ended he reverted to his permanent rank of captain. In 1857, Sibley was finally promoted to the permanent rank of major and in 1861, to colonel. His army record was outstanding in every respect. He was liked by his troops as well as by his commanders, and his military file was unblemished.

Sibley was not a "desk soldier," having seen considerable military action well before the Civil War began and in theaters other than Mexico. Earlier in his career, as a lieutenant, he served two terms in the "Second Seminole War" in Florida from 1838-1841, fighting bravely and twice being slightly wounded. As noted, his performance during the Mexican War was outstanding. He participated in the siege of Vera Cruz and somewhat later took part in the key battles at Cerro Gordo, Contreras, Cherubusco, Molina del Rey and the final battle for the capture of Mexico City. He performed in an outstanding manner, receiving several citations for his courage. His military experience continued beyond Mexico. In 1857, Sibley as a major was in charge of transporting supplies for the Utah expedition against the Mormons.

All of this lengthy and varied battle career, covering more than two decades, would serve him well in later years. There is no question that as hostilities erupted between North and South, Colonel Sibley was considered one of the brightest stars in the army. His services were coveted by both North and South.

This, then, was the experienced and brilliant veteran, Henry Sibley who reluctantly resigned his commission in the U.S. Army and headed for Texas at the end of May, 1861. It must have been particularly difficult for Sibley to leave New Mexico, because he loved the territory and had personally supervised location and construction of the many forts that now protected it. And like Jefferson Davis, Sibley believed that control of the West was the key to winning any war. He, too, understood what the naval blockade could do to the South, and understood the opportunity it afforded to neutralize the blockade through quick military action into California. "This might be a war between North and South," he once told an associate, "but it will be won or lost in the West!"

More painful for Sibley than simply leaving the area he knew and loved so well, however, was the leaving of friends and family. Sibley's second-in-command in New Mexico was Colonel Edward R. S. Canby, and Canby, an ardent Northerner, was Sibley's brother-in-law!

(One of the ironies of the Civil War was that it so frequently pitted brother against brother, and classmate against classmate. Thirty-nine men graduated from West Point in 1854, twenty-three of whom wound up as high-ranking Union officers during the Civil War, while fourteen fought for the Confederates, including the commander of West Point in 1854, Robert E. Lee, then serving his final year in that capacity. Of all the U.S. Army officers who in 1860 were at or above the rank of lieutenant, one-third would serve in the Confederate Army. Among them were many West Point graduates including some who would become prominent in the war: Stonewall Jackson, Robert E. Lee, Jefferson Davis, and such men as Hood, Beauregard, and Johnston.)

Canby had been serving as a groomsman for Sibley when the latter got married. During the days surrounding the wedding, Canby took an immediate and intense liking to one of the bridesmaids, who turned out to be Sibley's younger sister, Elizabeth. Soon, Canby and Elizabeth were dating seriously, and eventually Henry Sibley would serve as a groomsman for his junior officer, Edward Canby. (Modern historians still debate the relationship of the men; most believe they were brothers-in-loaw, but some believe that Canby married Sibley's cousin rather than his sister.) But the relationship between the two men was closer than simply being brothers-in-law. Sibley and Canby had also been classmates at West Point and they spent considerable time together outside the classroom. They had developed a close friendship long before the wedding.

And in addition to being brothers-in-law and West Point classmates, the men had fought side-by-side in several battles both in Mexico and against Indians in the West. As happens frequently with men in battle, this experience tied them together in an emotional way that is difficult to explain, but made them closer than many blood relatives. Thus, Sibley and Canby were relatives, classmates, friends and comrades-in-arms. And now they were being separated by political loyalties that dictated they become enemies on the battlefield.

That possibility, though, as painful as it may have been, did not deter Colonel Sibley from his duties as he saw them. Within days of heading to Texas Sibley was proposing a lightning strike by the Confederacy to capture the West (where Canby had remained). His fellow officers at the San Antonio headquarters for the Army of Texas liked the plan and encouraged him to take it straight to the top. With such support, Sibley sought, and was granted, an audience with President Jefferson Davis to explain his plan for conquering the West. Within days, Sibley was in Richmond, Virginia.

The South was already getting desperate because of shortages imposed on it by the war. The Union Navy had begun its blockade of Southern ports and the new Confederate government was withholding shipments of cotton in an effort to drive the price higher on European markets. Of the forty-three ships in the Union navy, twenty-two were patrolling the Atlantic seaboard and twenty-one were in the Gulf of Mexico, with orders to prevent ships from entering or leaving those harbors. In addition to all of that, the U.S. government had just purchased twelve more ships, leased nine others and contracted for an additional twenty-one to be built. All of these ships were to be used to totally blockade the South and prevent it from trading with the rest of the world.

Although the blockade was not fully effective yet, it was making itself felt. Early in 1861 Confederate agents had succeeded in purchasing substantial quantities of arms in France, but now could find no ships willing to try to take the weapons through the Union blockade. Jefferson Davis was among the first to recognize that unless a way could be found to make the blockade ineffective, the Union would soon strangle the Confederacy. The South simply could not fight and win a war unless it had trade with Europe. Such trade, as has already been noted, required safe seaports.

Colonel Sibley quickly pointed out what Jefferson Davis already knew: those safe harbors so desperately needed by the South already existed in California and Oregon. He emphasized that the Union did not have enough ships to blockade those Pacific

Ocean ports and even if they had such ships, they could not keep them afloat in the Pacific if California and Oregon belonged to the South. Where would the Union navy go for supplies?

Davis already knew the implications of the Union blockade. And he had just received a letter from Albert Sidney Johnston, the man responsible for Confederate operations in Missouri and Arkansas. Johnston was desperately short of weapons, and had learned that a shipload of rifles and ammunition had been seized by Yankee ships off the coast of Louisiana. He warned Davis that unless a way was found to get weapons through the blockade, "the South is doomed!"

At the same time, newspapers were carrying stories about General George B. McClellan's plan to bring the South to her knees. McClellan, now in charge of the Union army, told President Lincoln that he planned to "vigorously pursue" the war and bring it to a quick conclusion. This he proposed to do by carrying out what he called a comprehensive war plan. Under it, the Union would ". . . first and foremost, tighten the blockade to deny all commerce to the enemy."

All of these developments were weighing heavily on Jefferson Davis's mind as Henry Sibley outlined his bold plan to capture the West and seize a dozen new harbors for the South. But Sibley was promising more than just new harbors—something most others had not yet thought about. He could also deliver to the Confederacy vast amounts of wealth through the capture of the gold fields in Colorado and California!

The colonel proposed that he be allowed to raise an army of four thousand to five thousand men, which he would call the "Western Expeditionary Force." This command would also often be called the Army of New Mexico, and was sometimes known as "Sibley's Brigade."

Davis listened patiently and intently as Sibley laid out his plans to conquer all of the West. It was, as historians Hall and Davis wrote, "a somewhat visionary scheme, but not beyond the possibility of success." The Union commander in California had already warned Washington that if the Confederates ever got a toe-hold in California, it could have grave consequences for the United States.

Davis knew all of these things as he listened to Sibley outlining his plans for the conquest of the West. And now the colonel's genius for strategy came into play to answer unasked questions and allay unspoken fears. He had carefully thought through every detail necessary to make this huge land-grab work: how the troops must move, where they would get reinforcements and supplies, even the order of battle. Embarking from Fort Bliss in El Paso, Sibley told Davis, a group of these soldiers would quickly move westward along the Gila River Trail. Having captured that key artery they would thus control the main route between southern California and Texas. This was vital because it not only gave the Confederates safe passage all the way to the California border, but it also prevented Union troops from staging a California-based attack eastward into the Confederacy.

This initial strike force need not be large—since the enemy was not expecting such an attack and would thus be ill-prepared to stop it. He was also ill-prepared because virtually all army units that had not deserted the western forts for the Confederacy had now been recalled to Washington to defend the capital from rebel attack. There were almost no Federal soldiers remaining in the West! Sibley pointed out all of these shortcomings to Davis saying that Union forces were entirely inadequate, both in numbers and quality, to offer serious resistance, and anyway were thought to be divided in their loyalty.

Sibley's force would proceed swiftly to Tucson, a hot-bed of Confederate sympathy, and seize the city. It would serve as capital of what the Rebels would now call the Arizona Territory.

In addition to everything else that was working for the South, Sibley said that the civilians of northern New Mexico, predominately Mexican in composition, could be counted upon as being either pro-Southern or at least apathetic. Commercially and economically, New Mexico was generally dependent upon the slave states of Missouri and Texas . . . all of which meant that the conquest of New Mexico should go without a hitch!

Once having secured the Gila River Trail, Sibley proposed to take the bulk of his troops and march northward up the Rio Grande River. Along the way, he would seize dozens of lightly defended or totally abandoned Union forts and a dozen cities. Capture of these posts would provide the invaders with everything they needed in the way of food, weapons and other matériel of war. Through their capture, the Texans could remain adequately supplied with all their needs, making it possible for them to carry out the entire campaign without worry about overextended supply lines. If Davis or other Confederate planners recognized this portion of the plan as a potential Achilles' heel, they did not say so.

The initial objective of the invading Confederate army would be to seize Fort Union, a key military outpost in north central New Mexico. Fort Union was on the Santa Fe Trail, north-north-east of Las Vegas. The fort's position of control over the Santa Fe Trail was absolutely vital to prevent Union reinforcements from Kansas. It would also provide the Confederates with a jumping-off point for possible later attacks into Kansas. The mere presence of Rebel soldiers at Fort Union would force the Union to keep substantial numbers of Federal troops in neighboring Kansas, troops that might otherwise be sent to fight in the South or to reinforce federal positions around Washington.

Once Fort Union was secure, the Confederate forces would then head north again. They would capture Denver and the rich Colorado gold fields. The gold thus seized would fill the Confederate treasury and make it financially possible for the South to purchase warships, guns, ammunition, uniforms and food from Europe.

From Colorado, the Confederates would push on northward to Fort Laramie in the Nebraska Territory. Seizure of that outpost would also give Sibley's army control of the Oregon Trail. By dominating the Gila River, Santa Fe and Oregon Trails, the Rebels would control all transportation to and from the West. The vast frontier region would be isolated, and could be picked apart at the leisure of the Western Expeditionary Force.

Would four thousand or five thousand soldiers be enough to accomplish all of this? No, but Sibley also had an answer for that problem. With Confederate troops now occupying all the key points from El Paso north, Sibley proposed to begin recruiting an Indian cavalry unit. Commanded by Confederate officers, these Indians would be fierce fighters. And because of their lifestyle, the Indian army would also be highly mobile, with the advantage of having intimate knowledge of the area's geography. This highly mobile fighting force would not only make the Union think twice about attacking westward, it also could eventually be used, Sibley suggested, in a flanking movement against Union troops in the middle-West.

(Recruiting Indians to fight for the Confederacy fascinated Jefferson Davis; he later promoted Albert Pike, a Confederate General, to the rank of "Indian Commissioner" and gave him the responsibility of recruiting Indians to fight for the Confederates. Although Pike met with limited success, he did manage to recruit more than three thousand Indians who actually fought Union troops at the battle of Pea Ride, Arkansas; he is also believed to have contributed greatly to the scope and ferocity of the Great Plains Indian Wars that paralleled the Civil War years.)

But even that was not all! While the Indian cavalry was protecting a line from El Paso to Fort Laramie, other Confederate troops would occupy the Utah Territory, consisting of present-day Utah and Nevada, and the states of Oregon and California. The capture of the two states would give the Confederacy more gold for its treasury, thanks to the active gold mines in California and would supply the South with badly needed deep-sea ports. The ports would be safe from the Union blockade and make it possible for the South to engage in active trade with Europe. Beyond all of that, the capture would position the South to influence Great Britain and France to join the war on the side of the Confederacy, a key element of the South's long-term political strategy.

And the beauty of Sibley's far-reaching plan was not only what it promised in both immediate and long-term rewards for the Confederacy, but that it could be carried out with a minimum of existing Southern manpower. Most of the West, after all, had been deserted by the U.S. Military. Sibley iterated that half of the soldiers had already gone south to join the Confederacy and the remainder had been called back to Washington to help defend the Union capital from Rebel forces. The West was virtually unprotected, and capturing it would be almost embarrassingly easy!

As for local citizens in the sparsely-populated West, Sibley reinforced Davis's belief that they should pose no threat to the invasion. Persons in the New Mexico Territory were mostly of Mexican descent, people who had settled there when the area belonged to Mexico, he said. They were by and large still opposed to the United States. It was just common sense that very many of them resented the Union because of the Mexican-

American War, and these people should either be friendly toward the Confederates or at the very least, should offer them neither problems nor resistance.

The Nebraska Territory, in which Fort Laramie was situated, and the Colorado Territory were barely settled at all. There were no more than thirty thousand whites in the Colorado Territory and fewer than five thousand in the western half of the Nebraska Territory. Of these, many had Southern roots and Southern sympathies. In fact, the first gold miners in Colorado were men from Georgia, and the biggest town in the territory, Auraria, was named in honor of the town of Auraria, Georgia! Several pro–Confederate "cells" were operating in Denver, and more than two hundred of Colorado's men had already showed up in Texas to volunteer for the Rebel army.

The Utah Territory was settled primarily by Mormons who had their own reasons for harboring passionate hatred of the United States government. Their bitter feelings stemmed from previous military actions against the Mormons on two separate occasions; Sibley reminded Davis that he had personally participated (as superintendent of military supplies) in the most recent such campaign and had first-hand knowledge about how much the Mormons hated the United States government!

In the first confrontation with the Mormons, Federal troops drove them from land they had occupied in Illinois and Missouri. This was land the Mormons claimed God had given to them in a "vision" seen by Brigham Young.

Later, the Mormons settled the Utah Territory, formed the "State of Deseret," and applied for statehood. The U.S. refused the request on several different occasions, on grounds that the Mormons permitted bigamy. Eventually, President James Buchanan, who was determined to wrest control of the territory from the Mormons, ordered that Brigham Young be removed as territorial governor and replaced by Alfred Cumming of Georgia. To make that decree stick, Buchanan sent in Federal troops.

The Utah conflict suddenly and dramatically blew all out of proportion when residents of the area attacked a wagon train of pioneers whom the Utah settlers thought were invading soldiers. All of the adults in the wagon train were killed in what became known as the "Mountain Meadows Massacre." A leading Mormon, John D. Lee, was convicted and hanged for the murders, and U.S. troops occupied the territory and enforced Federal law from 1858 until the Civil War erupted. This "occupation" by the United States was deeply resented by the Mormons who still harbored bitterness toward Washington, and Sibley was completely confident they would help the South in the Civil War. As it turned out, Utah sent two companies of volunteers to fight for the Union and only a relative handful of men to battle for the Confederacy.

As for California and Oregon, said Sibley, these two states had been mostly fur-trapping areas until recently. Oregon had too few people to offer much resistance, and California, like Colorado, had attracted as many Southern gold miners as those from the North. In actual fact, said Sibley, the two states were virtually apolitical and probably had no desire whatsoever to get involved on either side in the Civil War.

All of these, Sibley told Jefferson Davis, meant that the conquest of the West would be quick and simple, and would result in even larger benefits to the South than previously anticipated by Davis. Politically, monetarily and militarily, this was a brilliant scheme on the part of the Confederacy, and it had staggering implications for the United States as well as the South.

As Sibley outlined his plans in great detail, President Davis was no doubt thinking of his own strong feelings for the West and of the all those years he had battled for a transcontinental railroad running from Mississippi to California. When Sibley finally finished speaking, Davis approved of the plan, saying it had potentially great rewards and no obvious pitfalls. He promoted Sibley to the rank of brigadier general on the spot. He also formally appointed Sibley as commander of the new "Western Expeditionary Force," and told him to report back to San Antonio to begin raising his army. The general's specific orders commanded him to "drive the Federals out of all of New Mexico. After that, you are to be guided by circumstances and your own good judgement"—a strong implication that once New Mexico fell, Sibley was authorized to continue on his own to capture the remainder of the West.

At the same time, however, Davis cautioned Sibley that the whole matter must be kept secret insofar as that was possible; even his recruiting was to be done quietly and without fanfare. A part of Davis's desire that no one else hear of the plan was to ensure that the element of surprise would remain on the side of the invading Confederates, but it also went a great deal further than that.

For one thing, the leaders of the Confederacy had already opened secret, preliminary talks with the government of Mexico. These negotiations were aimed at securing Chihuahua, Sonora and Lower California, either by purchase or conquest. That Mexico was willing to consider a possible outright donation of those states to the Confederacy should not be surprising. The territory was difficult to rule from Mexico City and was often in rebellion. Beyond that, the Mexican government hated the United States because of the Mexican-American War of a decade earlier, and would do anything to help her enemies. These factors translated into an eagerness to help the Confederates, even though a great many of the officers who led American troops in the Mexican War now served the Confederacy. The Mexicans held their grudge against the nation, not the individuals who waged the war.

A Confederate military historian of the day, Major Trevanion T. Teel (who was also one of General Sibley's senior officers), wrote, "The state of affairs in Mexico made it an easy thing to take those States, and the Mexican President would be glad to get rid of them and at the same time improve his exchequer."

General Sibley apparently told many friends that there was a secret understanding between Mexican and Confederate authorities regarding a change of ownership of the northern Mexican states. Teel quotes Sibley as saying that as soon as the Confederates gave evidence they would definitely occupy Northern Mexico, President Juarez would cede the territory. Teel wrote, "Juarez, the President of the Republic (so called), was then in the City of Mexico with a small army under his command, hardly sufficient to keep him in his position. That date, 1861, was the darkest hour in the annals of our sister republic, but it was the brightest time for the Confederacy, and General Sibley thought that he would have little difficulty in consummating the ends so devoutly wished by the Confederate Government."

At the same time that the Confederacy was holding these delicate and top secret talks with Mexico, the Confederacy was also busily trying to woo support from England, France and Germany. A part of the strategy was to portray the South as the victim of blatant Northern aggression, first by statute and later by military invasion. The South carefully cultivated a portrait of herself as being in a defensive position militarily.

It was important in the subtleties of diplomacy that nothing be done to change that image. Davis feared that Europeans would have found it difficult to "harmonize the fact of an invasion of the West with the Southern representations of a noble war for independence." If word got out that the South was preparing a major invasion, it could sabotage all of the diplomatic inroads made up until now by the Confederacy. In addition, Davis recognized that one of the great advantages enjoyed by the South was that her soldiers ardently believed they were defending their homeland from outside invaders, while the North had a much more difficult time drumming up passion for a defense of "the Union."

Of course, the requested secrecy suited General Sibley just fine. He high-tailed it back to Texas and set the wheels in motion to carry out his grand scheme for the invasion of the West. Sibley could not wait to get started.

To his delight, he learned that anti-Union sentiment had already surfaced in the land he was about to seize. Groups of civilians in the New Mexico Territory, under repeated urging from Colonel John Baylor and organized Confederate sympathizers, were about to "officially proclaim" themselves independent from the Union, and announce that they were now a part of the Confederacy. While the proclamations (issued at Mesilla on March 16, 1862, and separately at Tucson on April 11) had no legal status and had nothing to do with the legitimate government of the territory, they did indicate that Southern invaders would be welcome in the area.

Colonel John Baylor, already in New Mexico's Mesilla Valley to prevent any surprise attack on Texas from that direction, now issued his own proclamation from the village of Mesilla. In the proclamation, Baylor claimed that all of the New Mexico Territory lying south of the 34th Parallel was henceforth to be known as the Confederate Territory of Arizona. (The 34th parallel runs through Wichita Falls, Texas, and separates modern day New Mexico and Arizona roughly at their mid-sections.) Sibley rubbed his hands gleefully as he read the newspaper reports of "strong Southern sentiment" which had surfaced and "appears to be gaining strength" in New Mexico.

Equally pleasing was the news that Southern troops actually already occupied a small part of the New Mexico Territory. This was the first Sibley knew that soldiers under the command of Colonel John B. Baylor had already moved into the Mesilla Valley, just north of El Paso. They had also seized a number of former Union army forts, now abandoned by Federal soldiers.

Baylor was a hard-nosed—most accounts say "cruel"—Texan who had already established a reputation for giving no quarter to anyone who stood in his way. Stories about Baylor's dishonest and heartless nature were well known in the West. Alvin Josephy says that in spite of the plans by General Sibley and General Pike to recruit Indians to fight on behalf of the Confederacy, Baylor planned to murder Indians in cold blood whenever possible:

> John Baylor hated Indians, and severely chastised a subordinate who talked with Apaches in New Mexico, saying the Confederacy intended to "exterminate" the Indians; "The Congress of the Confederate States has passed a law declaring extermination of all hostile Indians. You will therefore use all means to persuade the Apaches or any tribe to come in for the purpose of making peace, and when you get them together, kill all the grown Indians and take the children prisoners and sell them to defray the expense of killing the Indians." Later, Baylor was accused of killing 60 Indians by deliberately giving them a bag of flour that had been poisoned.

Partly because of his reputation as a man who would stop at nothing to get his way, Baylor had encountered no resistance to his New Mexico land-grabs, either from the handful of Union soldiers they found there or from the local citizens. Even better, when the Rebels arrived at Fort Fillmore, some of the Union soldiers fled from the advancing Rebel forces and several others had actually surrendered and asked to join the Confederate army.

Unfortunately for Sibley and the remainder of the Confederate hierarchy, the easy capture of Fort Fillmore would lead him and others to the false notion that they would face virtually no resistance in the West. This premature and unwarranted Confederate euphoria would prove to be a fatal error.

PART TWO

Getting Ready for Battle

CHAPTER FOUR

FIRST COLORADO VOLUNTEERS

I am a private soldier, depending upon the rumors of camp for my information. I may often mistake; may censure where praise is due and vice versa. For this I must beg indulgence, for my vision comprehends only the rear of events as they pass out of sight. Besides, this diary is intended to mirror the feelings of the soldiers as faithfully as possible. If it is not always just, it will still, I trust, be interesting as exhibiting the present view of events contrasted with the hue they take from time.

Ovando J. Hollister, Sergeant
Company F, First Colorado Volunteers

Samuel H. Cook was one of thousands of men who flocked to the Colorado Rockies in search of gold in 1859 and 1860. He was also one of thousands who failed to find it. By late June of 1861, Cook and two companions were out of money, out of food, and nearly out of hope. They were hungry, cold, broke and dejected.

As they sat around a camp fire at their claim not far from Golden, Colorado, in May of 1861, Cook began reading though a recent edition of a Denver newspaper. In the paper he found an article which said that the United States government desperately needed troops to wage war and defend itself from "secessionist aggression." The article said that any man who recruited twenty-five or more volunteers to join up with him would be commissioned an officer and would lead his own troops in the service. To a hungry gold miner, that sounded like the best possible deal. Cook, by coincidence, was a personal friend of Colonel

Jim Lane at Fort Leavenworth, Kansas. The more he thought about it, the more Cook was sure he could round up twenty-five men easily, probably twice that many. There were that many starving gold miners within a stone's throw! He would enjoy working with his old friend, Colonel Lane, and would enjoy even more the prospect of regular meals, warm clothing and a comfortable bed.

Cook wrote a letter to Colonel Lane, outlining his plan to recruit down-on-their-luck gold miners. Lane quickly wrote back his approval, and appointed Cook as Captain of the "Colorado Volunteers." At Cook's request, his two gold mining partners were also made officers of the company: George Nelson as first lieutenant and Luther Wilson as second lieutenant.

The day after he received Lane's letter, Cook rode fifteen miles into Denver. There he had a printer prepare a number of recruiting posters. One day later, Cook began nailing the posters to trees, buildings and mining structures throughout the valley. To his surprise, he found the recruiting surprisingly easy; it seems that more men than he imagined were ready to give up on striking it rich. Would-be volunteers began showing up at Cook's tent the same afternoon and by the middle of August he had eighty-seven volunteers ready to ride with him to Kansas to join the Union army.

Now, a group of eighty-seven riders is somewhat unusual under any circumstances, but these men attracted considerable attention in a war-nervous society. Word quickly spread that this large group coming down out of the hills was headed for enlistment in Kansas. Colorado Governor William Gilpin heard the news as he reached his office on Thursday morning, August 20.

Governor Gilpin was not only a man of unusual intellect, he was also a man of great foresight and patriotism. A Pennsylvanian by birth, Gilpin's ancestors had distinguished themselves in England under Cromwell and in New York under George Washington during the American Revolution. Gilpin was an honor student at the University of Pennsylvania, and later graduated high in his class from the United States Military Academy at West Point.

As a soldier, Gilpin distinguished himself fighting Indians—first in Florida and later in the New Mexico Territory. He had also fought the Mexican-American War where he attained the rank of major.

After that war, Gilpin became an explorer and headed into the western territories. He was later sent back to Washington, D.C., elected by local citizens to represent them and plead for statehood for Oregon. While living in Oregon, Gilpin founded the city of Portland. On March 22, 1861—barely three weeks before the Confederates fired on Fort Sumter—Abraham Lincoln appointed Gilpin as governor of the Territory of Colorado.

When the first shots of the war were fired, Gilpin told friends he was dismayed to find "a strong and malignant secession element [in Colorado], which had been ably and secretly organized in November of the preceding year." And Gilpin wrote to the U.S. War Department that "extreme and extraordinary measures are required to meet and control [the secessionist] onslaught."

A few weeks later an ugly incident in downtown Denver began to polarize the citizens of the Colorado Territory. Wallingford and Murphy's Mercantile, the largest general store in the city, was run by transplanted Southerners, who were strong supporters of the Confederacy and secession. On the morning of April 24, 1861, one of the owners ran a Confederate flag up the pole atop his building. Almost immediately, an angry pro-Union crowd gathered in front of the store. Several hurled rocks at the building and as emotions began to build it appeared that the situation was about to turn decidedly nasty.

One of the men standing in front of the store was Samuel M. Logan, an ardent Union loyalist who was already thinking about enlisting in the army to fight Confederates. Logan squeezed past others in the crowd, climbed up on a hitching rail at the front of the building and swung himself onto the roof. There, he grabbed the offending Rebel flag and to loud shouts of approval from the crowd below, ripped the banner to shreds. The angry crowd then surged forward and seemed intent on demolishing the store, and, given the mood of the men, possibly harming its occupants. Only the timely appearance of the Denver town marshal and six heavily armed deputies finally persuaded the crowd to disperse.

But no one in the city was about to forgive and forget. The day following the incident, a Denver town meeting was held. Among the resolutions passed at the meeting was one which said:

Resolved that as for Colorado, she, with willing hearts and ready feet, will follow the flag and keep step to the music of the Union,

Resolved that the government of Washington is good enough for us—that it is the best government the world ever saw—that we will ever sustain it,

Resolved that the right inheritance of Constitutional Liberty—our forefathers, living, fought for and secured, and dying, blessed—we, their sons, should maintain at any hazard, even unto death,

Resolved that the flag of Colorado Territory is the "Star Spangled Banner." [Boyd, "Thunder on the Rio Grande," p. 3]

The flag incident seemed to galvanize first the city and later the entire territory. Miners, fur trappers, and ranchers began to openly choose up sides and it soon became apparent that while Northern sympathizers would dominate numerically, there were enough Confederates in the Territory to pose a serious potential threat.

Soon serious incidents were being reported around the territory. Captain Abram McKee, described as a former Texas Indian fighter, was arrested in Denver along with forty other men as they prepared to ride to Texas to join General Sibley's army. The men were held in Denver's jail for several weeks until most of them swore allegiance to the Union and were released. (This was the normal method of dealing with such problems, and it rarely worked, though it did seem to satisfy the local populace.)

Another local man, A. B. Miller, left Denver with a trainload of supplies destined for use by the Confederates. The wagon train was captured by Union troops in western Kansas and the goods turned over to the U.S. Army. Miller, himself, escaped capture and was never located by the Union.

Still another group of about thirty Coloradans who favored the Confederacy captured a U.S. government supply train near Fort Wise. However, the Rebels themselves were captured a short time later and were returned to Denver for trial. The return trip was a difficult one; the army escort and the 30 or so Confederate sympathizers set out from Fort Wise (later Fort Lyon), Colorado, for Denver and ran into a vicious blizzard. They rode for eighteen hours hopelessly lost and eventually found themselves back at Fort Wise. They set out again the next morning, this time completing the trip without incident.

Even before those incidents Governor Gilpin had been giving considerable thought to the threat posed by Rebel sympathizers in Colorado, and to the persistent rumors that the Confederacy had its eye on capturing the West. Some of those rumors said the Rebels actually planned to capture Denver and the Colorado Territory.

Gilpin was nervous enough about the rumors to have twice sent telegrams to Washington, one each to the War Department and to the U.S. Congress, which technically governed the Colorado Territory. His messages passed along the rumors of a pending Confederate invasion of the West and pleaded for help in defending Colorado from the planned attack. Official Washington, though, was far too busy with "more pressing" business to worry about rumors from the sparsely settled Colorado Territory.

In fact, Washington rarely paid any attention to complaints or warnings from Colorado or any of its other western territories. Alvin Josephy noted that:

> Washington displayed little interest in military problems of the remote southwestern Territory [New Mexico] whose barren wastes appeared to have no pressing relevancy to the war or the fate of the Union, and whose total non-Indian population—mostly poor, Spanish speaking former Mexican citizens—was less than 95,000. Fully preoccupied with the crisis in the East, the War Department could give [New Mexico Union Commander Edward] Canby no assistance, but pressured him, instead, to hurry the transfer of the 2,500 Regulars in his Department to Fort Leavenworth for assignment to the "more vital" eastern war zones.

The lack of concern in Washington, as evidenced by a lack of response to Gilpin's telegrams, left the governor in something of a quandary. Gilpin eventually concluded that if Colorado was to be defended from Rebel invaders, it was up to him to make it happen. And while he was trying to figure out exactly what to do in order to save Colorado for the Union and halt any possible Confederate invasion, he learned about Sam Cook and those eighty-seven volunteers passing through Denver on their way to Kansas.

The governor hastened from his office and began searching for Cook's men. They were not difficult to locate; the riders had congregated in downtown Denver to eat lunch, and their eighty-seven horses clogged Larimer Street. Gilpin quickly caught up with Captain Cook and offered to buy his lunch.

Over the meal, Gilpin outlined to Cook the desperate situation facing Colorado. Warming to the task, Gilpin also told Cook that the territory was planning to form its own military unit, a move which was specifically authorized by the territorial charter. Gilpin did not mention that the charter made no provision for funding such a military unit. He told Cook that this new military unit, to be known as the First Colorado Volunteers, was just as important to the Union as any other unit. Then he got to the meat of his discourse; he asked Cook to remain in the territory rather than reporting to Kansas as planned. When Cook hesitated, the governor sought to sweeten the deal by promising that if they remained in Colorado, Cook and his men would be "well mounted, armed and equipped, and will have active service with the United States Army."

That was enough to convince Captain Cook. He called a hasty meeting of his riders and placed before them the proposal from Governor Gilpin. The men soon decided that if pay and facilities were the same, it would be easier for them to remain in Colorado than to ride six hundred miles across the Great Plains to reach Fort Leavenworth and Colonel Lane. Besides, defending their home Territory made their mission seem more urgent and somehow more gallant! (It may also have seemed considerably safer!) Governor Gilpin promptly dubbed the men Company F, First Colorado Volunteers.

Then Gilpin quickly set about trying to find a place to house his newly recruited soldiers. Word spread quickly that the governor was organizing a group of volunteers to defend the Colorado Territory from a possible invasion and offers of help began flooding the governor's office. Whether spurred by patriotism or bad luck in the gold fields, eager recruits began appearing everywhere.

One offer to help came from prominent Denver attorney John P. Slough. Slough was a fast-rising politician in Colorado, having moved to Denver after being narrowly defeated for governor of Kansas in 1857. (He also had been kicked out of the Ohio state legislature after a fist fight with a fellow lawmaker on the floor of the House.) Possibly out of no motive other than patriotism (and possibly with an eye on any political advantage to be gained), Slough became an outspoken pro-Union crusader in Colorado. He donated substantial amounts of his family's money to help with the war effort. Slough also located a vacant building on the Platte River, the old "Buffalo House" hotel, and used his considerable influence to get it donated as a place in which to house the soldiers. In gratitude for all his help and his money, Governor Gilpin appointed Slough as a colonel and placed him in command of the burgeoning First Colorado Volunteers; such appointments in return for service to the government being common at the time.

Now things began to happen quickly. Colonel Slough threw himself into his new assignment with enthusiasm. He and Governor Gilpin set about finding other officers for their little army. They wanted dynamic leaders who could control the rugged out-of-work miners, cowboys, and the barroom crowd considered most likely to join the Colorado army. The first of these officer recruits was a military veteran and Colorado pioneer, Samuel F. Tappan. Originally appointed a captain, Governor Gilpin promoted Tappan to lieutenant colonel less than a month later when the size of the Colorado army blossomed to more than two thousand men.

Governor Gilpin next approached another friend, a prominent Denver preacher named John Chivington. Chivington was an elder in the huge, 1.5 million–member, Methodist-Episcopal church, and was responsible for church growth in the West. He was also a circuit rider who regularly paid visits to the rough and tumble mining camps and ranches that dotted the east face of the Rockies. As such, Chivington was thoroughly familiar with the ways of miners and cowboys, and was well-known throughout the region. He was as tough as any of them, but he was simultaneously gentle, well-educated and a natural leader. Gilpin asked the Reverend Chivington to join the army and serve as its chaplain. To his surprise, Chivington refused.

"If there's fighting to be done, I want to fight," the preacher told Gilpin. "There is no force more evil on earth than the Confederacy and its people" [Boyd, "Thunder on the Rio Grande," p. 4]. The governor admitted his surprise but responded by appointing Chivington as a major of the cavalry.

The fact that Chivington wanted to fight probably came as no surprise to the governor or anyone else who knew Chivington. The preacher led a rebellion in the ranks of the Methodist-Episcopal church a few years earlier when Chivington and others demanded that all church leaders from the South sell or otherwise get rid of any slaves they owned. The resulting battle broke up the church, and left Chivington as spokesman for the most conservative, anti-slavery element.

Preaching in Ohio in the late 1850s, Chivington spoke out against the evils of slavery. Three men in his congregation were said to have threatened to "tar and feather" him unless the preacher quit talking about slaves. The stories—apparently true—said that the following Sunday morning Chivington appeared in the pulpit, placed his Bible on the lecturn and then laid a pearl-handled revolver beside the Bible. He then proceeded to preach against slavery, and no man in the congregation dared challenge him!

And now recruits for Governor Gilpin's new army began flooding the Denver area. The turn-out of volunteers far exceeded anyone's expectations. By early September, 1861, twenty-seven hundred men were signed up for the First Colorado Volunteers. It was a gratifying turn-out, but the sudden and unexpected influx of volunteers presented some serious logistical and financial problems for the governor to solve.

The official U.S. Census, conducted nine months earlier by the United States Marshal's office at Denver, estimated Colorado's white population at 30,000 persons. The document said there were 18,136 white males over the age of 21; presumably at least a quarter of them were over the age of 45 (making them ineligible to volunteer). That would mean that the 2,700 volunteers who poured into Denver may well have represented twenty percent or more of those men who were of good health and of the right age to enlist in the army. It was an altogether astounding response, no doubt echoing both the highly inflated passions of patriotism in the wake of Fort Sumter and the more down-to-earth reality of unsuccessful gold miners who were simply looking for regular meals!

Immediately, these recruits ran into at least imagined trouble. Rumors began to circulate throughout the territory that surprise attacks were being planned by Confederate raiders or groups of Rebel sympathizers in Denver against the new Colorado recruits. Guards were posted every night at the Buffalo House Hotel, although no such attack ever materialized.

In the meantime, Governor Gilpin was struggling with a number of related, severe problems thrust on him by the unexpected flood of volunteers. He needed desperately to establish an actual military camp somewhere near Denver to house and train the volunteers; keeping them in an aging hotel simply was not the way to train an army. In addition, Gilpin needed to obtain arms and ammunition for the soldiers, as well as horses, wagons, tents, clothing, medical supplies and food.

As an entirely separate but closely related matter, the governor now decided to buy all firearms of any description then in the possession of Colorado citizens. This was not so much an effort to arm the First Colorado Volunteers as it was to prevent the weapons from falling into the hands of Confederate sympathizers. The pro-secessionists in the area were also trying to buy any available weapons for shipment to the South.

As it turned out, the governor's effort to procure all the spare weapons in the territory met with resounding success, far beyond his wildest expectations. Virtually every man in the region had one or more old firearms, and many were eager to sell them, especially if they were outdated. Territorial officials soon had collected hundreds, some sources say a thousand or more, old rifles, heavy shotguns, pistols of questionable value, and a handful of other weapons including swords and even a cannon!

The first cannon owned by the First Colorado was purchased for a reported three hundred dollars from one Charles Autobees, a trapper in the San Luis Valley. Where the cannon originated is a matter of conjecture; some said it had been abandoned by the Fremont expedition during the winter of 1848–49; others say it was transported by the army to fight Indians about 1850. Whatever the truth of the matter, the weapon wound up in the hands of trapper Autobees, who had mounted it on the roof of his cabin supposedly as a deterrent to hostile Indians. Autobees claimed to be thoroughly and unquestionably loyal to the Union. Because of his loyalty, Autobees said he was willing to sell the cannon to Gilpin at a "most reasonable" price. (His neighbors sent word that Autobees had made a similar offer to the Confederates!) Gilpin's agents bargained at length with the trapper and eventually purchased the weapon and sent it to nearby Fort Garland.

The overwhelming success of the official territorial arms drive did not mean that similar Confederate efforts were a failure. They continued to buy arms, too, and were also quite successful.

The most important result of the Colorado arms drive was that Rebel sympathizers were driven into the open. Printed notices began showing up at mining camps and other public locations, naming places and times where Confederates would pay "the best prices for rifles and shotguns, and for black powder." Gilpin made sure that pro-Union men attended all such meetings and recorded the names of all pro-Confederates in attendance.

As pro-Union and pro-Confederate sources struggled to control the local arms market, stories began to circulate regarding alleged Rebel plans to pillage Colorado. There were rumors that these Southern sympathizers planned to rob the Clark, Gruber and Company Bank and Minting Establishment in Denver to get ready cash that would be shipped to Dixie. In actual fact, Confederate sympathizers did manage to rob a couple of wagon trains on Colorado's eastern plains, but they obtained little of value for their efforts.

For Governor Gilpin, the real problem in effectively coping with these Rebel forces was that all of his counter-measures were costing a lot of money and Colorado's Territorial Treasury had no provision for spending money on such projects. Worse than that, the United States Government, which controlled the territory and its treasury, showed no inclination to help out. In fact, Washington was doing an altogether excellent job of ignoring Colorado and the repeated requests from Governor Gilpin for assistance.

Gilpin now found himself with a huge number of soldiers who rightfully expected to be on the territorial payroll, and to be fed and housed and clothed, and he had no way of doing so. Still, the governor reasoned that the federal government must ultimately come to its senses; after all, if he was able to prevent a Confederate takeover of Colorado and the remainder of the West, surely the United States government would be elated! The end would justify virtually any means in this time of insurrection.

Gilpin was a man of action. Based on his assumptions about the reasoning process in Washington, the governor approached a Denver printer. He ordered that $355,000 in United States Treasury Notes be printed and delivered to his office.

Now, $355,000 was a lot of money even in 1861; it amounted to more than the annual budget for the Colorado Territory as allocated by the U.S. Congress! Gilpin reasoned that by the time these "treasury notes" began to show up at the federal treasury in Washington, Congress would surely have seen the error of its ways. Reasonable men would then be glad that Gilpin had taken direct and forceful action to stem the oncoming Rebel invasion!

Gilpin made good use of the bogus federal treasury notes. First he bought land along the Platte River just two miles from downtown Denver. The availability of the land, which would be used as a camp and training area for the volunteers, was the result of personal efforts on the part of Colorado's Territorial Secretary, Lewis L. Weld. He convinced the current owners to sell the property at a bargain rate to the government of the territory. In recognition of the secretary's efforts, a grateful Gilpin named the new training grounds "Camp Weld."

Construction began at once. A month later, the *Rocky Mountain News* reported on progress at Camp Weld:

> The buildings, which consist of officers' headquarters, quarters for soldiers, mess rooms, guard house, hospital, etc., occupy four sides of what is nearly a square, and are built in the most substantial and comfortable manner. The building space occupied by each company is 180 feet, divided into mess rooms which are 30 by 18 feet, with huge fireplaces at either end, and sleeping apartments of the same size, capable each of accommodating 25 men [*Rocky Mountain News*, October 24, 1861].

Although most citizens seemed to support the governor and the troops, some local residents thought the accommodations somewhat lavish just to house a bunch of soldiers. Local editorial writers soon dubbed the First Colorado Volunteers as Governor Gilpin's "pet lambs." And just as the name "Baylor's babes" stuck with the Southern soldiers occupying a corner of New Mexico, so the Colorado soldiers would affectionately be known thereafter as the "pet lambs."

By now, full-scale military training was underway at the Camp. Quartermasters were busy spending Governor Gilpin's treasury notes to buy everything they needed, including food, uniforms, weapons, horses, wagons, and general supplies. Considerable amounts of the script also went to pay wages of the soldiers, carpenters, teamsters and others.

Unfortunately for Governor Gilpin, some of those treasury notes began showing up in Washington, D.C., much more quickly than he had anticipated. Startled federal officials disavowed any knowledge of the notes and began an investigation to determine who was counterfeiting United States bank drafts. It took only days to discover that the "counterfeiter" was Colorado Governor William Gilpin.

The news hit Denver like a thunderbolt! When Washington announced the notes were worthless and would not be honored, there was panic among Colorado merchants. Lumber yards, food suppliers and other Denver-area businesses found themselves holding tens of thousands of dollars in worthless paper. Many of the businesses suddenly found themselves unable to pay creditors or employees, and several were reported to have gone bankrupt as a result of holding the worthless script.

As for Governor Gilpin, the United States Congress would unceremoniously remove him from office four weeks later. Several congressmen prepared formal charges against the disgraced former governor, accusing him of malfeasance, counterfeiting and even treason. There was even one rumor that the bogus money was somehow tied to a Southern plot to destroy confidence in U.S. currency. At least two congressmen authored bills that called for Gilpin to be hanged, although no statutes existed under which capital punishment could legally have been imposed in the case and the proposed bills were never actually introduced in congress.

But anger and frustration over the phoney money was not confined to Colorado's merchants; there was no little unhappiness among the soldiers out at Camp Weld. Many of the men had been carefully saving their money, which they now found to be worthless. A near riot erupted at the camp. There was talk of forming a lynch mob to "go get Gilpin."

Into the midst of the mob waded Major John Chivington, using all of his considerable powers of persuasion to prevent serious trouble. Appealing for calm, Chivington talked quietly to the soldiers. He told them that if they were in the army only for the money, they had joined for the wrong reasons anyway. This is a war, he reminded the troops. "It is not about pay. It is about good versus evil. It is about saving our Territory. It is about protecting our wives and children. It is about saving the United States of America from an evil aggressor" [Whitford, *The Battle of Glorieta Pass*, p. 13].

There were a few "boos" and a lot of muttering among the troops, but the situation was no longer out of hand. Genuine calm began to return as Chivington continued an eloquent appeal to the men's loyalty to the Union, and to their sense of responsibility to protect the land and people of the territory. His impromptu lecture continued on for more than thirty minutes. When he finished speaking and walked away at last, many angry soldiers left camp and never returned. A considerable number of other men, however, returned quietly to their barracks as soldiers. And a few of the others remained confused and sitting on the fence, undecided whether to leave or stay.

When it was finally calm enough to count remaining noses, the officers were pleased with the end result; only 1,500 of the soldiers had left camp, or slightly more than fifty percent. It is a tribute to the strength and persuasiveness of John Chivington that 1,200 others chose to remain as soldiers, even without pay.

Those who stayed at Camp Weld continued to train for the eventuality they would someday face Rebel invaders. Somehow, Gilpin and others found a way to keep the troops fed although the soldiers remained critically short of ammunition, horses, blankets and supplies.

CHAPTER FIVE

DEALING WITH SPLIT LOYALTIES

Alcohol has a most interesting effect on the men. Take a little Oporto wine, one quarter; native wine, "tambien," red "rot" lo mismo—mix. Net result, patriotism!

Ovando J. Hollister, Company F
First Colorado Volunteers

*P*ro- and anti-Union conflict in Colorado began to escalate at a serious and dizzying pace, partially as a result of Gilpin's bogus money and partially because "war fever" now gripped the entire nation. Much of the bitter and growing rivalry in Colorado would ultimately lead to tragedy.

In early September of 1861, a dozen or so pro-Confederate men quietly slipped out of Colorado and headed for the South. The leader of this group was a once-prominent Denver business-man named W. P. McClure. He soon approached Confederate General Sterling Price in San Antonio and proposed that he be allowed to organize a Rebel army in the Colorado Territory. McClure was convinced that there was enough strong pro-South-ern sentiment remaining in the Territory, especially after the script fiasco, that he could "easily raise a Confederate regiment" there, perhaps two regiments!

General Price liked the idea. Not only did the South need sol-diers, they particularly needed men who knew the Colorado ter-ritory to help with General Sibley's planned invasion. He commissioned McClure a captain in the Confederate army, and made the dozen men with him lieutenants. They were ordered to return to the Colorado Territory and attempt to raise two full companies of Confederate soldiers and "be prepared to assist the Confederate Army at the appropriate time."

Somehow, news of McClure's plan leaked to Union authorities. Federal troops at Fort Garland were alerted and ordered to intercept the thirteen Rebels when they re-entered the Colorado Territory from Texas. The government intelligence was so good that they knew the approximate date and exact location at which Captain McClure and the others would re-enter Colorado.

Like the remainder of the West, Colorado was desperately short of real soldiers, but that did not stop the army's effort to "get" the thirteen Confederates. The army quickly organized a sizable band of friendly Osage Indians, who were commissioned to "intercept and destroy" the McClure band.

Little is known of the battle that ensued when the Indians finally found the thirteen returning Rebel soldiers, but it is known that the Indians were completely and gruesomely successful. Several days later they returned to Fort Garland with the heads of all thirteen Rebel soldiers in burlap bags!

At about the same time, forty-two additional Confederate sympathizers were seized by an angry posse of loyalists at Bent's Old Fort in southeastern Colorado. Seventy-three Union soldiers consisting of a captain, thirty escorts and forty-two "personal" guards were sent to get the Rebels. One guard was assigned to each Confederate prisoner. Each guard led a prisoner's horse by day and guarded him by night. No one was permitted to speak on the nine day trip back to Denver. The policy of strict silence was to keep the Rebels from plotting their escape, as well as to make sure they did not conspire to conceal the truth when questioned later in Denver about their plans against the Union.

During the long journey, the escorts accidentally discovered a small cannon hidden in a fodder stack on a ranch belonging to a suspected Rebel sympathizer. The soldiers seized the cannon and took it with them back to Denver. There is no indication where the weapon came from, although it was widely believed that it was to have been used by an invading Confederate army at some point in the future.

The killing of the dozen Confederate officers and the capture of forty-two additional Rebels, together with other incidents that occurred about the same time seems to have finally put a halt to overt southern support in the Colorado Territory. On October 26, 1861, just two weeks before leaving office, Governor Gilpin was prompted to report to Congress that "the core of the Rebellion [in the Territory] has at present withdrawn, to gather strength," presumably in Texas and the Indian Nation (Oklahoma), with a view to someday returning and capturing the West.

But even with the most blatant Confederate threat eliminated, Gilpin knew that he had only bought a little time. There were daily reports of sympathizers actively organizing and planning for the eventual take-over of Colorado. Worse, were the reports from reliable sources that General Henry Sibley was already training an army with which to invade the West. And there were those persistent appeals from General Edward Canby in New Mexico asking that Colorado send him some help.

In answer to those requests, the governor authorized the formation of two small companies of volunteers that were to be recruited and trained specifically to quickly reach and assist Canby in his defense of New Mexico. These companies were originally named the "Jefferson Rangers" and the "Denver Guards." Their recruitment was an emergency stop-gap effort to slow the rebel advance until the First Colorado was ready for action. In the late summer months of 1861 these two companies were organized in the Pueblo-Cañon City area, south of Pikes Peak and present-day Colorado Springs.

On August 29, James H. Ford was appointed captain and authorized to raise one of the companies, which the local press immediately dubbed "Jim Ford's Independent Company." At Ford's request, the governor named Alexander Robb as first lieutenant and Cyrus DeForrest, Jr., as second lieutenant.

One day later, Gilpin appointed Theodore H. Dodd lieutenant and authorized him to raise a second company of volunteers. Dodd did the better job of recruiting and was soon promoted to captain of what was then called "Captain Dodd's Independent Company." The name stuck and the original names for the units were never again used. Initially, Dodd's company consisted of about seventy men, Ford's of about fifty.

Because Gilpin specifically planned to send these men to New Mexico as opposed to raising a local army to stay in and defend the Colorado Territory, he announced that these two newest companies were to be the start of the Second Colorado Volunteers. As it turned out, they ultimately would be all that ever existed of the Second Colorado.

One of the early volunteers for the Second Colorado was Alonzo Ferdinand Ickis. Although sporting a limited education, Ickis maintained a detailed diary of his time in the army and of the battles he witnessed. His writing was good enough to later get him promoted to the position of secretary to Colonel Kit Carson's unit of scouts and he became the official historian of that group.

Ickis says that Dodd was not the first commander of what became known as Dodd's Independent Company. He says a West Point graduate and former army regular, C. D. Hendron, was the first captain, assisted by Lieutenant J. C. W. Hall. Hall was a professional hunter and was an outstanding recruiter.

After the unit was formed with Dodd as second lieutenant, several of the men, including Captain Hendron, became involved in a barroom brawl with a group of locals. During the fight, Private Loyd was beaten to death and all the other men from the Second Colorado, including Captain Hendron and Privates Piatt, Custard and Cate, were injured.

Hendron returned to camp, rounded up a large number of volunteers, and returned to town where he arrested the locals involved in the fight. The arrest was clearly illegal, and for this breach of etiquette Hendron was demoted and drummed out of the service. Lieutenant Hall resigned immediately thereafter and Dodd was promoted to Captain.

By December, both of these independent companies had their full compliment of men, Dodd with ninety and Ford with ninety-one men, and had concluded their hasty training. Although both were technically infantry units, they were also supplied with horses and therefore were able to move swiftly.

On December 7, 1861, Dodd's unit pulled out of Cañon City, crossed the rugged Sangre de Cristo pass, and headed for Fort Garland in the southern portion of the state, some one hundred and ten miles distant. A week later, on December 14, the unit was formally mustered into the United States Army for a period of three years, with Dodd to remain as its captain. Even as a federal unit, however, Dodd's company retained the designation Company A, Second Colorado Volunteers (or Second Colorado Infantry).

Ford's company was right behind Dodd's. Ford left Cañon City on December 12, arriving at Fort Garland on the 21st as Company B, Second Colorado Volunteers. His unit was also sworn into the United States Army for a three-year period.

On December 26, both of these units were ordered to "proceed with haste to New Mexico and there to join up with General Edward R. S. Canby" to defend the territory from anticipated invasion. Colorado was formally in the war.

Almost immediately, the units ran into severe travel problems occasioned by the winter weather. Private Ickis wrote that the snow was two to four feet deep, and the mules simply could not haul the wagons along the trails. Long ropes were attached to the wagons, and scores of men pulled at the ropes to help move the wagons through the drifted snow. The bitter cold was almost unbearable, and two dozen of the men suffered frostbite during the trip. It was a harbinger of the future for the First Colorado.

Back in Denver, city officials now organized two additional companies of soldiers known as the "home guards." They were sworn into their units for six-month tours beginning October 1, 1861. These home guards were known simply as Number 1 and Number 2. Later, when the First Colorado had been sent to New Mexico, these two units moved to Camp Weld and kept the base in "good repair" until the regulars returned to Denver. Numbers 1 and 2 were formally recognized by the Department of War, and were paid as Union troops until they were mustered out of service in 1862.

At the same time, the ten companies of the First Colorado Volunteers were now engaged in rigorous training at Camp Weld. Although the massive desertions following the "federal treasury note" debacle had depleted the ranks of some of the companies, most still numbered between seventy and one hundred men.

Companies A, B, C, and D consisted primarily of men recruited in Denver's bars, although Company C also had about a dozen miners from the old Buckskin Joe area.

None of the recruits, however, had been in Colorado more than two or three years: all had come to the territory as miners, trappers or ranchers. The official records show that Company A, for example, consisted of seventeen men originally from New York, four from Pennsylvania, nine from Ohio, seven from Ireland, six from Canada, five from Vermont, four from Scotland, three from Illinois, two each from Germany, England, Virginia, Indiana, and New Jersey, and one each from Rhode Island, Maine, Maryland, Massachusetts, Michigan, Missouri, Iowa and Wales. The average height of the men in Company C was five-feet eight-and-a-half inches. The tallest man in the company measured six-feet three-and-a-half inches.

Company E was made up exclusively of former gold miners from the Oro City and Laurett areas. Company F was made up primarily of recruits from the South Clear Creek mining district, while Company G had men out of the Nevada, Empire City and Clear Creek mining camps.

Company H was recruited from Central City, Company I from Central City, Denver and the Clear Creek mining districts, and Company K from Central City and Denver.

While the numbers of men in this Colorado army were not especially impressive compared to the number of Confederates then planning to invade the Territory, their physical fitness made up for a lot of the numerical differences. They were, as one historian noted, "uncommonly hardy and well seasoned, and not in the habit of being afraid." Virtually all of the men had worked for months or years in the outdoors, dragging heavy rock and ore out of mines in the high mountain country; they were said to be unusually fine physical specimens. And because virtually all of the men were accustomed to hunting deer, elk and antelope for food, almost all were excellent shots. These attributes would serve the men well in the weeks and months to come.

But even the formal establishment of military units in Colorado, and the imprisonment or killing of known Southern sympathizers, did not completely halt the bubbling and churning division of loyalties in the area. On orders from Fort Leavenworth (the military headquarters for the Territory), Colorado's Company F was sent to Fort Laramie, Wyoming, to get badly needed military supplies that could not be obtained locally. Colonel Alexander, who was the base commander at Fort Laramie, was an outspoken and ardent supporter of the Confederacy.

Although Fort Laramie had a surplus of everything the Coloradans needed, he refused to permit the visitors to sleep in military quarters, and denied their requests for arms, ammunition and clothing. He eventually did supply them with food, but only with "wormy, condemned bacon and stale bread." He also refused to lend them any wagons with which to return the questionable food stuffs to Denver. As a result, soldiers had to ride all the way back to Denver, 180 miles away, where they picked up empty wagons and returned to Fort Laramie for the supplies.

In spite of the difficulties, however, training continued and gradually the units at Camp Weld began to take on the appearance of an army. At last, in early December 1861, as Henry Sibley was poised to invade New Mexico from the south, the Colorado soldiers appeared ready for battle. Three of the companies were sent to Fort Wise (later known as Fort Lyon) in eastern Colorado to "guard those approaches to the state." The remaining units were held at Camp Weld "in a high state of readiness."

Their readiness would soon be tested.

CHAPTER SIX

THE WAR BEGINS

At our first camp, on St. Vrain's Creek, a dispute occurred in the party as to whether bacon, used to oil firearms, would or would not make them rust. Little Hawley had ten dollars that said bacon grease was the best that could be used. Judge, on the other side, would bet ten dollars, but he had not got it with him. He put up five, the balance to be staked at the time of trial. As soon as the money was up, the crowd adjourned to an adjoining grocery, procured two buckets of milk and a gallon of whiskey, and bound the bet by drinking the stakes. The bettors joined us, and as neither ever mentioned it again, the merits of the case are still in the dark!

Ovando J. Hollister, Company F
First Colorado Volunteers

*C*hristmas, 1861. It had been a grim year for Americans on both sides of the Mason-Dixon line. Closely following the secession of eleven southern states, Rebels had shelled Fort Sumter on April 12, 1861. Three days later, President Lincoln called for 75,000 volunteers to defend the Union.

Despite the Confederate attack at Fort Sumter, things at first seemed to go quite well for the Union. On April 19, the president formally proclaimed a blockade of the South, and ships of the Union navy began to effectively cut off shipping to and from Southern ports. As the Yankee blockade took hold, trade with the rest of the world became increasingly difficult for the Confederates. They were already beginning to get desperate for food, arms and other supplies and it became increasingly urgent that General Sibley launch his western expedition and obtain those safe new harbors in California and Oregon.

For the North, things did not look so bad at that point in the war. The Union had 71 percent of the nation's population, 81 percent of its bank deposits, 72 percent of the railroads and, most important, 85 percent of its manufacturing capabilities. Most Yankees were supremely confident not only that the South could be whipped, but that the whipping could be administered with a minimum of difficulty and in a very brief period of time! Many residents in and around Washington thought the war was a frivolous lark, and they were eager to witness the first battle so that they could see a Union force quickly defeat those upstart Southerners.

In New Mexico the picture was not as bright for the Union. On June 16, Colonel Canby ordered Major Isaac Lynde to abandon Fort McLane on the Texas state line and move his command to Fort Fillmore, near the town of Mesilla, and closer to Fort Craig. John Baylor's incursion from Texas into the extreme southeastern corner of New Mexico was the only Confederate invasion of Union territory anywhere in the country. And of course, Washington paid little attention to the fact that a "handful of Rebels were sitting in the uninhabited desert of a western territory." The area was just too remote and too thinly populated to be of concern in the East.

On June 17, the Union inaugurated a new reconaissance technique; a hot air balloon soared aloft and sent back to the White House the first message telegraphed from an airborne soldier; a note that the point of observation commanded an area nearly fifty miles in diameter! Congressmen were duly impressed, and said the balloon was another of the modern weapons in the Northern arsenal which promised to help make short work of the Southern insurgency.

On June 27, in an effort to make soldiering more tolerable and attract more volunteers, the Confederacy announced it would raise soldiers' pay from eleven dollars a month to eighteen dollars a month. Two days later, the U.S. War Department announced pay in the North would be raised to sixteen dollars a month, "payable in spendable currency," an obvious jab at Confederate money that was beginning to circulate in the South and which had questionable value.

Soldiers on both sides were preparing for conflict with great difficulty. Both had trouble getting adequate clothing; many of the uniforms were made of "shoddy" (rewoven) wool, which had a tendency to fall apart whenever it got wet. Confederate soldiers had even more trouble getting shoes, and many of them would fight the war barefooted, even in snow and bitter cold weather.

Food for the troops was also a problem. The armies on both sides tried to keep the soldiers supplied with flour, corn, pork, beans, coffee and sugar. When they were on the move, the soldiers were issued salt pork and hardtack biscuits, and coffee. Most often, though, poor handling and refrigeration techniques meant the meat was rancid and the vegetables spoiled long before they reached the troops. Within weeks of the start of the war, soldiers for both Union and Confederacy were usually just living off the land: stealing chickens, sheep and pigs and picking whatever crops they could find along the way on which to exist.

It was July 1861 before the seriousness of the war began to finally be realized in the North. On the 21st of that month, as hundreds of Washington spectators watched, Union troops were completely defeated and routed after the first battle of Bull Run. Suddenly much of the early lighthearted euphoria disappeared and the Civil War became a serious matter. If it was difficult for Governor Gilpin to get the attention of Washington before Bull Run, it was completely impossible now.

By August, General Sibley was in San Antonio raising and training his Western Expeditionary Force. By early September, nearly five thousand Confederate recruits were undergoing basic training. They were well armed and outfitted, probably better than any other Confederate troops then in training. After all, Henry Sibley knew where to get anything he needed to carry out his critical assignment; much of it was the material and supplies brought South from those abandoned Union forts in New Mexico and elsewhere in the West. Besides, his was to be an elite unit undertaking a mission crucial to the survival of the South, and they would be denied nothing.

In the New Mexico Territory, days were especially dark and forboding for the beleaguered Union forces. In Mesilla on March 4, Confederates held a huge outdoor rally where passionate speeches were made, urging citizens to join the Confederacy. One of the speakers told the crowd, "The hell of abolitionism glooms to the north; the Eden of liberty, equality, and right smiles upon you from the South. Choose between them!" The citizens responded by holding a referendum at which they agreed to join the Confederacy, providing only that their territory could join as an independent state and not as a part of any expanded Texas!

At Taos in August, a crowd of pro-Confederate sympathizers gathered in the town square and sang anti-Union songs. Finally, they pulled down a long cottonwood flag pole and ripped the United States flag from the pole, preparing to put a Confederate flag in its place.

Kit Carson happened into town at precisely that moment. He fired his pistol into the air to get the attention of the crowd, then ordered them to back away from the flagpole. Carson sent a man in the crowd (whom Carson apparently knew to be a Union supporter) into the town hardware store to obtain a hammer and some nails. When the man returned, Carson nailed the Union banner to the pole, and asked for volunteers to help him raise the pole. A dozen men stepped forward and the pole was raised without incident. When the pole was firmly in place once again, Carson turned to the crowd and said, "New Mexico has been Union since the Territory was won from Mexico and Union she will stay!" The crowd quietly dispersed.

At about the same time Edward Canby, the senior officer in the area, in Sibley's absence, was formally promoted to the rank of brigadier general, and told to "defend the Territory." With what? Obviously, defending New Mexico was easier said than done.

For starters, there were virtually no troops left in the region with which Canby could defend anything. Those soldiers who had not gone to join the Confederacy had been called back East to join the Union army. Worse than that from Canby's point of view, when they pulled out of New Mexico the soldiers had taken with them all the weapons, ammunition and supplies they could carry. They also took horses, mules and wagons. Defending the Territory without men, arms, or transportation was a tall order.

The War Department kept reassuring General Canby. They had permitted a small number of veteran soldiers to remain in

New Mexico, and pointed out that two companies of the Second Colorado Volunteers were also on hand. In addition, the New Mexico territorial government had promised to support the Union by committing five companies of militiamen to the effort. Those five companies consisted of about two thousand five hundred men, and the War Department felt that was a sufficient number to discourage any enemy thoughts of invasion.

But General Canby knew what the War Department did not know; those five companies of New Mexican volunteers were inadequate in every respect: they had no training, terrible weapons, and questionable loyalties. Many of them still deeply resented the United States for having wrested the territory from Mexico a decade earlier. Canby doubted they could be counted on in the event of hostilities.

(Whether the later failure of many of these units was a self-fulfilling prophecy remains a question. Alvin Josephy says the New Mexico troops were poorly trained and widely distrusted by Anglos, and they suffered tremendously because of the language barrier; most of the New Mexicans spoke only Spanish and most of the Union regulars spoke only English. As a result, says Josephy, "many of the native militiamen had no heart or interest in the Anglo's fight; twice the troops mutinied and deserted." Throughout the campaign the few Union soldiers were as suspicious of the New Mexico militiamen as they were of the Confederates and Confederate sympathizers.)

And hostilities were coming. By June 16, a Rebel invasion of southeastern New Mexico appeared imminent. Canby ordered Major Isaac Lynde to hasten his departure from the poorly constructed Fort McLane, situated virtually on the Texas state line, and move quickly to the larger and more defensible Fort Fillmore near the town of Mesilla. The general sent Lynde wagonloads of ammunition, weapons and other supplies, everything he could spare, to make certain Lynde could hold out against any Confederate threat.

Canby also sent another letter to the Colorado Governor William Gilpin, requesting that he send more reinforcements immediately. Canby's letter stated that although he was not technically authorized to request the support, a failure to do so would almost certainly result in a Confederate victory in New Mexico, followed shortly by an invasion of Colorado.

Canby's predictions began coming true about the time his letter arrived in Denver. On July 25, Confederate Colonel John Baylor arrived outside Fort Fillmore with the lead elements of the invading Confederate army. These were the men who had already been dubbed "Baylor's babes," and they were eager to prove themselves in battle. Baylor had with him only a vanguard of 258 men and knew that he was outnumbered by Union soldiers in the area. But Baylor also had information that local Union commanders were jittery and felt that they might succumb to a brazen bluff.

Colonel Baylor camped within a quarter-mile of the fort and sent a messenger to Lynde warning that unless he surrendered at once, the fort would be reduced to rubble with all the Union soldiers still inside it. Major Lynde, who had seven hundred Union regulars and New Mexico militiamen with him, believed he was heavily outnumbered. Confused and frightened, Lynde did nothing in response to the note.

Colonel Baylor assumed that Lynde's delay meant that the Union commander had chosen to fight. Knowing that he could not take the fort by force, Baylor then retreated back into the town of Mesilla. A short time later, Major Lynde cautiously sent about three hundred men toward the town in an effort to find out what was going on. The Confederates spotted the approaching Union troops and opened fire, killing three men and wounding six others. The Yankees turned and fled back to the base.

Lynde was not totally convinced that a huge Confederate army was about to overrun his position. He now ordered his men to pack up and pull out as fast as they could do so; by 1 A.M., all of the Union soldiers were on the trail heading for Fort Stanton some 140 miles to the northeast. Unfortunately, before they left the fort many of the men broke into the post's stock of whiskey and filled their canteens with the alcohol. The liquor may have tasted good and given the men courage during the night, but by the middle of the next day the temperature had reached 100 degrees and the men began to suffer terribly from a lack of water.

Major Lynde and some of the soldiers finally arrived at the village of San Agustin Springs, but the remainder of his troops were strung out for ten miles behind him.

The pursuing Confederates under Colonel Baylor soon overtook the Yankee stragglers and took them prisoner. By early afternoon, five hundred Yankee soldiers were in Baylor's custody and the Confederates had surrounded the town where Lynde and the remaining Union forces were stopped. Lynde later complained that he could not find one hundred men who were sober and willing to fight. As a result, he surrendered his command, giving the Confederates their first major military victory in New Mexico without ever having fired a shot!

Baylor lined up the captured Union soldiers and lectured them about their options: they could either march back to Texas and be placed in prisoner-of-war camps, or they could join the Confederate army. Most of the Union soldiers did not hesitate to add insult to the injury of their surrender; they quickly switched sides. It was said that virtually all seven hundred of them volunteered to join the Rebel forces.

General Canby now occupied Fort Craig, a sizable old fortress situated on the west banks of the Rio Grande about halfway between El Paso and Albuquerque. Behind the fort rise the foothills of the southern Rocky Mountains, densely covered with scrub oak, pine trees, sagebrush, and populated by hostile Apache Indians. In spite of the Indians, it would be good land to get lost in, to escape in, if one had to do so. Canby made note of the possibilities.

To the front of the fort the land sloped gently down to the river some two hundred yards away. One of the major north-south trails passes between the fort and the river; another trail parallels the river on the far side. On the opposite shore, a hill rises sharply so that the east bank is really a cliff soaring two hundred feet higher than the water level.

The fort itself, like most of the others in the region, had been constructed under the watchful supervision of that master and detail-oriented soldier, Henry Sibley. He knew everything there was to know about the fort: its strengths and weaknesses, escape routes, placement of guns and portals.

The fort was originally built as quarters for two full companies of dragoons. It was constructed of thick adobe, with holes left in the walls so that soldiers could fire their rifles without exposing themselves to the enemy. At the time of construction, it was assumed that any enemy would be Indian, and the fort was certainly more than adequate to keep Indians at bay. However, the adobe offered little protection from weapons larger than rifles and arrows, weapons such as howitzers or artillery. Canby knew that heavy guns could knock down the walls one big chunk at a time. In any case, as defense against a modern army the fort was almost worthless.

Several miles downstream from Fort Craig is the little town of Paradero, and three miles in the other direction is the town of Valverde (sometimes misspelled "Val Verde"). And just beyond the latter town is the point at which the trail that parallels the river on the east side crosses the stream to join the main trail on the west. The crossing point is called North Ford, and it soon would become the focal point for troops on both sides.

Despite poor communications, Canby was well aware that Confederates were already operating south and east of Fort Craig. He knew, too, that many of his soldiers had deserted and joined the Rebels at Fort Fillmore.

The one reliable, trained helper still available to General Canby was Kit Carson. Carson had already forged a reputation for himself as an army scout and Indian fighter. He was loyal to the Union and eager to fight Rebels. That spirit, plus his unquestioned ability with a rifle made him a most valuable ally to the hard-pressed Canby.

Carson asked to become a regular soldier in the Union army. Canby was happy to oblige, and swore Carson in for a six-month enlistment. And using the power of his rank, General Canby appointed Carson lieutenant colonel and "second-in-command of United States forces in New Mexico Territory." (That grand title was neither particularly meaningful nor especially surprising since Carson represented the only other regular soldier at Fort Craig.)

The two men then set about trying to find a way to offer some resistance to the oncoming Confederates. Carson spent his days concentrating on scouting out trails, villages, and, most importantly, places where a small number of soldiers might lie in ambush and have a reasonable chance of inflicting serious damage to large numbers of enemy soldiers.

Canby spent his time recruiting and training local farmers and villagers. Because of the shortage of both arms and ammunition, the volunteers were told to provide their own weapons and they showed up with an interesting variety of fire power. These New Mexico militiamen were armed with rusty old shotguns, a handful of muzzle-loading rifles, battered revolvers, and a number of cavalry sabers.

The training itself was sporadic and difficult to accomplish, even with help from the Second Colorado Volunteers who were also based at Fort Craig. Although the local residents apparently were sincere about defending their Territory, they also had other responsibilities that must take precedence over training. After all, they had crops to tend or cows to milk or businesses to run and could spend only a little time each day learning how to soldier.

General Canby, therefore, must have been sorely tempted to take up the "generous" offer from his brother-in-law that Christmas holiday. Canby received a letter from General Sibley, warning him that New Mexico was about to fall into Confederate hands and suggesting that Canby get quickly out of the area. There was no hint of sarcasm in the letter; it was a genuine warning from friend to friend, or brother-in-law to brother-in-law; get out while you still can! Canby ignored the implied threat, but must often have wondered whether anyone cared whether he stayed or left for safer environs elsewhere.

After obtaining the blessings of Jefferson Davis, Sibley returned to Texas to begin recruiting his Western Expeditionary Force. In August, he appointed another former Union officer— Henry C. McNeill, as his lieutenant colonel. McNeill began recruiting men. One of his first volunteers was William R. Scurry of DeWitt, Texas, a prominent attorney and secessionist. Like McNeill, Scurry was named a lieutenant colonel. Also among the early volunteers were Colonel (later General) Thomas Green, Captain (later Major) John S. Shropshire, Major Samuel Lockridge and Private Joseph D. Sayers, a future governor of Texas. (It was highly unusual that Sibley appointed his own officers; Confederate law, like Union law, permitted the volunteers to elect their own officers. Sibley said, however, he had to appoint his own officers to be certain he had the right men in each post.)

By late September, 1861, Sibley had well over three thousand soldiers, most sources believe many more, fully trained and ready for the invasion. Historian Alvin Josephy, Jr., says Sibley had more than 3,500 men with him at this time and some sources say the Confederates in the Western Expeditionary Force numbered closer to four thousand. (Throughout the campaign, the number of men in Sibley's command would fluctuate greatly—growing lower because of battle casualties, sickness and desertions, and climbing higher with new recruits attracted from conquered territory. As a result of these constant changes it was difficult at any given time to know how many men were participating in the Rebel invasion of New Mexico.)

His army, which had trained in a camp five miles northeast of San Antonio on the highway to Austin, consisted of three regiments of infantry, five additional companies of cavalry under the command of Colonel Baylor, two batteries, and three independent companies.

These units would shortly unite with the six companies of Colonel Baylor's 2nd Texas Mounted Rifles and another company of Texas "Brigands," which operated as an independent company. These seven additional companies swelled Sibley's force by another twelve hundred or so men.

Sibley soon dispatched one of these companies westward to secure the Gila River Trail across the southern end of the territory, and to officially occupy the town of Tucson. Although they were not needed as an occupying force, since Tucson had already officially voted to join the Confederacy, their presence so near the California state border would discourage any Union troops from coming eastward out of California to interfere with Sibley's planned northward drive. The main body of Sibley's invasion force was gathered at Fort Bliss in El Paso. At that moment, El Paso was the westernmost outpost of the Confederacy.

In addition to his troops, Sibley was well prepared in other ways to carry out his invasion of the West. He had well over three hundred wagonloads of supplies (some say closer to four hundred wagons) everything needed to carry his men all the way to Fort Laramie. There were wagons loaded with food, wagons loaded with spare rifles and pistols, wagons full of black powder, several with kerosene for lanterns, and a number with a variety of other goods such as medical supplies, spare clothing, blankets, tents, and the other wares required to support the soldiers. The troops were accompanied by more than eighty mounted cannons of various size and descriptions, and they, in turn, by caissons of ammunition. In addition, Sibley had a herd of fifty or so steers that would follow the troops and provide beef to feed them.

Virtually all of the Confederates were mounted, since a foot soldier could hardly be expected to walk from Fort Bliss to Fort Laramie and from there to Los Angeles! And in addition to the four thousand or so saddle horses there were another eight hundred to one thousand horses and mules that were to pull the wagons. In addition to government-issue weapons, the Texans carried hunting weapons of all types, including shotguns.

On November 7, the men in Sibley's brigade were told to make ready for departure. Twenty-four hours later, Colonel John Reily told the assembled troops, "You are on the eve of leaving a land that many of us may never again see. You have bid adieu to your friends, home, and happy firesides to fight in the field in the defense of your country's honor. You are soldiers together. The people of Texas expect much from you. Much is to be done. Much will be done; I am confident of the result." Reily closed his speech with a prayer.

General Sibley also spoke to the troops, but he was not a polished speaker and aroused little emotional support. There is no official record of his remarks. At the close of the ceremony, the ladies of Nacogdoches presented General Sibley with a regimental flag.

Then, companies A and F, 1st squadron, under Captains William Hardeman and James Crosson had the honor of leading the procession out of camp toward New Mexico. Two days later, Colonel Scurry, assisted by Major Charles Pyron, pulled out with companies B, G, D and H of the 2nd and 3rd squadrons, and companies C, I, E and K of the 4th and 5th squadrons. The last of the recruits, the third regiment under Colonel John Sutton, marched out of San Antonio on November 28.

In one final attempt to avoid hostilities in New Mexico, General Sibley issued a proclamation on December 20, 1861. The document pointed out that because of geography, common commercial interests and "future destinies," New Mexico was rightfully a part of the South. He urged the citizens of the territory to denounce their allegiance to the United States and join the Confederacy. The document also sought to win any soldiers who might have wavering Union loyalties or latent Southern sympathies. Sibley appealed in the "name of former friendship to my old comrades in arms still in the ranks of the Union's defenders, to renounce allegiance to the usurpers of their government and liberties." He promised that the men would be well received in the Confederate army, and said, "I am empowered to receive you into the service of the Confederate states, the officers upon their commissions, the men upon their enlistments." Then, Sibley ordered his army to begin its campaign to capture the West.

After issuing the proclamation Sibley, too, left San Antonio. Many of the Confederate units marched directly to Fort Thorn, New Mexico, located on the Texas line and which had already been abandoned by Federal troops. Sibley and some of the remaining Texans went first to Fort Bliss, near El Paso, leaving there for the Mesilla Valley of New Mexico on December 12. On Christmas morning, the Texans occupied the town of Mesilla where they were warmly welcomed by local citizens.

During the march from San Antonio westward, Private Robert Pinkney, described as the "Brigade clown," was court-martialed for speaking disrespectfully to an officer and threatening to physically attack a noncommissioned officer. Pinkney was sentenced to twenty days in the brig at Fort Bliss.

Two other privates, James Tobin and Thomas N. Harvey, got into an argument that ended when Harvey pulled a knife and killed Tobin. After the troops arrived at Fort Bliss, Sibley ordered a court martial for Harvey. He was quickly convicted of murder and ordered executed by firing squad. Harvey took a two-inch-square piece of white paper and pinned it to his breast, and asked the men of the firing squad to aim carefully at the target. Harvey said he did not fear death and did not care to live; he was executed and buried at Fort Bliss.

As disquieting as those incidents were, something far more ominous happened about the time the troops finally arrived at El Paso. More than a dozen men came down with the measles and soon more than a hundred were infected. Fifteen of the men eventually died, and a number of others were physically unfit to participate in military action for several weeks.

Even worse than the measles, smallpox now broke out among the troops camped in southeastern New Mexico. Before the campaign ended, several hundred Confederates would be sickened by smallpox and more than one hundred killed by the disease. At times, smallpox was so rampant as to seriously compromise the effectiveness of General Sibley's troops. In ten days, he would battle Union forces at the North Ford, and would be able to field only about two-thirds of his soldiers.

Still another serious problem cropped up while the men were in El Paso and the Mesilla valley. Already they were facing a growing and increasingly severe shortage of supplies. Private Theophilus Noel wrote in his diary, "Forage there was none; commissary supplies were getting scarce; the cold season was coming on, clothing was being needed; all of which the country afforded none. Our quartermaster brought no supplies with him and none was to be had in the territory." General Sibley was aware of the shortages, but assured his troops that there would be plenty of everything as soon as the troops captured Fort Craig, Albuquerque and Santa Fe.

On January 14, soldiers under the command of Major Charles Pyron captured the old Federal camp at Alamosa, lying on the Rio Grande 32 miles south of Fort Craig. They had expected to find the little fort defended by Union soldiers and were disappionted to find that it had already been abandoned. Worse than that, all of the supplies on which the Texans had counted were long gone. Most were carried away by retreating Union soldiers; what they could not carry, they scattered. The streets of the town were literally covered with coffee, rice, sugar, flour and beans.

That night, a band of Apache Indians raided the Confederate camp at Willow Bar, and stole about eighty horses and another eighty mules. Major Pyron ordered a large patrol to pursue the Indians and recapture the animals. The Texans chased the Apaches for two full days, but finally lost them altogether in the hill country. They returned to camp empty-handed three nights later, exhausted, hungry and thirsty.

On February 3, the 1st Regiment arrived at Fort Thorn on the east bank of the Rio Grande. On February 5, the 2nd regiment arrived, and on the 12th, the 3rd regiment. Smallpox broke out at Fort Thorn on February 7.

(On February 6, Union forces under the command of General Ulysses S. Grant captured Fort Henry, after most of the Confederate defenders had fled to Fort Donelson. The seizure of Fort Henry opened the Tennessee River to Union gunboats as far south as northern Alabama.)

Citizens of El Paso lined the streets on the morning of February 6, waving flags and tossing flowers at Sibley's troops as they made their way from Fort Bliss, through the city, and northward toward New Mexico. Excitement gripped civilians and soldiers alike as this grand parade passed in review. It was, indeed, a formidable force. Interestingly, it did not include Henry Sibley himself; the general had ridden to San Antonio for some last minute conferences before the campaign actually began.

The troops who crossed from Texas into the Mesilla Valley were under the command of Lieutenant Colonel William R. Scurry, Sibley's second-in-command and a veteran front line officer. Scurry was a member of a noted Texas family, originally from Tennessee. He had fought under General Zachary Taylor in the Mexican War and returned to Texas to take up the practice of law. He served as a district attorney in Texas until the Civil War erupted, whereupon he was commissioned a lieutenant colonel and assigned to Sibley's Western Expeditionary Force.

The Confederate troops under Colonel Scurry marched into the center of the valley and made camp, just as cold, wind-driven rain began to fall from dark, low-hanging clouds. The Rebels pitched their tents and awaited the arrival of Sibley. It proved to be a long wait.

The camp was a place of misery for the keyed-up soldiers, eager for the start of battle. The weather was awful and the tension made everything much worse. They needed fires to keep warm, but firewood was scarce and what little they found was soaked with water. The horses suffered from the cold and a shortage of food as much as the men, and several animals were lost during the cold winter storm. Smallpox broke out in the camp on the third day.

For nine long days the cold and unhappy soldiers waited and mumbled and cursed their officers as soldiers are wont to do. By the time General Sibley finally rode into the camp, the Western Expeditionary Force could hardly wait for the fighting to begin!

PART THREE

Bloody Confrontation

THE NEW MEXICO CAMPAIGN
Fort Union
Santa Fe
Glorieta
Albuquerque
Rio Grande
Peralta
North Ford (Valverde)
Fort Craig
NEW MEXICO TERRITORY
Fort Thorn
Fort Bliss
El Paso del Norte
MEXICO
TEXAS

CHAPTER SEVEN

THE BATTLE OF NORTH FORD (VALVERDE)

Several serious incidents occurred between local authorities and the military, and the army declared open season on [Denver]. Soldiers roamed wherever they wished, stealing whatever they found. Major Chivington said, "they only came back to camp to get their meals."

Ovando J. Hollister, Company F
First Colorado Volunteers

General Canby was moving as fast as he could to prepare for the oncoming Confederates, but he knew in his heart that he could not offer them much of a battle. On paper, the two opposing armies may have looked reasonably well matched; Sibley with somewhere in the vicinity of 4000 to 5000 soldiers and Canby with a force numbering about 3600.

The similarities, however, stopped at raw numbers. Canby's 3600 "soldiers" were mostly local volunteers who were poorly trained and inadequately armed. There was not even any assurance the volunteers would bother to show up when the battle was finally joined. And because they were only part time volunteers, they were under no obligation to obey Canby's orders. Canby viewed these men as well meaning, but of little real value when it came to fighting.

As for "regulars," Canby was blessed with fewer than five hundred men. They included about three hundred soldiers left behind when the remainder of the troops either left for Washington, or headed for Dixie. He also had his friend Kit Carson, plus two "independent" companies of Coloradans from the Second

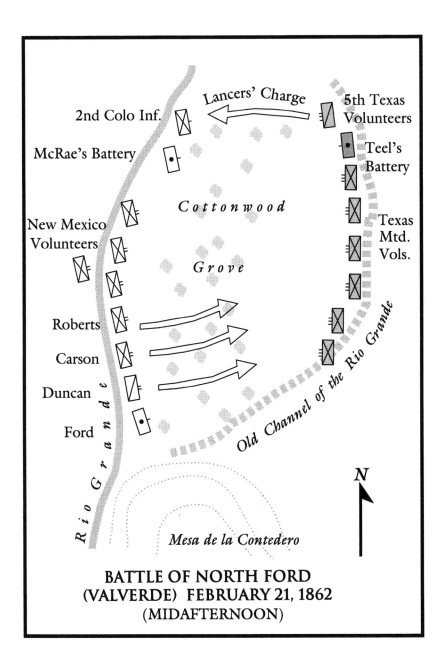

2nd Colo Inf.

McRae's Battery

New Mexico
Volunteers

Roberts

Carson

Duncan

Ford

Cottonwood

Grove

Lancers' Charge

5th Texas
Volunteers

Teel's
Battery

Texas
Mtd.
Vols.

Old Channel of the Rio Grande

Rio Grande

N

Mesa de la Contedero

**BATTLE OF NORTH FORD
(VALVERDE) FEBRUARY 21, 1862
(MIDAFTERNOON)**

Colorado Volunteers. (Historian Josephy says Canby had 220 regulars and possibly as many as 720 men of the Second Colorado.)

The New Mexico Territorial government believed there was no way that Canby and his handful of followers could possibly stop the Confederate invasion. Governor Henry Connelly had already abandoned his offices in the territorial capital building at Santa Fe and moved thirty-five miles east to Las Vegas. It was said he kept his suitcases packed and a wagon with a fine team of horses ready at all times, in the event it became necessary to make a hasty retreat from Las Vegas and New Mexico.

But as desperate as his situation was, Canby was determined to do everything possible to stop the Confederate invasion. He rounded up as much of a force as he could muster and raced out to meet the oncoming enemy.

Sibley was also having his troubles. Many of his horses and mules had already escaped and wandered to the Rio Grande to get water. There they were captured by natives and turned over to the Union forces. The loss of these animals was a severe blow to Sibley, and some sources say that the Confederates soon became so short of horses that they had to burn many wagons filled with provisions and personal property. In addition, nearly a quarter of all the Confederate soldiers were sick and unable to go to battle.

On top of all that, there was the personal animosity between John Baylor and Henry Sibley. Jealous of one another's command they made no effort to disguise their dislike of each other. And Josephy says that Baylor considered Sibley a "coward and a disgrace to the South," and says that many of Sibley's own soldiers "considered him a drunk."

On the morning of February 7, General Sibley began moving northward with 2515 men who were prepared for battle. Some of his remaining soldiers were on guard duty at the two captured Union forts. Some had gone to Tucson, and several hundred were ill with smallpox, or were otherwise not set for battle. It didn't matter. Sibley was confident he would meet nothing more than token resistance. His troops quickly seized another unmanned and undefended Union Fort, simply by walking inside and running a Confederate flag up the pole.

Then, Sibley headed north once again. Besides his troops, Sibley was accompanied by fifteen pieces of artillery and about one hundred wagonloads of supplies. (He had emptied or burned the remainder of the three hundred wagons with which he left El Paso. It would have made little difference even if they had still contained supplies, however, because so many horses had died or escaped that there were no animals available to pull any additional wagons.) The Confederate campaign to capture the West was formally underway, and the troops were in high spirits.

In the Union camp, Canby began hearing rumors that the Texans were actually underway and headed for Fort Union. Reports from citizens and from several of Canby's scouts said the Confederates were on the east side of the Rio Grande, and had begun moving north along the main trail that would take them to Albuquerque and Santa Fe. Canby wished for additional time, but knew he would not have that luxury. Fortunately, Kit Carson knew just the place to set up an ambush of the Texans. Canby rounded up all available volunteers and raced for the trail.

The Confederates camped eight miles south of Fort Craig on the night of February 15. On the following morning, Sibley ordered his toops to march forward "prepared for battle"; he fully anticipated meeting his brother-in-law sometime during the day.

Crossing the river at the North Ford near Valverde, Colonel Canby took the Union troops southward along the trail for three miles. There, the trail passed over a steep hill that was lined with rocks and trees—the perfect place for a Union ambush. Canby positioned his soldiers along the crest of the hill and waited nervously for the oncoming enemy. It would not be a lengthy wait.

Two hours later, the vanguard of Confederate troops obligingly showed up, riding along the trail straight toward the waiting Yankees. Several hundred Union soldiers and volunteers, virtually none of whom save for Canby and Carson had been tested by fire, aimed their rifles and waited.

Unfortunately for Canby's plan of ambush, the volunteers did not wait long enough. One of the militiamen fired his rifle at the Rebels, even though the enemy was still a good quarter of a mile distant. As if the shot were a signal, scores of other volunteers immediately fired their weapons in a meaningless assault on the air that separated the armies.

The surprised Confederates milled around for a few seconds in confusion. Despite Sibley's admonition, they had not anticipated an attack and were uncertain as to how to handle it. However, the veteran officers quickly regained their composure and began firing artillery and long range minié rifles at the Union troops. Every tenth man was ordered to the front and told to stay there "at all hazards."

The enemies exchanged gunfire without significant result for more than two hours; only one Texan was slightly wounded and the Union forces suffered one man killed. The Union victim was seventeen-year-old Private Hugh Brown, a member of Company B in Dodd's Independent unit. Brown, "the youngest and smallest boy in our company," was hit by grape shot and critically wounded. He was carried back to Fort Craig but died the following morning, the first Coloradan to die in battle with the invaders.

As for the exchange of gunfire, nothing significant was accomplished by either side. However, had the Texans charged the little Union force during the battle it appears likely that the Yankees would have turned and fled. (Some accounts say most of the New Mexico militiamen fled anyway; Josephy says several hundred vanished during or after this initial confrontation.) In fact, the Rebels did not attack. Most dismounted and sought shelter, while a rider was sent back to warn the main body of troops. While the messenger was searching for General Sibley, darkness fell and the engagement was broken off.

For some reason that was never explained, Canby pulled his troops out of their position on the ridge as soon as it got dark. He led the soldiers back to Fort Craig, where they were fed their supper and bedded down for the night. Night attacks were rare during the era and perhaps Canby felt there would be no action before daylight anyway. Or perhaps the general felt that fresh troops would fight a better battle on the morrow. Whatever the Union commander's unshared reasoning, it did not work.

The Confederates assumed that the Yankees had been forced to retreat, and dutifully reported that they had soundly whipped the Yankees. The Texans were elated to find the enemy such an easy foe, and there was great celebrating that night in the Confederate camp.

The following night, the Union force scored a strategically important victory of sorts. Army scouts slipped into the rear of the Confederate camp and stole 164 of the enemy's mules. Between the losses to Union raiders, attacks by Indians and starvation due to the lack of forage, Sibley's New Mexico campaign was soon severely crippled by a lack of horses and mules.

About the time of the Confederate invasion of New Mexico, the U.S. Army authorized a veteran soldier, Captain James Graydon (known as "Paddy" to his friends) to organize a completely independent military spy company. Graydon's men dressed in civilian clothing and frequently posed as farmers or shopkeepers in the towns through which the Confederates traveled. Graydon's group operated free from any normal military restraints; they were asked only to provide as much information as possible about the enemy, and when the occasion permitted it, to "harass the enemy by sabotage or other available means." The men who served in the spy company thoroughly loved the assignment. They would prove their value again and again as the South's campaign unfolded.

After Canby withdrew his volunteers to Fort Craig on the night of February 16, Graydon undertook a sabotage effort that nearly ended in tragedy for his soldiers. The captain and three of his men obtained two large wooden boxes. Into each box they stuffed six of the 24-pounder howitzer shells after first trimming their fuses. Then Graydon's men "borrowed" a pair of old, broken-down mules from a nearby farm. The boxes of explosives were strapped to the mules, making the animals living bombs.

About the middle of the night, Graydon and his companions, together with their mules, swam across the Rio Grande a few miles south of Fort Craig. Reaching the opposite bank, they worked their way through trees and brush until they were within a few hundred yards of the sleeping Confederates.

Having successfully reached the enemy camp without being spotted, Graydon quietly ignited the fuses. Then he slapped each of the mules on the fanny, assuming they would gallop forward in fright, running directly into the middle of the Confederate camp. The resulting explosion would most certainly raise havoc, possibly inflict some casualties, stampede the Confederate's beef herd, and definitely demoralize the enemy.

Unfortunately for Graydon, he had failed to learn the habits of the mules he had recruited for the suicide mission. The animals had been trained to follow after their master without halter or tether. When Graydon and his men turned and began running from the edge of the Rebel camp they were startled to find the mules with their burning bombs trotting along right behind them.

The panicked Union soldiers shouted at the mules and raced for their horses, but had barely mounted when the mules blew up. All of the Yankees were knocked to the ground, and one of the horses was slightly injured. Fortunately, all of Graydon's men managed to escape and return safely (although somewhat bruised) to Union lines a few hours later.

That day, the eyes of the world were focused on Fort Donelson in Tennessee. Bad weather continued to hamper Union troops. General Grant ordered gunboats to demolish the fort, and a fierce bombardment was underway; the fighting—which involved 27,000 Union soldiers and about 15,000 Confederates—raged for several days, and news of the battle was front-page news in papers of all the major cities of the North.

At dawn the following morning, General Canby and his little band of New Mexican volunteers returned to the trail where they had confronted the Confederates the previous evening. They were startled and disappointed to find their previous position of ambush was now occupied by the Confederates!

But this time it was the Rebels who fired prematurely, sending a cannon ball crashing into the trees behind and west of the oncoming Union soldiers. Canby quickly sized up the situation, recognized that he was now the one at a disadvantage, and beat a hasty retreat back past Valverde and across the Rio Grande.

The Confederates sent scouts out to question local farmers and the citizens of Valverde. They soon determined that the Union force opposing them consisted mostly of untrained and poorly equipped New Mexican militiamen. The information reinforced General Sibley's earlier conclusion that Canby's volunteer army posed no real danger. Yet the Rebels were slow to take advantage of the enemy; Sibley took a full day to bring up the remainder of his troops and supplies and prepare to continue the northward march.

Despite reports detailing the type and size of the volunteer units at Fort Craig, Sibley seemed a little uncertain as to exactly what kind of Union force was entrenched there. And even with all of the optimistic reports he could not be sure that Canby did not have a strong force of regulars at the fort. Some civilians reported that many men in army uniforms had been spotted in the area. On the other hand, the fort might not be defended at all, based on the fact that Canby seemed to be fighting with only a handful of local farmers. Sibley decided that he needed to test the fort's defenses before moving northward.

On February 16, Union forces under Ulysses S. Grant finally took Fort Donelson and captured between 12,000 and 15,000 enemy soldiers. In addition, the victorious Union troops seized 20,000 rifles, 48 pieces of artillery, 17 heavy guns, about 4,000 horses, and large quantities of commissary stores. The victory was a cause for great celebrations throughout the North.

On the morning of February 20, a Confederate cannon mounted on the hill opposite Fort Craig belched fire and smoke just as the sun broke over the horizon. The cannon ball crashed into the back wall of the fort, taking a huge chunk out of the adobe wall.

The shot was apparently simply intended as a wake-up call. As startled Union soldiers raced to the front wall of the fort they spotted hundreds of enemy soldiers lining the hill across the Rio Grande. Then they saw another Confederate soldier, riding under a white flag of truce, coming up the trail toward the front gates of the Fort.

The enemy soldier was a Texas Ranger, who bore a note from General Sibley to his brother-in-law. General Canby walked from the fort to meet the Texan and stood on the path leading to the river as he read the letter.

The note from Sibley warned that a "huge and powerful Army of the Confederacy"—the "Western Expeditionary Force"—was across the river, prepared to reduce Fort Craig to rubble. Sibley invited Canby to take his Union volunteers and beat a hasty retreat, "rather than face certain and total defeat." But Sibley also recognized that his brother-in-law was not likely to run from confrontation, or to surrender without battle, regardless of the odds against him. As an alternative to fleeing, therefore, Sibley offered to have his forces confront the Union army "on an open plain immediately east of the river and the fort."

Canby recognized that meeting the well-organized and heavily armed Texas invaders in the open would be certain disaster for his troops. He politely declined the invitation, sending back a note to Sibley that "we will choose our own place and time to confront your army."

When the note was returned to Sibley, the Confederate general took no immediate action. He seemed a little confused and mildly irritated that the note did not spell out Canby's plans. From the wording on the note, Sibley still could not be sure about the size of Canby's army, whether he could defend the fort, and whether he could actually put up a battle should the two armies meet. However, he concluded that Canby would make good his promise to choose the time and place of battle, and apparently spent the remainder of that day preparing his troops for some surprise attack from the Union force.

Late in the afternoon, the Confederates began moving slowly northward again. Their pace was greatly hampered by the elements. The trail was rough and extremely hilly, and the ground was wet from melting snow and rain. Wagons sank in the mud to their axles, and horses began to collapse from a lack of food. Men, too, were tired and hungry and now encountered a new problem. Although there was plenty of water less than two miles away in the Rio Grande, the troops were ordered to stay well clear of the river to avoid a confrontation with the enemy. As a result, the men had no water to drink and the animals were limited to whatever puddles they could find in roadside ditches.

General Canby was also busy that day. He rounded up all the volunteers he could find from neighboring farms and villages. Shortly after dark that night, he pulled all of the troops out of Fort Craig. The Union commander returned to the North Ford and there, on the heavily wooded east bank, prepared to meet the Confederates.

Well before dawn on the morning of February 21, Canby was in position among the trees and heavy underbrush on the west side of the Rio Grande, one hundred miles south of Albuquerque and six miles north of Valverde. Kit Carson and about three hundred New Mexican militiamen anchored the left, or north, side of the Union line, while Canby and about two hundred and fifty additional local volunteers held the center. The two independent companies of Colorado volunteers and most of the Union regulars were positioned on the far right, the side on which the main trail approached the river on the opposite bank.

The morning of February 21, 1862, dawned clear and cold. There was no breeze whatsoever, giving the false impression of complete serenity. The lack of a breeze would soon prove to be a serious problem for both armies.

When the sun peeked over the eastern horizon that morning, General Sibley's army of just over twenty-five hundred ablebodied men were already up and preparing for battle. They would be accompanied by fifteen pieces of artillery. They fully expected to be attacked during the day. They also knew it was likely that the Union attack would be planned in such a way as to prevent the Texans from reaching water, which was becoming a critical problem. Many of the soldiers had been thirty-six hours without water and the Confederates knew they could not last much longer without solving the problem of the water shortage.

A large advance unit of seven hundred soldiers, under the command of Colonel William R. Scurry, set out well ahead of the main body of Confederate soldiers. Scurry was assisted by Colonel Thomas Green and Major Samuel Lockridge, two brave and veteran soldiers. With them was the 4th Texas Mounted Volunteers and five light howitzer batteries. This vanguard would be followed at a considerable distance by the remaining Texans and the rest of their artillery and by about one hundred wagonloads of supplies, and the Confederate beef herd.

A few minutes after 9 A.M., the lead units of the advancing Confederate army, under the command of Major Charles Pyron, topped the hill on the east bank and started down the trail toward the Rio Grande. Opposing them, directly across the river, was Lieutenant Colonel Benjamin S. Roberts, the man once jailed for reporting Confederate treachery at Fort Craig. Roberts had with him a mixed group of two hundred and twenty Union soldiers. They were soon reinforced by a group of Colorado Volunteers under Captain Henry R. Seldon, and by Kit Carson's New Mexican Volunteers.

The selection of the battlefield was not a particularly wise one from the Union point of view. In the first place, the Rebels occupied the high ground, and were able to shoot downhill, always a marked advantage in close combat. In addition, the battlefield contained seven sand ridges running parallel to the river and lying fifty to one hundred yards apart. These ridges formed excellent natural breastworks, giving the Texans ample protection from Union gunfire and a great series of walls from behind which they could pour gunfire into the Union lines.

Once again, though, nervous and untrained New Mexican Volunteers opened fire without orders, while the enemy was still a considerable distance away. Thus warned, the Confederates quickly spread out across the narrow valley on their side of the river and the first major battle of the New Mexico campaign got underway. The Rebels immediately brought up their artillery under Teel, Riley and Fulcrod, and commenced shelling the Yankee positions.

Soon, cannons on both sides were lobbing shells at their respective enemy, and riflemen were scurrying from tree to rock as they sought favorable positions from which to shoot at the foe. As the battle raged, thick clouds of smoke engulfed the battlefield, making visibility difficult and adding to the confusion of the fight. Both sides swore at the smoke and prayed for a gust of wind to clear the area. It was not to happen throughout the long day.

About 9:15 the Yankees launched an attack toward the Confederate right; the assault was hurled back. Then the Texans counterattacked, charging down the center of the valley; they came under heavy fire and were also repulsed.

As time wore on, casualties began to mount on both sides. During the occasional lull in shooting, wounded men could be heard crying for help or begging for water. No one had the courage to race onto the battlefield and try to aid these poor, helpless victims of war; many of them would die slow and agonizing deaths while the battle raged around them.

About 10:30 a large unit of the 5th Texas Volunteers charged on the right. Two companies of mounted lancers managed to get within a hundred yards of Captain Ford's Independent Company, which was anchoring the Union line left of McRae's Battery. At least twenty-nine of the attackers were shot from their horses, however, and the squadron retreated.

Private Ickis was among the men of Company B, who were at the forefront of that battle. He reported that the Texans knew from the unique Colorado uniforms that the Union force were not "regulars"; they assumed that they would be battling New Mexican Volunteers and apparently anticipated an easy victory.

Ickis wrote that "Three companies of Lancier Rangers, each armed with a long lance, made a charge upon our Company of 71 men, armed with musket and bayonet." As soon as the Confederates launched the attack, the Coloradans knew they were in trouble. They were outnumbered by perhaps six to one and were not in a position to send for help, even if help had been available.

In a letter to his brother, Ickis wrote:

On came the enemy; not a word in our ranks. All were still but our brave little Captain [Dodd], who gave his commands in so cool and determined a manner as to make all breathe easier and every nerve to become steady. Our captain stepping in front said, "Steady there my brave mountaineeers. Waste not a single shot. Do not let your passions run off with your judgement. Steady, men. Steady. Do not fire until I command." Not a sound in our ranks. I could hear my own heart beat. On came the enemy with their lances poised in the air, ready for the conflict. Each lance was tipped with a small secessionist flag. Oh, what suspense! They are now within 40 yards of us. Our captain is in front, gazing first at the enemy and then at us. "Steady, men. Guns to faces, but wait for the command to fire." Every eye is on the Lanciers. Our captain now commands, "Fire!" We sent forth a volley which sent many brave Texans to bite the dust; many horses were riderless. The enemy wavered for a few moments—precious moments to us. We were again loaded when they got to us and we gave them a second volley, then grasped our guns firmly and rushed upon them with bayonet. They appeared bewildered and did not appear to know how or what to do. Soon they were butchered; I can not call it else. Only one man out of three companies [of Texans] escaped uninjured. His horse had been shot from under him at our first volley and he was taken prisoner.

The Texans staggered back, but soon another attack was ordered, and when the first men began running forward Colonel Green ordered the entire Texas line to charge. A sizeable number of Texas infantrymen gained control of a ridge near the edge of the Rio Grande on the south side of the crossing. They were only about twenty-four yards from the nearest Union soldiers. Canby shifted some of his riflemen to assist the Colorado regulars who were trying to hold that side of the line, and a fierce fire-fight ensued. In moments, the Texans were driven back after apparently again having suffered high casualties.

A short time later the Texans tried to regain the same ridge. They formed a skirmish line and marched toward the river as the Yankees poured artillery and rifle fire into their midst. Eventually the Texans were driven back by the withering gunfire. Three more times over the course of the next two hours, the Confederates tried to regain the water's edge, and three times they were repulsed.

Colonel Roberts believed at this time that the Confederates were preparing to mount a new assault against his left, and sent all available men upstream to meet the challenge. These troops, most of them Colorado volunteers, tried to cross the Rio Grande, and were immediately challenged by about an equal number of Confederate soldiers. The Texans raced into the water and caught the Union forces in midstream, unprepared for combat. A fierce struggle ensued, with soldiers on both sides using their bayonets. In moments, the river was red with blood and choked with bodies of the victims.

The Texans were eventually repulsed and retreated back up the hill, but were immediately replaced by a charge from the 5th Texas lancers. The fresh Rebel troops swept down the hill, directly toward the weary Union soldiers, who were still standing in the bloody water.

Historian Josephy described the ensuing struggle this way: "Coming at full gallop, the troopers, armed with nine-foot-long wooden lances tipped with three-inch-wide steel blades, nearly panicked the Coloradans. But [the Coloradans'] commanding officer, Captain Theodore H. Dodd, coolly closed up his ranks and shouted, 'They are Texans. Give them hell!' A volley shattered the Texans' front line, knocking men and horses to the ground." Some of the Texas lancers "came near enough to be transfixed and lifted from their saddles by bayonets," a Colorado private wrote, "but the greater part bit the dust before the lances could come into use. Only three Texans escaped unharmed; the survivors fell back to their own lines in disorder. All others were shot or bayoneted. My friend G. Simpson ran his bayonet through one and then shot the top of his head off!" [Josephy, *The Civil War in the American West*, pp. 107–08.]

Encouraged by this success, Colonel Roberts ordered all of his troops to cross to the east side of the river. In retrospect, this did not appear to have been a wise move. Within seconds, the Union had formed a new line and was struggling to advance even further uphill toward the Confederates. The Union batteries on the right flank of the Federal lines were now badly exposed. Heavy fighting raged from one side of the valley to the other.

Captain Dodd's company of the Second Colorado was at the center of this fighting and, according to Canby's official report on the battle, "fought like seasoned soldiers." But the Coloradans paid a high price for standing their ground; they lost thirty dead and thirty more wounded before 1 P.M., a casualty rate of approximately 50 percent.

At this point in the battle, General Sibley reported that he had become suddenly ill and was unable to remain on the battlefield. He placed Colonel Thomas Green of the 5th Texas in over-all command of the battle and headed back down the trail toward Valverde. Aides said Sibley was running a fever and was weak, symptoms of smallpox which was rampant among his troops. Even so, it would later be alleged that Sibley actually returned to his private coach and spent the remainder of the day drinking there. One of the Confederate officers later wrote that, "the commanding general was an old army officer whose love for liquor exceeded that for home, country or God." Colonel Baylor charged that Sibley spent the remainder of the day "cowering in an ambulance." (It is not clear whether these charges were made at the time of the incident, or after the entire Confederate campaign had failed and the South had mounted an effort to discredit the commanding officer.)

On the opposite bank, General Canby had taken personal command of the Union force. He recalled Kit Carson and those 2nd Colorado troops still upstream. He ordered them and the 2nd New Mexico to charge a ridge held by the Texans on the east bank. The Confederate unit was under the command of Major Henry Raguet.

The Coloradans and Kit Carson charged up the hill, but the 2nd New Mexico not only refused to obey the order, they actually retreated back across the river. Private Ickis recorded in his diary that "At 4 P.M., the enemy emerged from the ravine suddenly and made a charge upon our batteries—or rather, sections of batteries. Major Lockridge with 1500 men charged our section of six small guns, supported by 250 men. The Mexicans ran at the first sight of the enemy without firing a shot." This panicked and apparently cowardly retreat left the Union force unacceptably small, and Major Raguet was quick to take advantage of the situation. Two hundred Texans charged down the slope, expecting to have a comparatively easy time driving back the little Union force.

To their surprise, the relative handful of Coloradans fought fiercely and refused to give ground. The Texans' charge was stopped and then hurled back. By the time the Texans had regained their ridge, they had lost forty men killed or wounded. However, the Coloradans knew that they were not now in a position to capture the Confederate lines. They withdrew to a clump of trees at the edge of the water.

It was now approaching late afternoon. Confederate Colonel Scurry called for volunteers to charge the Yankee position in an effort to capture the cannons being fired by Captain Dodd's company. More than a thousand Texans volunteered for the mission, even though they knew they would have to race through the concentrated gunfire which had already claimed too many of their companions. Scurry selected 750 men under the command of Colonel Green and ordered them to carry out the assault.

A Texas officer "leaped to the top of an embankment and shouted, 'Take the battery or lose the day!'" As he dashed down the trail waving a sword, other Rebel troops poured out of concealment and also raced at the Yankee lines.

Union soldiers all along the front now rose to a standing position and began firing at the line of charging enemy soldiers. The Rebel charge faltered, halted and finally degenerated into a rout back up the trail. Now it was the Union forces who raced forward and charged up the hill in hot pursuit of the retreating Confederates. In seconds, most of the Texans had regained the relative safety of a small ridge. Stopping, they turned to face the charging Yankees behind them who were now in the open, treeless valley.

Now it was the Texans who opened fire and the Union forces who faltered, milled about in momentary confusion, and finally raced for their lives back down to the river. In that exchange, however, the Texans had suffered unusually heavy casualties, mostly as a result of deadly fire from Union artillery, especially one cannon at the far right end of the Yankee line. The cannon was under the command of Captain Alexander McRae, a former

Pueblo, Colorado, businessman, and former Union regular who had been stationed at Fort Craig.

The Texans knew they either had to retreat and give up all the ground they had secured thus far in the battle, or they had to capture the Colorado artillery. They chose the latter. In a few moments the Confederates organized still another frontal assault on the Yankee cannon. When there was next a momentary lull in the firing, scores of Texans suddenly leaped to their feet, poured over the embankments and raced seven hundred yards down the hillside to the Union position.

A number of the Coloradans were caught by surprise by the Rebel assault, and several were killed or wounded before anyone could get off an answering shot. In seconds, the Texans overran the Union lines and fierce hand-to-hand fighting erupted all along the front. The Texans were firing their pistols at point-blank range and clubbing Union gunners with rifle butts, or slashing them with bayonets.

Captain McRae rallied his surviving troops and continued to pour grape shot and canister at the enemy. Dozens of the attacking Texans fell, but the rest kept on coming. Within a matter of minutes, the Rebels had crossed the ground separating the two armies and were in amongst the Union soldiers. By that time, fifteen of ninety-three Coloradans who were still working the guns had been killed and about an equal number wounded.

The Texans' charge into the teeth of the withering Union rifle and cannon fire was commanded by Major S.A. Lockridge. Throughout the attack and the bitter, hand-to-hand fighting that followed Lockridge could be heard shouting encouragement to his troops as he and his men struggled for control of the big gun.

This was one of those cases in which officers on both sides were former close friends and comrades-in-arms. Both the Union captain, McRae, and several of the Confederate officers had once been Union regulars. All of them had been assigned to Fort Craig just a few months earlier. McRae and several of the Confederates recognized each other as they battled nose to nose. Major Lockridge shouted, "Surrender, McRae. We don't want to kill you!"

McRae, whose arm was already shattered and whose leg had been pierced by two bullets, leaving him barely able to stand up, leaned against the hot barrel of his cannon and replied, "I shall never forsake my guns!" At that precise moment, both Confederate Major Lockridge and Union Captain McRae were killed by rifle fire. Texas Captain Marinus van der Heuvel and Private Charles Sutton were also killed in the exchange.

(Interestingly, when the Confederates later sought to honor Lockridge posthumously for his bravery in that battle they discovered that he was not Lockridge at all. His real name was William Kissane, and he apparently had a minor criminal record in Cincinnati. He also had participated in the burning of the steamship *Martha Washington* in Cincinnati in the late 1850s, one of the first Southern acts of defiance against the United States government.)

Private Ickis was among the handful of Union soldiers who successfully retreated from the battle. He said that at the height of the fighting:

> . . . our men stood their ground firing as fast as possible. At every shot the enemy's ranks would be opened but they were soon filled by other men. We gave them the balls as fast as possible. Colonel Canby was near us, cheering the men but it was of no avail. They were now on and around the battery when one of our boys jumped upon a magazine withstood at the side of the guns, drew his pistol, cried "Victory or death!" and fired his pistol into the ammunition. One loud report and it was all over with that brave boy and many of the enemy who had been crowded around the battery.

Ickis also said that during the fight, Patrick H. Duphy of Company B had his leg shot off below the knee with grape; Frank Kenton was shot in the arm. Both men were close friends of Ickis.

After the fighting at the North Ford ended, the armchair generals would say that the turning point in the battle was the capture of McRae's cannon by Lockridge's Texans. They would also argue that had other Union troops in the area, specifically meaning the 2nd New Mexico, which had literally run from the battlefield, fought adequately, the Confederates would never have been able to cover the seven hundred yards from the ridge to the river where McRae and his men were positioned. In an angry letter to the United States War Department a few weeks later, New Mexico Governor Henry Connelly blamed both the New Mexico volunteers and a handful of regular Union soldiers:

It is painful to relate that of the forces in position for the protection of [McRae's] battery, not one company advanced to its relief or even fired upon the enemy as he approached. The force consisted of two or more companies of regular troops and one regiment of New Mexico volunteers. The regulars were ordered—nay, implored—to charge the enemy, by Colonel Canby, Major Donaldson and Colonel [William O.] Collins, superintendent of Indian affairs, who were all three present, in immediate contact with the troops and within 20 yards of the battery when it was taken. The regulars having refused to advance, the volunteers followed their example and both retired from the field, recrossing the river and leaving the battery in possession of the enemy!

The capture of McRae's cannon seemed to take the wind out of the Union sails. Dozens of New Mexico militiamen who had been fighting nearest the captured battery now threw down their arms and ran for their lives. Scores more, all along the line, soon followed suit.

Kit Carson is said to have fired several warning shots into the air over the heads of the panic-stricken militiamen, but was unable to stem the tide. In a few seconds, only a relative handful of army regulars and Colorado Volunteers were still on the battle line for the Union. Their position was hopeless; they were outnumbered perhaps as much as eight to one.

As General Canby watched the complete rout of his troops, his horse was shot from beneath him. Regaining his feet, Canby ordered all remaining troops to withdraw "as rapidly as possible." Most of his soldiers did not need to be encouraged; they threw down their weapons and fled. As the Yankee soldiers hastily pulled out of the area, victorious Confederates raced across the river and laid claim to all of the abandoned Union cannons and the other weapons and ammunition the retreating army left behind.

For the Confederates, there was another bonus associated with the rout of the Yankees. All of the Union soldiers carried canteens, many of them filled with whiskey, and each man carried a knapsack filled with food. The soldiers who ran flung these items to the ground in their haste to get away. The Confederates quickly recovered the knapsacks and canteens from the dead and wounded as well as those abandoned by the retreating soldiers and are said to have eaten better that night than at any other time since entering New Mexico.

It may have been a fortunate thing for both sides that the Union forces fled when they did. Confederates later reported they were preparing to charge across the river in another all-out attack when the Union army retreated. The Texans were confident that such an attack would have destroyed the Yankees, but probably at a high cost to themselves. Men crossing the river would have been easy targets for Union rifles.

Although the Confederates clearly won the battle, it is difficult to say which side suffered most in the long run. *Colorado Volunteers in New Mexico* claims that two hundred Texans were killed and another two hundred wounded in the Battle of the North Ford (the Confederates called it the "Battle of Valverde"), compared to the sixty-four Union dead and one hundred Yankee wounded. This account says the Texans also lost five hundred horses and mules "killed, escaped or captured," and said the loss of the animals forced the Confederates to later abandon thirty wagonloads of supplies and convert a cavalry unit to infantry because of the shortage of animals.

Union Captain Gurden Chapin, writing to the War Department, reported that the Union lost 62 dead and 140 wounded. General Canby placed the number at 65 soldiers dead with 157 wounded, "of whom a substantial number died soon afterward." He also said one officer and 34 enlisted men were missing and "either killed, taken prisoner, or gone AWOL."

Private Ickis said that the Union loss was 48 killed that day, with 30 more to die in the days and weeks following the battle. He reported 350 Union soldiers wounded and 21 taken prisoner. He placed the Texans' losses at 400 killed and 600 wounded. Ickis says that Captain Dodd's company of 71 men lost 40 killed or wounded and 7 prisoner, noting "it was the most of any one company in the field; we were first in action, last from the field. Many of the boys with whom I was acquainted in the mountains are dead or wounded."

The United States battle surgeon who accompanied the Union troops that day, Dr. E. I. Bailey, reported counting the bodies of fifty-seven Union dead on the battlefield. Dr. Bailey said at least seventeen additional U.S. soldiers died in his field hospital a short time later.

General Sibley reported to San Antonio that he had lost "40 men with about 100 others wounded." That report appears to be extremely conservative and possibly deliberately misleading. Sibley would demonstrate in later battles that he was not above doctoring figures substantially to make him and his troops look better. Some other reports filed by Sibley's officers listed up to 300 dead and 450 wounded, which seems exaggerated on the high side. Alvin Josephy—without citing his sources—says that Sibley lost 36 dead, 150 wounded, and 1 missing. Josephy also says Sibley lost "many" wagons, horses and supplies.

Actually, battle casualties were difficult to ascertain with any degree of certainty throughout the Civil War. And casualty figures were frequently and deliberately misrepresented by commanders. Figures were either minimized to keep the enemy from knowing how effective they had been, or to keep superior officers from knowing how badly a particular unit had been mauled, or to claim a greater victory. With the same reasoning, reports of enemy losses were frequently exaggerated. Official reports nearly always overestimated the number of troops in an enemy unit.

One thing was certain: staggeringly high casualty counts were reported on both sides in most Civil War battles. Unlike more recent conflicts, a huge percentage of wounded battle survivors died soon after a Civil War battle. The high death rate was due in part to the length of time between injury and medical attention, which was often substandard at best, reflecting the primitive state of medical science.

The minié balls fired by weapons of both sides inflicted grievous injuries that shattered bones, opened gaping wounds and destroyed organs. In addition, infections were rampant. Records indicate that up to a quarter of all the men listed as wounded in battle would die within a few days; in World War II that rate was cut to 4½ percent, by Korea it was down to 2½ percent and in Vietnam barely more than 2 percent. As for those listed as "missing in action," the majority of them were also killed in the fighting, their bodies overlooked by burial parties who worked mostly at night, with poor lighting and under great stress.

Following the Battle of North Ford, General Canby and about one hundred regulars and Colorado Volunteers returned to Fort Craig. Early the following morning, the fort was approached by three Confederate soldiers, riding under a flag of truce. The Confederates were Colonel Scurry, who had played a key role in the previous day's fighting and who would later become on of the South's best cavalry generals; Captain D. W. Shannon, who would soon be taken prisoner by the Yankees; and Lieutenant Tom P. Ochiltree, who would later become a United States Congressman.

The Rebels demanded that General Canby surrender Fort Craig and all the men remaining under his command. They warned that unless the Union soldiers surrendered, Confederates would begin shelling the fort and would not stop until the fort was reduced to rubble. Canby is said to have replied that if Sibley thought he was strong enough to capture the fort, "let him try it!"

Whether the Confederates decided they were not strong enough, or simply concluded that its capture was insignificant is difficult to say. In his official report, Sibley later claimed that the capture of the fort was meaningless. But whatever their reasoning, the Rebels never attacked Fort Craig; they simply by-passed it and continued on their northward march toward Albuquerque, Fort Union, and, ultimately, Colorado.

In a touching letter to his family, Alonzo Ickis wrote:

We came out second best. In America this is a day of great rejoicing. All join in celebrating the anniversary of the birth of the immortal George Washington. Alas! How different it is with us. The shrieks of the wounded and dying together with the ghastly appearance of the dead form an impression upon our minds time will never erase. On the morning of February 22, I visited the "dead room" at Fort Craig to search for one of my friends [Private John McKee], who was missing and had not been recognized when the dead were brought in. I went into the room where they were piled, one upon another. I climbed over the dead bodies, turning some over but could not find John. [Six weeks later, McKee's body was found in the Rio Grande; he had been shot through the head.—Ed.] The wounded were in every room of the fort and such scenes as I there beheld I hope are seldom seen. Men mutilated in every conceivable manner. Never did I expect to go into a room where there were fifty men piled one upon another, climb over them, rolling them over, seeking a friend, and this without a shudder. Who will say war is not degrading!

Ickis added in his diary: "Of our wounded, they filled every room [at Fort Craig]. One poor fellow was shot with an ounce ball; it went in at the point of his nose and came out at the back of his neck. Dr. Basil Norris says he will get well."

Immediately after the battle, the Confederates sent a note asking for a three day suspension of hostilities to enable them to bury the dead and dress their wounded. The Confederates found it particularly difficult to care for their wounded. They were already short of medical supplies because of the outbreaks of smallpox. In addition, a raid by Apache Indians had resulted in the destruction of great quantities of medicine and medical instruments.

Four days after the battle, the Confederates sent a note identifying Union soldiers who had been taken prisoner. Among them were six men from Dodd's Company B: Privates John Ames, Sylvester Gilson, Jacob Martin, and William Withington, Quartermaster Sergeant Sydenham Mills and Corporal Samuel Westerfield. The note from the Texans also reported that another of Captain Dodd's soldiers, private Harrison Berry, had gone "up the country," meaning he had deserted.

The note from the Confederates was accompanied by a letter from Private Ames to his best friend, Private Alden Cate. Ames said he was being "kindly treated to the best the Rebel camp affords." He noted that the Texans referred to their Union prisoners as "abbs," apparently meaning "absentees."

Private Ickis by this time was bitter about the New Mexico volunteers who deserted at the time of the battle. He noted in his diary that "we would have been a damned sight better off if they had all been in hell before we came into the [New Mexico] territory!"

General Canby, Colonel Carson and other Union regulars who survived the battle and were inside the fort when the Texans threatened to demolish it, now escaped out the rear exit of Fort Craig. Taking to those tree-covered slopes in the distance, the survivors began working their way northward to attempt another defense of the Territory, this time from Fort Union.

General Sibley and the Confederate command were confident that all the fight had been taken out of the Union forces, that only a handful of soldiers remained anywhere in the territory. Texas spies said that the only enemy force remaining in New Mexico was at Fort Union, about eight hundred New Mexican volunteers and a hundred or so regulars "who are not eager for battle."

The conquering Confederate forces spent the next several days camped on the east side of the Rio Grande about two miles from Fort Craig. This delay was to permit recuperation from the bloody battle at the North Ford, and also apparently to savor the victory. Sibley was obliged to send several wagonloads of badly wounded soldiers back to the town of Valverde. The Rebels commandeered a Catholic Church in the town to serve as a Confederate hospital.

Ickis later reported that three hundred enemy wounded were taken to Fort Fillmore, four miles south of Las Cruces and forty miles north of El Paso. The fort had been seized by the Rebels just after they entered the territory. He reported that another two hundred and ten were hospitalized at Socorro, and said that between three and eight of those men were dying every day.

On February 26, the Texans finally resumed their leisurely march northward. They expected to be greeted as conquering heroes by people along the way and were both surprised bitterly disappointed at the coolness with which they were greeted by civilians. In fact, many citizens were openly hostile to the invaders, and the Texans resented their reception.

On February 27, the Texans arrived in Socorro. Several local volunteers came down the road to challenge the Texans, but fled after a few shots were exchanged. No casualties were inflicted by either side, although Confederate battle records insist that three Union soldiers were killed and two wounded in the brief encounter. Entering the town, the Confederates found it nearly deserted, and everything that might have been of value to the invaders was gone, apparently having been shipped to Fort Union. In angry retaliation, the Confederates burned several buildings.

They also seized a large Roman Catholic church to serve as another field hospital. There, about fifty more of the seriously wounded men from the fighting at North Ford were hospitalized.

On March 9, the ironclads U.S.S. Monitor and C.S.S. Virginia battled to an inconclusive draw, only one day after the Confederate ship had wreaked havoc on Union vessels in the harbor at Hampton Roads, Virginia. The battle pushed all other war news off the front page of papers throughout the world; it was immediately clear that a new era in naval warfare had arrived.

As they moved northward, the Texans could see columns of smoke rising from ahead of them and feared that the Yankees were burning everything of value before retreating. The fears were justified.

The Texans formally occupied Albuquerque on March 2 and Santa Fe on March 10. The capture of the cities was anticlimactic, however. Both were nearly deserted and almost everything that might have helped the Rebels was long gone, either shipped to Fort Union or burned in the huge bonfires. Among the items taken or destroyed were all guns, black powder, blankets and spare clothing.

Again, the Confederates were not amused to find the cities already stripped of valuables. Just as they had extracted revenge from farmers between Valverde and Albuquerque, so they now took revenge on those living in the cities. The Confederates looted businesses in both cities, and burned several stores belonging to known or suspected Union sympathizers. Those merchants who could be identified as having cooperated with the Yankees or who sent valuables to Fort Union were forced to pay various amounts of money to the Rebel soldiers. There are unconfirmed reports of civilians being brutalized by the invaders.

Although the stories of Confederate atrocities to local civilians were too rampant to have been entirely fictitious, there is some question whether they were as bad as recorded by the victims. One historian wrote that, "Sibley's Confederates swept north, leaving many folktales of chapels being used as stables, wine casks broken, and women raped or threatened by drunken soldiers. Perhaps few of these tales could be substantiated; invaders are always so accused. But these family legends, passed down through the generations, have edged New Mexico tongues with the tone still heard in the word 'tejano.'"

Another writer said, "Wherever the Southerners went, they pillaged recklessly, seldom being concerned with whether or not the goods they were stealing belonged to a Confederate or a Yankee. This increased the already existing hostility of the native population."

There is no hard evidence that General Sibley condoned or was even aware of the ransoms being extracted, or the looting and other alleged attacks on civilians carried out by his soldiers. On the other hand, there is no evidence that Sibley did anything to check on or control the troops once they reached the two cities; as commander, such was his responsibility. The General had seized a villa near Albuquerque to serve as his temporary headquarters and rarely ventured outside the building. Later, when there was an official effort to discredit Sibley, it would be widely rumored that the general spent much of his time in a drunken stupor. Again, there is little hard evidence to support those accusations.

Actually, the Rebels did quite well for themselves in Albuquerque despite the earlier effort to ship all valuables in the city to Fort Union. When news of the advancing Texans reached town, the local Wells Fargo office prepared to ship nearly a quarter-million dollars in gold bullion to Kansas City for safekeeping. Unfortunately for Wells Fargo, a blizzard closed the Santa Fe Trail and the gold couldn't be taken out of town. Confederate soldiers found the gold shortly after entering Albuquerque and seized it on behalf of the Confederacy. General Sibley was able to send it all to San Antonio a short time later, along with a note saying the gold was just a start, and that he would be sending much more as soon as he had conquered the Colorado gold fields.

It is said General Sibley thought the seizure of the gold vindicated his decision to by-pass Fort Craig on his way northward. He felt that seizing the gold for the Confederacy was far more important that crushing his brother-in-law's pitiful little army either at the fort or in the Battle of North Ford.

But the Rebels did not stop with simply looting Albuquerque and Santa Fe. They sent raiding parties into villages as far as seventy miles west of Albuquerque searching for anything of value. And at one such village, the Texans struck it rich. A number of New Mexican militiamen fled when they heard the Confederates were coming and left behind great stores of food and ammunition. Looting of the town of Cubero provided twenty-five wagonloads of commissaries and a reported twenty-nine thousand rounds of ammunition. (These supplies were probably stockpiled in the campaign against Indians and were never intended by the Union for use against Confederates.) Before leaving the cities a few days later, Sibley would be able to dispatch three-dozen wagonloads of valuables back down the trail to El Paso for safekeeping.

But the good news was tempered by bad. Food for horses was still simply not available, and the Confederates were now losing up to a hundred animals every day because of a lack of forage.

Half of each regiment had now lost their horses, and General Sibley ordered many of the soldiers to give up their horses so that the animals could be used to pull the wagons and artillery pieces.

Nearly two-thirds of the Confederates were without horses by the time the Texans were ready to leave Santa Fe. All of the 1st regiment was now dismounted as was half of the 2nd; within days, half of the 3rd would also be forced to surrender their horses.

The horses were not government property; each man had brought his own animal with him from civilian life. When Sibley ordered the men to turn the animals over for wagon-hauling duty, he gave each soldier an "IOU," promising that the Confederate government would pay a fair and reasonable price as soon as the victorious Rebels returned to Texas. Most of the soldiers carried the IOUs with them for the remainder of the war, but the Confederates never made good on the notes.

While General Sibley was trying desperately to deal with the problem of his horses dying from the lack of available food, similar problems plagued the surviving Union forces at Fort Craig. Private Ickis noted in his diary that "the lack of forage is a serious problem; a detail of one hundred men is sent every morning into the mountains to dig hay (collect mountain grass) for our animals."

And there were other problems. On March 7, Ickis told his diary: "Forty of Kit Carson's New Mexico volunteers deserted during the night, taking ponies and arms with them." The good news was that Union scouts that same night managed to capture a dozen horses and sixty head of steers, stolen from the camp of the Rebels.

On March 16, Ickis wrote in his diary, "I wish Christianity would come to the base. The American Bible Society [should] send a missionary here. There are no class of men who are more profane than the officers and soldiers of this garrison. The "Bread of Life" is seldom seen, while the history of the four kings—poker—is a constant study!"

On March 17, a huge war party of Navajo Indians, numbering perhaps three hundred men, ran off forty of the Union head of mules after a brief gunbattle at the corral. Ickis was on hat (guard) duty that day and got involved in the gunfight. His companion, Private Jordan of F company, was wounded in the leg, but not seriously hurt. Ickis covered Jordan with a jacket and sent a New Mexico volunteer back to the fort to get medical help.

On March 26, friendly Pueblo Indians brought in 250 mules stolen from the Confederates. The Indians said twenty braves were killed in a battle with the Rebels before the horses were stolen. They negotiated for the sale of the animals, and Colonel Paul paid the price demanded.

Captain Graydon came to Fort Craig on March 28 with forty captured Texans and ninety-one mules. He reported that 200 more Texans had been captured and two guns seized by New Mexico volunteers in a skirmish near Santa Fe.

Denver in the 1860s. *Colorado Historical Society*

Brigadier General
Henry H. Sibley.
*Colorado Historical
Society*

General William R.
Scurry. *Colorado
Historical Society*

Christopher Carson.
*Colorado Historical
Society*

William Gilpin.
*Colorado Historical
Society*

O. J. Hollister.
*Colorado Historical
Society*

Colonel John M.
Chivington. *Colorado
Historical Society*

Major General
Edward Canby.
*Colorado Historical
Society*

Bridge in Apache Canyon. *Colorado Historical Society*

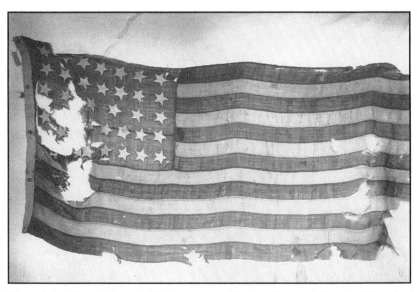

Flag of the First Colorado Volunteers at Glorieta Pass. *Colorado Historical Society*

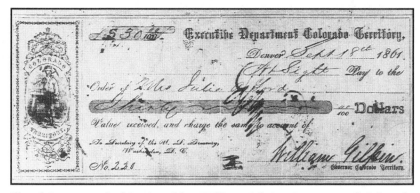

Illegal "treasury draft" printed by William Gilpin, Governor of Colorado Territory, to pay for the First Colorado Volunteers. *Colorado Historical Society*

Kozlowski's Ranch, 1957. *Colorado Historical Society*

CHAPTER EIGHT

COLORADANS RACE TO THE RESCUE

The view from this point [Raton Pass] is magnificent. Mountains meet the eye wherever it turns. Away to the west the Spanish Peaks rise grand and towering, their bold temples silvered with snowy lines like the gray hairs of some old-time Anaks—their crowns encircled with a wreath of storms, they seem the natural guardians of this wild region, the august witnesses of a grander order of things now passed away. At their feet, a small park spread its soft, turfy carpet as if to woo the reluctant sunshine, or charm to its embrace aught that lives and breathes to dispel the awful solitude hanging on the unhewed hillsides, crouching in the dark shadow-haunted chasms, or sighing in the storm-nursed pines.

Ovando J. Hollister, Company F
First Colorado Volunteers

*I*f things were going badly for General Canby—and indeed they were!—they were also going badly for the First Colorado Volunteers, although for entirely different reasons. While the General was waging his losing battle against invaders at the North Ford, the First Colorado was killing time at Camp Weld and Denver. And soldiers who have nothing to do frequently find ways to get in trouble.

Soldiers of the First Colorado were filling their idle hours with activities that were not generally appreciated by citizens of the Territory. For example, the quartermaster of F Company is said to have sold most of the unit's supplies of food, blankets, clothing and first-aid goods on the black market in Denver. The men in Company F were aware of what was going on, but did not want to be in a position of reporting their sergeant to authorities. Since they were the most severely impacted by the resulting shortage of supplies, this reluctance to tattle put the men in a strange position.

Eventually there was talk among the soldiers of F Company about deserting en masse. Some suggested they should ride to Kansas, where they had originally planned to go anyway, there to enlist with the U.S. Army in hopes of actually participating in a battle.

Several men eventually carried out the plan. Private Ovando J. Hollister was among those who slipped out of camp one weekend with every intention of never coming back. About a dozen soldiers headed for Fort Leavenworth where they planned to enlist and "get to see some action." However, ten miles east of Denver Hollister's best friend became ill and the men had to turn back to seek medical attention. Hollister had not been missed during his brief absence and apparently never again tried to leave Camp Weld.

However, ten other men did not come back and presumably rode on to Kansas to rejoin the army. Many other soldiers also left Camp Weld, some to enlist elsewhere, others to return to mining or seek their fortunes elsewhere. The large-scale desertions of men from the First Colorado soon became a serious matter. Eventually, Colonel Slough filed formal charges of desertion against Captains Charles P. Marion and J. W. Hambleton of Companies K and G; both men were drummed out of the service.

The military action against the two captains slowed the frequency of AWOLs for some time. It also provided a temporary diversion and some mild entertainment for the troops. Soon, however, the men were again fighting boredom and getting into all kinds of trouble in town while waiting for a chance to fight the Rebels.

In fact, the soldiers were soon causing so much trouble in Denver that an open split developed between the soldiers and citizens of the community. The Denver city council hired extra police officers to deal with the growing "military problem."

In late December 1861, the soldiers at Camp Weld decided they wanted to give themselves a huge Christmas party. Of course, they had few supplies necessary for such a party; even those that normally would have been available had now been sold by crooked quartermasters. As a result the soldiers had to go on "procurement raids," which meant they sneaked into town and began stealing items needed for the celebration.

Hollister commented that one party of raiding soldiers had worked a long time trying to pick the lock of a hen-roost door before noticing that the door was barely fastened to the shed with leather hinges. "Another, with great labor and no little risk of detection, carefully carried a 40-gallon barrel of vinegar to their quarters, supposing it to be whiskey." But Hollister defended the raids into Denver by saying ". . . we had been dogs now for four months without pay. No money in the company, either. We couldn't live over Christmas on [a continued diet of] bread and beef; it already stunk in our nostrils like quails in those of Israel."

Soon, serious problems with soldiers became a daily routine. The *Rocky Mountain News* reported that soldiers only returned to Camp Weld for their meals, and spent the remainder of their time causing trouble in the city. One soldier was arrested shortly after Christmas, but other soldiers took him by force from the two police officers who had him in custody. The soldier was returned to Camp Weld, but was soon convinced by his officers to return to Denver and give himself up to authorities. The soldier did so and was convicted of disorderly conduct. He was ordered to pay a fifty-dollar fine and was ordered to be held in jail until the fine was paid. Of course, since Governor Gilpin's treasury notes were no good, the soldiers were not being paid at all and there was no way the convicted man could earn money for his freedom. The town marshal recognized the absurdity of the situation and after giving the soldier a stern lecture, released him from jail.

Occasionally, incidents involving the army were more serious. One private, Charles Henderson, was arrested on charges of spying for the Confederates and of plotting to burn down the barracks at Camp Weld. Henderson had talked openly of someday deserting and joining the Confederate army, and he frequently criticized President Lincoln and the U.S. government. However, evidence against him on the specific charges of spying and planned arson appeared shaky at best.

Nonetheless Henderson was tried by court-martial, convicted, and sentenced to death. Colonel Slough, a lawyer in civilian life, felt the sentence was too harsh and the evidence too shaky to warrant a death penalty. Slough refused to give the necessary confirmation of the sentence, and met privately with each member of the court-martial board to discuss their verdict. Within a week, four of the officers had rescinded their agreement on the death penalty, although the other three members continued to insist on it. While the debate raged, Private Henderson was killed—shot to death one morning by a guard who said Henderson had been trying to escape from the stockade.

There is no telling how serious the growing conflict between civilians and the military might ultimately have become had it not been for General Sibley's January invasion of New Mexico. As soon as the Confederates moved into the Mesilla Valley of New Mexico, the Colorado military units were put on full-scale alert. That seemed to sober everyone up, and the units got down to the serious and now-pressing business of training hard and preparing for the expected Rebel invasion of Colorado.

On February 10, Lewis Weld, the acting governor of Colorado while William Gilpin was in Washington trying to answer questions about his "treasury notes," received a telegram from General David Hunter at Fort Leavenworth, Kansas. The wire, which was read to the assembled troops, said:

> Send all available forces you can possibly spare to reinforce General Canby, commanding Department of New Mexico, and to keep open his communication through Fort Wise. Act promptly and with all the discretion of your latest information as to what may be necessary and where the troops of Colorado can do the most service. [*United States War Department Records*, Ser. I, IX, 630–32]

Four days later, Weld sent a wire to General Canby:

> Am dispatching the First Colorado under Colonel John P. Slough to your aid. You will find this regiment, I hope, a most efficient one and of great support to you. It has had, of course, no experience in the field, but I trust that their enthusiasm and patriotic bravery will make amends, and more than that, for their lack of active service in the past. [ibid.]

The soldiers at Camp Weld cheered loudly when each of the telegrams was read to them. Hollister wrote that "extraordinary bustle and cheerful activity now prevailed and all were ready to march by the appointed time in the face of the great difficulties then existing."

On the evening of February 22, Colonel Slough received still another wire, this one reporting the first sketchy information about the bloody battle at North Ford. Many of the soldiers in camp had been personally acquainted with Captain Alexander McRae, and news of his bravery and death was the talk of the camp. The fact that a real person, a friend, had been killed in battle was sobering to the troops and they reacted to the news by training harder and resolving to "get even."

First reports from the New Mexico battlefield (later proved to be erroneous) stated that of Captain Dodd's company all but two men had been killed in the fight. These were grim reports, and the camp suddenly took on a somber, professional air of quiet determination.

Several of the companies were temporarily dispatched to Fort Wise, situated on the north bank of the Arkansas River in southeastern Colorado. The fort had been built to control Indians in the area, and was isolated from almost everything else. However, it was the first military outpost north of Fort Union, and was not far from the Santa Fe Trail. As such, the fort was strategically located and of great importance to the defense of Colorado.

At Fort Wise (soon renamed Fort Lyon), the Colorado soldiers discovered that military life was not always as easy as what they had experienced at Camp Weld.

Fort Wise consisted of a dozen buildings constructed of mud and rocks, with dirt roofs and floors and virtually no furniture. When the soldiers arrived, it had been snowing heavily and the buildings were cold. Faced with the situation, the men stole their own army wagons and used the boxes for bunks. Other wagons were broken up and used to build furniture, or to feed the fires built to heat the buildings.

There was not enough food available at Fort Wise to satisfy the hungry soldiers, and several soon broke into a nearby store. The store was rumored to be owned by a secessionist, who was said to be sending money and supplies to the Rebels. After the break-in, the owner complained to the base commander and a full scale investigation was ordered. Private Hollister said that the men of Company F did not participate in the burglary, but did help themselves to some stolen candy. They were quickly spotted and arrested. Fortunately, he says, the army investigated and exonerated itself, so all the men were released!

In Denver, Colonel Slough now received a direct order from incoming Governor John Evans. Slough was to take the First Colorado Volunteers and proceed "as rapidly as possible to New Mexico, there to act independently if unable to contact General Canby." And the orders went on to specify that Slough and the First Colorado were to "locate, engage and harass the enemy." The wording of that final line was to become a bone of contention within a few weeks.

Early the following morning, March 1, 1862, 900 officers and men of the First Colorado Volunteers set out from Camp Weld; the other 300 men of the unit were now stationed at Fort Wise. Still plagued by a shortage of horses, only 400 of the men were mounted; the cavalry unit was led by Major Chivington. Colonel Slough traveled by carriage, but the remaining 500 soldiers walked. They were followed by 37 wagons loaded with their baggage, and with supplies and food. They also brought with them a half dozen small, brass cannons, including the one purchased earlier from Charles Autobee and the one found in the fodder stack in southeastern Colorado.

At first, the southward trek of the First Colorado went very well. The soldiers marched smartly south along the South Platte River, and when the river turned toward the mountains they continued due southward toward the Monument Divide. By midafternoon they had reached the summit of Monument Hill and started down the tree-covered south side slope of the divide. They camped that night some forty-five miles south of Denver, and were in high spirits. The men talked constantly of the upcoming confrontation with the Confederates and wondered what it would be like to be under fire and shoot an enemy soldier.

The following day, the soldiers continued to move rapidly southward although there was noticeably less chatter among them. Even though the men were tough from hard-rock mining and from months of training at Camp Weld, the long march with heavy field packs began to take a toll. That night it was a weary group of soldiers who pitched camp a few miles southeast of Pikes Peak.

Shortly before midnight on March 2, a vicious spring storm blew out of the nearby Rockies and engulfed the First Colorado's campground. Wind was estimated at fifty miles an hour, driving snow pellets nearly sideways. The pellets stung when they hit a man's face, and made eyes water. Beards and hair were soon coated with ice. Even soldiers inside their tents were uncomfortable from the bitterly cold wind. They built fires in their Sibley stoves, presumably unaware that the stoves had been invented by the enemy troop commander! And to make matters worse, many of the tents collapsed under the constant pounding by the wind.

Ovando Hollister wrote on the first night of the vicious storm:

> Viewed from a station beyond their influence, snowstorms may be superlatively charming, for all I know—but watching a camp through the long, sullen hours of darkness, when the cold wet snow is driven into one's face almost to smothering, is no place to appreciate their beauties. From 11 o'clock till morning I crouched on the leeward side of a tent, blinded by clouds of smoke from the damp remains of our camp fires.

Most men thought the storm would end with the arrival of the morning sun, as a majority of Colorado snowstorms are wont to do. This one, however, had not yet spent its fury. The storm continued for three full days, piling snow into drifts five feet high. A number of the First Colorado horses and mules died in the blizzard and a half dozen of the soldiers were so severely frostbitten that they had to be returned to a hospital at Colorado City, unable to continue the journey.

Perhaps it was frustration over the storm, or perhaps it was simply time for a long-simmering dispute to fester and burst into the open. Whatever the reason, Major Chivington and Colonel Slough got into a heated shouting match the first night of the storm, an argument so loud it was overheard by scores of the men. Slough apparently wanted to turn back because of the storm, arguing that it was foolish to risk men and animals when Colorado City was only a few miles back up the trail. Major Chivington thought that any pullback was cowardly, disobedient to orders, and a victory for the evil Southerners. He wanted to simply stay in camp until the storm abated, then push on as fast as possible, perhaps even making up any time lost because of the blizzard.

In the heat of the debate, Colonel Slough was heard to shout that Chivington was "a crazy preacher with the idea that you are

Napoleon!" Chivington's answer was not recorded, but the argument halted at that point. Slough stormed out of the tent, got quickly into his enclosed private coach and set off for Colorado City, where he apparently spent the next few days in safety and comfort.

There were already hard feelings against Colonel Slough. Most of the men felt he was aloof and haughty. He was from money and well educated, while most of the soldiers were poor, and few of them had more than a third grade education. Slough was different in other ways, too. He dressed in carefully tailored uniforms while the men wore shoddy, ill-fitting garments. Also Slough never trained with the men, spending his time in headquarters, or in town "for conferences." Now the argument between Slough and the popular John Chivington solidified the men's dislike and distrust of their colonel. No matter what Slough did from that point onward, he was viewed as an outsider and not one of the men.

When the storm at last abated on the morning of March 6, Major Chivington quickly began to rally the troops. Walking from tent to tent, Chivington offered encouragement where needed, stern lectures where warranted, and a helping hand where possible. Two hours later, the half-frozen troops struggled out of camp.

They battled through the drifted snow, trying desperately to keep on the trail that was now virtually invisible. Time after time wagons slipped into ditches or overturned in creeks. The men strained to right the wagons, reload them and push on. Several times one or more horses got stuck in snow drifts and it took several men to drag the frightened animals to safety. But each time the soldiers overcame the latest difficulty and pressed onward, encouraged by John Chivington who seemed always there to lend a hand.

By noon they had traveled something less than ten miles, and when they stopped for lunch the men were simply too tired to go on. They drank deeply from the clear, icy water of Greenhorn Creek and hoped that their officers would permit them to stop for the day. Chivington would not hear of it; in thirty minutes, he had the troops moving again. By sundown they had pushed their way another ten miles along the snow-covered trail, camping that night on Dry Creek.

By the time they finally got their tents erected and their fires built, some of the soldiers were close to rebellion. Even John Chivington's charm could not end the sullenness and hostility that now pervaded the camp. The men were tired, hungry and frustrated. There was open talk of desertion, and no one knows how nasty things might have gotten had not a messenger arrived in camp just then.

The rider had been sent from Colonel Tappan, who commanded the three hundred First Colorado Volunteers then at Fort Wise. The messenger reported that, based on reliable reports from civilians fleeing the area, troops under General Canby had been completely defeated in the battle at North Ford. Not just defeated, but completely crushed. For the first time, the Colorado troops learned that most of the New Mexico volunteers at North Ford had thrown down their weapons and fled, and that only a few hundred regulars remained in New Mexico to face a Rebel army that could number as many as four thousand men.

Colonel Tappan's message was to the point; "For God's sake, you must hurry on. I fear that we may already be too late. The only hope for Canby and for New Mexico—and, ultimately, for the United States—is your timely arrival at Fort Union." Tappan's message went on to report that the victorious Texans had already seized Albuquerque and Santa Fe and would soon be marching to Fort Union. Even if General Canby had managed to get to the fort ahead of the Rebels, he could not possibly have enough troops or weapons to stop the Confederates. If Fort Union fell, warned Tappan, its vast military stores would fall into the hands of the enemy, and then there would be no stopping the Texans until they reached Fort Laramie. Tappan said he and the three hundred troops under his command were leaving Fort Wise at once and would meet the remainder of the First Colorado at Fort Union.

When he had finished reading the message to the troops, Major Chivington stood in silence for several long seconds. Then, speaking in a quiet but determined voice, he told the soldiers he would not belittle them by repeating what had just been said. But he added, "The disaster that will follow a Confederate victory at Fort Union will be our personal disaster. If the Rebels get Union, there'll be no stopping them in Colorado."

He paused once again for effect, a technique he had polished during all those years in the pulpit, and the silence was almost eerie. Finally Chivington asked if the men were willing to endure the fatigue of forced marches "in order to save the honor and property of the republic." There was a chorus of "Yes, sir!" from the gathered soldiers.

"May God have mercy on us," said Chivington, who then commanded the troops to abandon everything except their weapons, one spare shirt, an extra canteen, enough hardtack and coffee for two days on the trail, and two blankets. He ordered the teamsters, driving the supply wagons, to pick up the men's cast-off baggage and "catch up with us when you can." Then the major turned again to the soldiers and warned them, "We will make 65 miles every 24 hours until we reach Fort Union. It is the only way!" [Whitford, *The Battle of Glorieta Pass*, pp. 16–17.] To their credit, none of the soldiers so much as murmured any displeasure or offered resistance.

And they followed through on their promise. The following night, the determined volunteers camped sixty-three miles closer to Fort Union. Yet, even that herculean effort was not enough.

The weary soldiers had been in their bedrolls less than five hours when another messenger rode into camp. This one was Captain Will Garrison, Chief of Subsistence at Fort Union. His message contained even more ominous news than had the first. Confederates, he said, had not just been victorious at North Ford, they had wreaked utter destruction on Union forces and then had ravaged Albuquerque and Santa Fe. Civilians had been mistreated, buildings burned. There were reports that General Sibley had replenished all of his supplies with goods taken from the cities, and that he was now well equipped to march all the way to Denver without serious shortages of any kind. More discouraging were the reports that scores, perhaps hundreds, of New Mexico men had volunteered to join the Confederate Army. "You are our only hope," the message said. "Unless you can stop them before they reach Fort Union, Johnny Reb will soon own the entire West."

Chivington again rallied his troops. He ordered the men to abandon everything except their rifles, one spare shirt and their two blankets, and then to race onward "as fast as you can go" toward Fort Union. Even though the men had been dragged out of a deep sleep and were still exhausted from the previous day's march, the weary soldiers once again accepted without complaint the seemingly impossible order. Within minutes, the column was again pushing toward New Mexico.

The following day, March 5, the soldiers hurrying south from Denver met up with the two companies that had been dispatched from Fort Wise. That brought the Colorado contingent back up to full strength, approximately twelve hundred men.

But the soldiers from Fort Wise brought bad news. Forty-two Confederate soldiers who had earlier been captured and held at Fort Wise had escaped federal custody. They most likely had reached General Sibley by this time, and the escapees had full knowledge that the Colorado soldiers had been dispatched to stop Sibley's invaders. They also knew that the Coloradans numbered only about one-third his own troop strength. The escapees had thus effectively eliminated the element of surprise as well as any possibility of bluffing the Rebels as to the size and strength of their units!

Now in desperation, the Colorado soldiers began to steal horses and mules from ranchers along the way. They argued that the thefts were justified under the circumstances. Private Hollister said, "If we gave offense in this unavoidable proceeding, it should be attributed to the pressure of the circumstances." He added that he hoped the good citizens of Colorado would understand.

Private Hollister and other soldiers, who already disliked Colonel Slough, now began to openly hate him. Up until now he had been held in formal military respect at the very least. Many of the soldiers tried their best to actually like him although Slough did not seem very "military," and always separated himself from the men as if he felt socially superior to them.

The soldiers had discussed Slough many times before, comparing the Colonel to Major Chivington, who was always friendly with the men, always fair, always willing to lend a helping hand. Until now, however, no one was openly hostile to Slough. The final straw that forever ended Slough's ability to command the First Colorado occurred that evening.

The exhausted soldiers had once again made camp and were gathering for dinner. Colonel Slough came riding past the gathered privates, apparently to meet with Major Chivington. A spontaneous cheer went up from the soldiers. They were cheering Slough to show their support, their loyalty to both him and the Union, their determination to meet and whip the enemy at any personal price. It should have been a heart-warming moment for Slough. Instead, the Colonel looked surprised. He blinked in amazement at the men, finally touched the bill of his hat, and rode on.

Hollister spoke for the men when he wrote in his diary that evening:

> How little some men understand human nature! He had been our colonel six months; had never spoken to us; and on the eve of an important expedition, after a long absence, could not see that a few words were indispensable to a good understanding. He has a noble appearance, but the men . . . lack confidence in him. Why, I cannot tell—nor can they, I think. His aristocratic style savors more of Eastern society than of the free-and-easy border to which he should have become acclimated, but that it is bred in the bone!

Before sunrise on March 9, the soldiers were met by several mule-drawn flat-bed ambulances, hauling seriously wounded Union troops northward out of New Mexico. These were soldiers who had been evacuated from the battlefield at the North Ford, but whose conditions were now deteriorating due to infection. It was believed that should they fall into the hands of the Confederates they would simply be allowed to die without medical attention, or such basic necessities of food and water. Thus, even though many of the men were desperately ill and near death, they were being moved from Fort Union to anywhere in Colorado they might find help.

Major Chivington talked with several of the ambulance drivers, then again addressed his troops. "We are only 120 miles from Fort Union, and the enemy has not yet arrived there. Abandon everything now except your rifles and ammunition. We must race faster than ever before to secure the Fort before the Rebs arrive." Surprisingly, the soldiers responded immediately. It is amazing the physical hardships men can endure when they set their minds to it. The soldiers tossed down their heavy backpacks of blankets, extra shirts and food, leaving it all for the wagon drivers to pick up and bring along at some later date.

The four hundred mounted soldiers under Major Chivington now left the main body of troops and made a dash for Fort Union. The foot soldiers followed behind as quickly as they could. By the time they halted eighteen hours later, Major Chivington's mounted troops had covered more than one hundred miles and the infantry had covered an incredible sixty-two miles over rough, hilly terrain. During that long day, several horses dropped dead from "overwork and underfeed." Hollister noted with disgust that Colonel Slough rode in a coach the entire way.

On March 10, snow and strong wind again hampered both columns of Colorado soldiers. Major Chivington gave up his favorite horse, a big gray, because it was needed to pull a wagon loaded with ammunition. Chivington switched to a saddle mule. That evening, both animals died of exhaustion. The good news, however, was that the cavalry was now only ten miles from Fort Union.

Because of the storm and their exhaustion, the infantry covered only ten miles that day, and was still forty-five miles from the fort. They camped near Reyado on a ranch owned by Lucien Maxwell. Maxwell was an ardent supporter of the Union and could not do enough for the soldiers. He fed them, helped them make beds in the barn after his house was completely filled with tired soldiers, and then he gave them 160 pounds of sugar, 100 pounds of coffee and other supplies needed to sustain their efforts.

On the morning of March 11, Major Chivington's cavalry finally reached the front gates of Fort Union shortly after dawn. As they topped the final hill they were relieved to see the American flag fluttering from atop the pole.

Fort Union lies in the middle of a small valley, about four miles across. To the east and west of the fort are tree-covered ridges. A small stream runs along the floor of the valley during the wet months, but is dry the remainder of the year. Journalist/soldier Hollister said the fort is:

> . . . a simple field-work of moderate size, with bastioned corners surrounded by dirt parapet and ditch. The armament is poor, consisting mostly of howitzers, but the supply of ammunition is deemed sufficient for any emergency. It has bromb-proof quarters in and surrounding it, forming part of the works, sufficiently large to accommodate 500 men besides the necessary room for stores.

Inside the fort, a nervous New Mexico Governor Connelly and Colonel Gabriel Paul were both waiting anxiously for the Coloradans. After the new arrivals dismounted, Governor Connelly formally welcomed them to New Mexico. He commented enthusiastically about the speed with which the Coloradans had made the trip, and thanked the men profusely for coming. Strangely, however, he made no mention of the North Ford Battle nor of the enemy, now encamped in Albuquerque and Santa Fe. The Coloradans thought it extremely odd! The omission was never explained.

It was twelve hours later, 9:00 P.M., when the infantry soldiers arrived so exhausted they could barely walk the last mile, even though the fort was in sight. When they found the sutler's store already closed for the night, the soldiers broke down the door and helped themselves to cheese, champagne and other food. Many of the men drank themselves to drunken oblivion in the corral alongside the weary horses, while some others collapsed and spent the night on the ground in front of the barracks. The majority, of course, made it into the barracks where they collapsed gratefully onto available cots.

The drinking that night did lead to a distasteful incident. Sergeant Amos Philbrook of Company K became inebriated, loud and boisterous. After he was warned several times to quiet down, Lieutenant Isaac Gray of B Company placed Philbrook under arrest for drunkenness. Philbrook whipped out his revolver and shot Lieutenant Gray in the face. Fortunately, the bullet struck the lieutenant a glancing blow, taking a chunk of skin from his nose and cheek but inflicting no lasting damage.

A mob of angry soldiers quickly surrounded Philbrook and might have lynched him on the spot, given the popularity of Lieutenant Gray. Fortunately, cooler heads prevailed and Sergeant Philbrook was merely hauled off to the stockade on charges of attempted murder.

Historian Alvin Josephy says the forced march to Fort Union demonstrated the physical strength of these Colorado mountain men and may help explain their toughness in the battles that followed. Said Josephy, "The 1st Colorado was a rough, brawling outfit, composed largely of miners, frontiersmen and the denizens of Denver's saloons. Bored by inaction in their Colorado camps, the troops were spoiling for any kind of a fight.

Their swift march south across the high plains and over the Raton Mountains in freezing weather put the hardiest of them to the test" [Josephy, *War on the Frontier*, p. 217].

The following morning, General Canby arrived at Fort Union, accompanied by the remainder of the Second Colorado Volunteers and about three hundred volunteers from the New Mexico militia. There were joyous reunions between men of the First and Second Colorado, and many a tear shed over those who were missing from the reunion.

One day later, the baggage abandoned by the First Colorado back on the trail during their forced march toward Fort Union finally arrived at camp. Soldiers were reunited with missing shirts, blankets and other personal items.

That same afternoon General Canby issued arms, ammunition and new clothing to the Coloradans. In many cases, the rifles they received were far superior to those weapons with which they left Denver. It would now be a far better equipped First Colorado that finally challenged the enemy!

On the morning of March 14 a messenger arrived at Fort Union with a report that some of Canby's pickets had captured a large wagon train of supplies headed for General Sibley. The pickets managed to take 150 Rebel soldiers as prisoners, and brought them to Fort Union for incarceration. The prisoners seemed to take their capture lightly and indicated they were convinced they would soon be set free by the Confederate army. Several of the captured Texans boasted that Sibley was rapidly swelling his ranks with volunteers who became eager to join the Confederacy after seeing the whipping administered to the Union forces at the North Ford.

One of the difficulties facing officers and men of the Union army was that their isolation made it difficult for them to receive any reliable news of what was going on. Rumors also begin to circulate through camp that a huge Union relief column was on the way to Fort Union from somewhere in Kansas. The relief column never materialized and apparently was never more than a figment of someone's imagination.

CHAPTER NINE

THE STRUGGLE TO CONTROL NEW MEXICO

On the inside, the houses are neat and cozy; the walls nicely white-washed; the fireplaces small and handy, shaped like the half of an old-fashioned beehive, with a small flue leading out for a chimney. Their mattresses, made of wool, are doubled up during the day and form a pleasant settee, ranging round the sides of the apartment. A table, two or three rude stools, a skillet, a coffee-pot and frying pan comprise the furniture, while ornaments, even among the best class, consist wholly of ordinary prints of sacred subjects, mounted in tin frames, and images of saints, roughly carved in wood.

Ovando J. Hollister, Company F
First Colorado Volunteers
(Describing the homes of Las Vegas, New Mexico)

*T*he bitter feelings toward Colonel John Slough that started at Camp Weld and grew on the long march from Denver to Fort Union mushroomed into full scale hatred at the latter place. Slough never seemed to know when to keep his disagreements with fellow officers secret. The latest incident, the one that finally turned all remaining Colorado officers and soldiers firmly against Slough, occurred while the men were waiting at Fort Union for further orders.

Slough and veteran U.S. Army Colonel Gabriel Paul seemed instantly to dislike one another. Unfortunately for Slough, it was readily apparent, even to the greenest recruit, that Paul was many times better at soldiering than was Slough. Paul had made the army his career. He was a graduate of West Point, a veteran of Indian campaigns and the Mexican-American War, and had acquitted himself well in all those actions. He had also been one of the few Union stalwarts at the recent Battle of North Ford.

The prolific Hollister described Paul this way:

Colonel Paul of the fourth New Mexican, is a sterling officer—one of the few never cursed by the soldiers. The best tactician in New Mexico and a strict disciplinarian, he combines so much judgement and tact in the discharge of his duty as to seldom give offense. His pluck is indomintable as was proven on the bloody fields of Mexico, and his men place all confidence in his thorough devotion to the cause of the Government. Of a medium size, the severe regularity of his features, his silvery hair and gentlemanly carriage compel respect. He dresses in citizen's clothes, puts on no unwarrantable airs, but quietly attends to his own affairs. From close observation, I caught the impression that Paul is a man of deep and earnest convictions, endowed with the courage to follow wherever they lead—as a soldier, brave and true, quick to decide and prompt to execute. He will attain a much higher rank before the war is over if justice is done to his deserts.

Yet Colonel Slough loudly let it be known that by virtue of his appointment by Governor Gilpin as commanding officer of the First Colorado Volunteers and due to the fact that the vast majority of troops at Fort Union were from Colorado, that made him the superior officer on the base. Except for General Canby, Slough said he would answer to no man at Fort Union. While Paul must have known that General Canby or virtually any other commanding officer would overrule Slough, he chose not to contest the issue at the moment. Some of the men had overheard Slough's outburst and were furious that the unlikeable Slough won the argument and the command.

As it turned out, it was probably a good thing that he did so, for the real basis of the argument between Colonels Slough and Paul centered on battle tactics for the approaching showdown with General Sibley. Colonel Paul said that the really important thing for the troops to do was to remain at Fort Union and wait for the Confederates. He believed the Coloradans and New Mexico volunteers on hand could hold out indefinitely against a frontal assault by the Rebels. Had Paul's plan been adopted, the troops likely would have been massacred by the big artillery of the advancing Rebel army.

Slough, on the other hand, did not want to hang around Fort Union. Fudging a little on the wording of his telegram from Governor Evans, Slough told Paul, "My orders are to act independently against the enemy. If we advance over the same route he is most likely to pursue in coming toward the fort, we can both defend the fort and simultaneously better harass the enemy, obstruct his movement and cut off his supplies."

Slough told General Canby of his plan to seek out the enemy and attack while Sibley was least expecting it. Colonel Slough agreed (for once) with Major Chivington, who wanted to head straight for Santa Fe by the shortest possible route and try to catch the Texans while they rested in the community and were unprepared for battle. General Canby liked the plan and gave his approval. Thus, on the afternoon of March 21, Colonel Slough sent word to the troops that they were to be prepared to march the following morning, Saturday, March 22.

The men knew that the order meant combat was near. Some of the soldiers, perhaps most of them, decided to have a last fling that evening. The soldiers again broke into the sutler's store and stole all the alcohol they could find. Some sneaked off base and went to the little town of Lome, about five miles away, and drank until the bars closed well after midnight. Several were arrested on charges of "drunk and disorderly," and were still housed in the town jail when the rest of the army moved out the next day. Major Chivington dispatched a special envoy to plead with town officials to release the soldiers because they were needed for battle; the town officials agreed and freed the men from jail.

Private Hollister said that the men stole so much liquor they could not drink it all that night. He wrote in his diary that the men "drank some, lost some, sold some, buried some for later parties which were never to be."

Colonel Paul requested that at least a token force be left behind to guard Fort Union against a surprise attack, but Slough would not hear of it. He would take all of the First Colorado, Captain Ford's company of unattached Second Colorado, and as many volunteers as would accompany them. When the army set out the following day it numbered 1,342 Coloradans and about 300 New Mexico militiamen—a total of 1,642 men, of whom about 400 were mounted.

Their departure was not without the usual "hurry up and wait" confusion common to military actions. The troops were lined up and prepared to march out of the fort at 5:00 A.M., then were ordered to stand down, supposedly because a message had been received from General Canby. At mid-morning, they lined up again, only to stand down again thirty minutes later. They finally got underway shortly after noon.

At Albuquerque, meanwhile, some of the Confederate soldiers who had escaped from Fort Wise now arrived at General Sibley's headquarters and briefed him on the advancing First Colorado Volunteers, whom they thought to still be somewhere in Colorado. They also said it appeared the Coloradans planned to merely assume a defensive position at Fort Union. Since Sibley, himself, had superintended the building of the fort he knew full well its strategic importance to his campaign. If Sibley held the fort, he would dominate New Mexico and have an excellent base of operations for his planned invasion of Colorado. If the Coloradans took the fort, they could seriously delay and hamper the Confederate movement into Colorado.

Accordingly, upon hearing that the Coloradans were coming, Sibley ordered his own army to prepare to move out of Albuquerque on Saturday morning, March 22. They were to march to Santa Fe, consolidate with soldiers in that city, and then move en masse to Fort Union. Sibley believed that the Coloradans, most of whom were on foot, were most likely still somewhere in the middle of Colorado heading south. It appeared to the general that he had plenty of time to capture Fort Union and then hold a surprise welcoming party of the "pet lambs."

Capturing the fort and lying in wait for the Coloradans could only be accomplished, however, if the Southerners moved without delay. Sibley had originally planned to follow the main trail from Santa Fe eastward to Las Vegas. The main trail swung well south of Santa Fe in order to traverse a gentle pass over the Sandia Ridge, and it would be about a four day march for the Confederates.

On the other hand, there was a more direct route, straight up Glorieta Pass, which ran almost due east out of Santa Fe. The pass is not unlike thousands of others in the Rocky Mountains; narrow and deep in places, wide and shallow in others. At both ends of the pass, La Glorieta is extremely narrow with sheer rock walls that rise a thousand feet or more nearly straight up. At many points along the passage, however, the walls of the canyon pull back, leaving flat, rocky glens as much as twelve hundred feet wide.

The road up Glorieta Pass was narrow and rough, and it would be hard to get the artillery and some of the wagons up the trail. Yet, the army could cut two full days off the trip to Fort Union by taking the more direct route. Sibley ordered that his army prepare to move by way of Glorieta Pass.

March 23. The advancing Union army crossed the El Rio Gallinan, the most northerly branch of the Pecos River. Advancing a few miles along the south bank, the soldiers came eventually to Las Vegas, New Mexico, the temporary location of the New Mexico government. Writer Hollister wasn't impressed: "It has the appearance, at a distance, of a clump of bushes or rocks—and improves but slightly on closer acquaintance!"

The people of Las Vegas seemed to know little of the war being fought only a few miles from their homes. There was a vague awareness that the Confederates were in New Mexico, but most local residents were surprised at this Union army marching to engage the Rebels. The villagers seemed apolitical, and were not eager to get involved on either side. Nonetheless, they treated the Colorado soldiers as their guests, sharing generously of their food and opening their homes for the soldiers to sleep in that night.

After their camp was established, some of the soldiers sought to take advantage of being in a town. They set out to find entertainment, or something worth stealing. Hollister said "both were distressingly scarce; there was precious little to steal and as to the women, the sight of them was more sedative than stimulating. If there chanced to be one that by any possible stretch of courtesy could be termed decent, there were enough around her to eat her and then go off with empty stomachs!"

On the Morning of March 24, the First Colorado left Las Vegas at sunrise and almost immediately entered rolling hill country. By noon they had passed through Teculote and crossed another branch of the Pecos. By sundown they were at Ojo de Vernal, also called Vernal Springs, at the very edge of the Sandia Ridge. Just a few miles ahead of them were the mountains and beyond the hills lay Santa Fe and the Confederates. Most of the

Coloradans were ordered to stop for the night, although Company F was sent eight miles further to camp at San Jose and see if they could pick up any news about General Sibley.

On March 25, the advance units of the First Colorado passed though the village of Pecos and halted at the Kozlowski Ranch near the top of Glorieta Canyon. Major Chivington's four hundred cavalrymen made camp a half mile from the nearest building and then sent a messenger up to the ranch house to let the residents know that the Coloradans intended them no harm.

The rancher, Martin Kozlowski, turned out to be an ardent Union supporter who welcomed the troops, invited them to his home and fed them. Very soon, his ranch would be turned into a field hospital where wounded troops from both armies would spend the next several months recuperating from their wounds. The ranch would also play host to teams of Union doctors and officers who used it as their New Mexico headquarters for the next several months. But Kozlowski never complained; he felt it was his duty to help in every way possible.

For the duration of these arrangements, Martin Kozlowski would be a most gracious host, and the men treated him with respect and admiration. In that regard, it was an unusual arrangement; troops on both sides of the war sometimes did not treat civilians with either respect or honesty. Noted one historian, "Kozlowski alone, unlike others who encountered troops from either side, had no trouble with the soldiers who stayed at his ranch for a total of about 60 days. Kozlowski, a Polish immigrant and U.S. Army veteran, later wrote, 'When they camped on my place and while they made my tavern their hospital for over two months after their battles in the canyon, they never robbed me of anything, not even a chicken!'"

But, while the rancher welcomed Major Chivington and his troops, he also had a bit of bad news for them; advance elements of the Confederate Army were already in the immediate vicinity. Several Texans had been at his camp just an hour earlier, apparently scouting the shortest way to Fort Union. Based on what the Rebel scouts had told him, Kozlowski feared that as many as six hundred Rebels could already be in the area. And based on what he had been told by several of the Confederate scouts who had stopped at the ranch house for water, a lot more enemy soldiers would be there within a day or so.

It may have been bad news to Kozlowski, but it was good news to the Coloradans; they had come all the way to New Mexico specifically to find and do battle with the Confederates. Major Chivington ordered Lieutenant George Nelson to take twenty men and try to locate the Confederate scouts.

Nelson soon picked up the trail, leading to the Pigeon Ranch, which stands at the top of the pass that leads from the high plateau country down the Sandia Mountains to Santa Fe. The pass actually consists of two parts, the upper canyon called Glorieta Canyon, and the lower, known as Apache Canyon. Together, they were called Glorieta Pass.

The Union patrol searched the ranch without finding the Confederates, but as they started back down the trail toward the Kowlozski Ranch they spotted four men riding toward them in the moonlight. The four were Confederate scouts, who mistook the Lieutenant Nelson and the Coloradans for Confederate troops and rode directly into their midst before recognizing their error.

The four Rebels were taken prisoner without a shot being fired. Disarmed and with hands tied behind them, they were hustled back to Major Chivington's command tent for questioning. Two of the captured Confederates were officers: Lieutenant Charles McIntyre and Captain Wayne Hall. Lieutenant McIntyre had originally been a Union officer and had served under General Canby at the Battle of North Ford only to switch sides after the Union army was crushed there. Captain Hall was a former Denver businessman and was personally acquainted with his captors, including Major Chivington.

The captured Confederates seemed not at all dismayed to have been taken prisoner. They boasted to their captors that General Sibley's invasion force was so powerful that there was nothing the Coloradans could do to stop it. "If you know what's good for you, you'll turn us loose and high-tail it back to Denver," said McIntyre to Major Chivington.

"You couldn't stop us if there were five times as many of you," added Captain Hall. Then he added, "One Confederate soldier is worth five Yankees any day."

Because of the disdain for their captors, McIntyre and Hall talked freely about what was going on at the Confederate headquarters, including the Rebel plan to march up Glorieta Pass, capture Fort Union and then take the remainder of the West. They also casually mentioned that the Rebels probably would start up the pass the following morning, Wednesday, March 26.

Major Chivington dispatched a rider to race back and alert the Colorado infantry that the Confederates were starting up the canyon the next day. He also sent word to Colonel Slough that he intended to meet the Rebels in the canyon and try to delay them until the remaining Colorado troops could arrive on the scene.

General Sibley now received word that sizeable numbers of Union soldiers had apparently passed through Las Vegas, heading for Santa Fe. That was somewhat puzzling, since those Colorado soldiers should still be several days away. Sibley assumed the soldiers who had been in Las Vegas were local volunteers, New Mexico militiamen. While they were troublesome, they had already shown themselves to be poor soldiers and Sibley was not overly concerned just because some of them were still operating in an area through which he intended to pass within twenty-four hours.

Sibley ordered Colonel Scurry to select about five hundred troops and take them to the top of Glorieta Pass. They were to secure the route for the artillery, supply wagons and foot soldiers who followed, and were to scout the country to make certain there was no serious enemy activity in the area. If the enemy were found, they were to be "engaged and destroyed" by this sizeable scouting party of Scurry's.

Colonel Scurry, who also had direct responsibility for the Confederate artillery, passed along a portion of his responsibility to Major Charles Pyron, another veteran of the Mexican War. It was Pyron who would actually take the five-hundred-man vanguard up Glorieta Pass the following day. Scurry would remain behind to help haul the clumsy artillery up the steep and rough canyon road.

On the evening of March 25, the entire Confederate army of perhaps as many as 3600 to 4000 soldiers made camp at the foot of Apache Canyon. Until General Sibley was certain that the canyon was secure, he planned to keep the bulk of the troops and all the supplies safe at that location.

While Pyron and his five hundred horsemen rode up the canyon the following day, Sibley and the remainder of the men would establish a base of operations at the bottom of the pass. True to his military training, Sibley wanted the camp to be correct and neat in every detail.

The general met with his junior officers that evening and told them exactly how he wanted the camp laid out. The supply wagons were to be lined up side-by-side, wheels nearly touching, and were to be parked facing the trail so that they could be easily accessed during any battle, or when the time came to move. A nearby box canyon would serve neatly as a corral for the hundreds of mules and horses that normally pulled the supply wagons. Another small box canyon would serve as a temporary prison in the event any Union soldiers were taken prisoner. Sibley also pointed out the area in which two huge hospital tents were to be erected, and the area for the mess tent and the general camp ground for the troops.

Sibley was fastidious and expected the camp to be perfect in every detail. He inspected progress several times to make certain the camp was exactly as he wanted it. It was not until almost midnight that the general was finally satisfied with the camp and permitted his tired soldiers to go to bed.

Without knowing it, General Sibley had just set the stage for his ultimate and complete defeat.

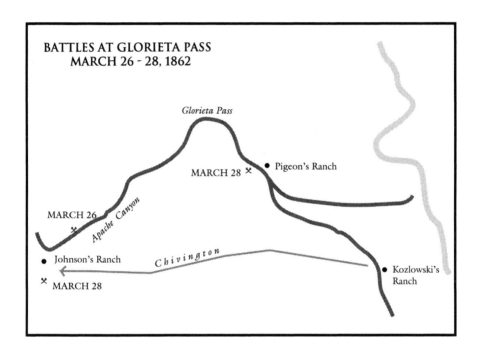

BATTLES AT GLORIETA PASS
MARCH 26 - 28, 1862

Glorieta Pass

MARCH 28 ✗ ● Pigeon's Ranch

MARCH 26
✗ *Apache Canyon*

● Johnson's Ranch

Chivington

✗ MARCH 28

● Kozlowski's
Ranch

CHAPTER TEN

THE BATTLE OF GLORIETA PASS, PART I

We thought it likely we would meet a force of Texans during the day, but it is doubtful if many [of us] realized the issues involved in the meeting. If he had, we would have stolen a longer and tenderer look at some of our comrades, whose countenances were soon to be robed in death.

Private Ovando J. Hollister, Company F
First Colorado Volunteers
(Preparing to march down Glorieta Pass)

At 8:00 A.M. on the morning of March 26, Major Chivington took a mixed group of cavalry and infantry, including Company F, and began the trip down Glorieta Pass from Pigeon Ranch. The Union force was led by approximately 190 cavalrymen, followed closely by 225 infantrymen. Several mounted scouts were sent ahead of the main party. Rumors begin to circulate among the troops that the enemy was already in the canyon and possibly only a short distance away.

At first, the men were tense and even fearful, but as time passed with no sign of the enemy they began to loosen up. By late morning it appeared that all the rumors were false and no enemy was any closer than Santa Fe. Some of the soldiers actually began to enjoy the scenery in the canyon, especially the deer and the eagles, both of which seemed everywhere.

At noon, the soldiers took a relaxing lunch break. By 12:30 they were underway again, seemingly carefree as they resumed their march down the canyon. One soldier wrote in his diary that "the day was so pleasant that it hardly seemed we could be marching to battle, possibly to death. Only that nagging reality kept the day from being perfect."

A dozen Union scouts were riding about a mile ahead of the main body of troops. At precisely 2:00 P.M. this group of pickets rounded a sharp curve in the trail and were surprised to suddenly find themselves literally in the middle of a group of thirty Texas scouts. The Texans had been riding in advance of Major Scurry's five-hundred-man vanguard. The Rebels were so startled by the sudden appearance of the Coloradans that none had time to even draw a weapon. All of the Confederates were taken prisoner by the Yankees and then hustled back up the trail to Major Chivington.

Chivington briefly questioned the prisoners who, like the four prisoners captured the previous night, made light of their situation. They believed that the few men they saw with Chivington was the entire Colorado army, and gleefully boasted that "Old General Sibley will make short work of these Pike's Peakers!" The prisoners told Chivington that they were followed closely by "about a thousand men"—a figure roughly double the actual number of troops accompanying Colonel Scurry up the pass. They suggested that the Union soldiers "should turn around and run all the way back to the hills of Colorado" if they wanted to live another day.

Chivington had already learned from the captives what he wanted to know, that a sizeable Confederate vanguard was in the canyon and heading toward the Coloradans. He ordered that the prisoners be taken back to the top of the pass and held at the Kozlowski barn where the four earlier prisoners were already housed. The major also told his guards to inform the remainder of the First Colorado that Chivington's advance force was about to engage the enemy somewhere in Glorieta Pass.

One of scouts assigned to this guard duty now turned to the men with Chivington. "We've got 'em corralled this time. Give them hell, boys. Hurrah for the Pikes Peakers!"

Hollister recorded what happened next: "Instantly the ranks closed up, the cavalry took open orders by fours and we rushed forward on the double-quick. Knapsacks, canteens, overcoats and clothing of all kinds were flung along the road as the boys stripped for the encounter." That first clash with the Texans was only minutes away.

Major Scurry's Texas vanguard consisted of between four hundred and five hundred men, which included the 2nd Texas Mounted Rifles and four companies of the 5th Texas. This entire unit was late leaving camp that morning, having delayed their departure to help wrestle some of the heavy supply wagons into place beside the trail as ordered by General Sibley. As a result, they had marched only an hour before breaking for lunch at about the middle of Apache Canyon. As soon as they finished eating, they set out again. By 1:00 P.M. they reached the top of the lower portion of the pass, Apache Canyon, crossed a mesa and began the climb up Glorieta Canyon.

The march was difficult for the Confederates, not only because it was constantly uphill, but also because of the altitude. The middle of Glorieta Canyon was more than a mile above sea level, surrounded by peaks that jutted more than two miles into the sky; the summit of the pass itself was over seven thousand feet above the sea.

At about 2:00 P.M., they entered a wide place of the canyon, a glen, really, about 250 yards wide and perhaps 600 yards long. The glen was nearly treeless and was reasonably flat except for occasional boulders that littered the canyon floor. On either side, the rocky walls rose sharply higher. The ground nearest the canyon walls were heavily covered with piñon pine, scrub oak and assorted other trees and bushes.

Through the center of this little valley ran a deep arroyo, crossing completely from one side of the canyon to the other. This gully had been carved by thousands of years of fast-moving water cascading off the steep mountain walls and racing toward a little stream on the far side of the glen. The arroyo was any-where from eight to twenty feet wide, and from fifteen to twenty-five feet deep. It was impossible to cross the arroyo except by way of a narrow wooden bridge at about the center of the glen. The bridge was sixteen feet long, and just wide enough to permit passage of a standard wagon.

Colonel Scurry led his troops across the bridge to the east side of the arroyo, and then ordered them to take a break. The weary soldiers, who had been pushing uphill for something more than three hours were grateful for the rest. They dropped in their tracks, panting for breath. Many of the soldiers lay on their backs staring at the sky and enjoying the warmth of the mid-day sun, their rifles carelessly dropped in the grass nearby.

They had been thus resting for no more than a minute or so, when suddenly the upper entrance to the glen was filled with Union soldiers, led by Major John Chivington. The startled Confederates, of course, had expected to be warned by their advance scouting party if any enemy soldiers were operating in the area. The appearance of the Coloradans came as a complete surprise.

Regardless of the surprise, though, the Rebels recovered quickly and "unfurled in defiance its red flag, on which was displayed the emblem of Texas, the 'Lone Star,' and planted in the road its artillery, two fine howitzers, guarded by mounted infantry." (Hollister saw the Lone Star banner as "a saucy little red flag emblazoned with the emblem of which Texas has small reason to be proud!")

The Confederates were already battle-tested and reacted quickly to the appearance of Major Chivington's troops. Within seconds, the Rebels had opened fire with rifles and howitzers, sending minié balls and grape shot ricochetting off the rocky canyon walls.

The untested First Colorado, under fire for the first time, milled about in confusion, or dived for cover. About half of the mounted troops leaped from their horses and fled into the trees on either side of the canyon, while the infantry spread out across the canyon floor, hiding behind rocks and ridges for protection from the enemy gunfire. It seems likely that had the Texans launched a full-scale attack at that moment, they would have overwhelmed the Union forces with minimal loss to their own troops.

They did not launch a charge, however. They stood and fired. Their failure to rush the Union line gave Major Chivington an opportunity to get his troops calmed down and organized. In seconds he was shouting orders that sent soldiers into fighting position. The remaining mounted men, those who had not abandoned their horses, were sent to the rear under the command of Captain George W. Howland.

There were just over one hundred of these mounted troops and Chivington ordered them held in reserve unless the Confederates were forced to begin a retreat. In that case, the mounted troops were to pursue the enemy as quickly as possible.

Chivington ordered Captain Samuel Cook to join Captain Howland in reserve. As he turned to lead his troops back up the canyon, however, Cook, who had been the first recruit and the first officer of the First Colorado Volunteers, was hit in the right thigh by a "one ounce ball and three buckshot"; he thus has the dubious honor of also being the first known casualty of the Battle of Glorieta Pass. Cook was not knocked from his horse, however, and continued to lead and organize his troops in spite of the painful injuries and his continued bleeding.

Captains Wynkoop and Anthony deployed their infantry companies as skirmishers among the trees on the left side of the canyon; they were soon joined there by Captain Charles Walker. Captain Downing headed into the trees on the right, and the remaining troops were scattered out across the canyon floor seeking shelter wherever they could find it.

The hilly, rocky terrain nullified much of the effect of the Confederate artillery. Most of the cannon balls sailed over rocks and ridges and crashed harmlessly on the surrounding hillsides. The Coloradans, firing their rifles and smaller cannons from the uphill position and shooting into the line of Confederates who had not sought shelter, were soon inflicting heavy casualties on the Rebels. In moments, Major Pyron's position became untenable and he ordered his soldiers to begin to withdraw.

Under heavy covering fire, the Rebels raced downhill and back across the narrow wooden bridge. Once below the bridge, Pyron ordered the six howitzers to concentrate their fire on the approaches to the bridge. That, he presumed, would hold the Union on the far side of the ditch. The remainder of the Confederate troops now spread out behind rocks and the few trees along the west side of the arroyo and poured their deadly fire at the Coloradans.

The heavy exchange continued for several minutes with neither side appearing to gain any distinct advantage. Each side had soldiers spread out from side to side across the floor of the canyon, and neither was in a position to either advance or withdraw without exposing themselves to murderous enemy fire. For a time it appeared as if the fighting would degenerate into a bloody stalemate, with each side possibly waiting to withdraw until after darkness.

But that suddenly and dramatically changed. Major Chivington appeared at the front of the mounted Coloradans at the upper end of the glen. He was holding a pistol in each hand, and had another shoved under each arm, and a fifth and sixth shoved into the waistband of his trousers. The Major shouted "God save our country. God save Colorado," and suddenly spurred his horse forward.

Aroused and encouraged by Chivington's one-man attack, 103 other mounted Coloradans in Captain Cook's unit also began racing forward. On they came, shouting and shooting as their horses thundered across the rocky canyon floor and headed for the Confederate lines. Major Chivington, riding a considerable distance ahead of the others, was dressed in "full regimentals [and] was a conspicuous mark for the Texan sharp-shooters." A number of Confederate soldiers tried to shoot him out of the saddle but, incredibly, none of their shots struck him; it was as if the leader of the Coloradans was under some magical protective charm. Later, a frustrated Confederate Lieutenant was taken prisoner by the Coloradans. He complained over and over again that he had emptied three revolvers at Chivington and then ordered his company to fire a volley at him; he could not understand how it was possible for Chivington to have escaped injury.

On they came, thundering eight and ten abreast, the horses seemingly flying over the ground as they headed for the arroyo. It was an awe-inspiring sight and the Rebel soldiers could hardly believe their eyes. Almost as if under some spell of their own, the Confederates stopped shooting and stood as if transfixed to watch the Union charge.

On rode Major Chivington and the Colorado cavalry at breakneck speed, on to the edge of the arroyo, and then the horses leaped high into the air. Of the 103 riders, 102 landed safely on the Confederate side of the gully. Only one horse failed to make it across the arroyo; horse and rider crashed to the gully floor and were dashed on the rocks below.

The remaining Union soldiers were in among the Confederates, shooting and slashing with sabers. As the Rebel soldiers rose to defend themselves from these mad horsemen, the remaining Colorado troops leaped to their feet and began pouring across the now-ignored wooden bridge. The Union soldiers were "cheering at the top of their lungs; a battle sweeping down the canyon like a hurricane."

Then it was the Texans who seemed to panic as their casualties began to mount rapidly. Some threw down their weapons and ran from the battle. Many others tried to retreat in a more orderly fashion, firing as they backed down the canyon. The important point was that they were all backing up. All across the glen the Texans were retreating, frequently in full-scale rout. As they pulled back, the Coloradans gave chase, stopping now and then to kneel and fire, then leaping to their feet and racing forward once again.

Most of the men of both armies had gone well past an old, deserted cabin before someone in the Colorado group thought to look inside the building. There he found fifteen armed Texans, who threw down their weapons and surrendered when the Coloradan walked inside. As the Union soldier led his fifteen prisoners back outside, someone shouted "Shoot the sons of bitches." "No," he replied defiantly, "I'm damned if you do. You didn't take 'em. I took these prisoners myself, prisoners of war, and I intend to keep 'em." He marched the Confederates back up the canyon and didn't stop until he arrived at the Pigeon Ranch. There the newest prisoners were turned over to guards who hustled them to the Kozlowski Ranch, where the Texans who had been captured earlier were being held.

Eventually, Major Pyron got his panicked troops under control again. The routed Texans crested a small ridge and took up defensive positions firing at their pursuers. The sudden and concentrated enemy gunfire stopped the Coloradans, who scurried for cover. Almost immediately, the battle again degenerated into a stalemate of infantrymen exchanging most ineffective gunfire.

Then on the right side of the canyon a large group of Texans, perhaps numbering thirty men, had been cut off from the main body of Confederate troops and were surrounded by the Coloradans. The Rebels hoisted a white flag and were taken prisoner by Captain Wynkoop's company. At almost the same time Company F took another group of about twenty prisoners, prompting Hollister to write ". . . they forgot that one of them was equal to five of us!"

One Colorado horseman was racing down the trail when his horse stumbled and fell, badly wrenching the soldier's knee.

The injured soldier, Private George W. Lowe, scurried from the middle of the trail to an embankment. He leaped over the dirt wall for shelter and found himself suddenly face to face with a Confederate captain. The Texan cocked a pistol and pointed it at Lowe, saying "I reckon this makes you my prisoner." But Lowe was not ready to be taken prisoner. He leaped on the Texan, and the two men tumbled to the ground in a life-and-death struggle. After a few minutes, Lowe was able to disarm the Texan. He quickly marched the Rebel soldier to the rear as another prisoner of war.

Still another Coloradan, Private C. W. Logan, was shot in the face and fell beside a large rock. He was badly wounded and losing blood, but not consciousness. Deciding he must crawl to a spot more out of the line of fire, Logan moved several feet to his right. There he spotted a Texas sharpshooter, leaning against the far side of the same rock. Logan cocked his pistol and pointed it at the Confederate, but the Texan called out that he was badly wounded and wished only to surrender. Logan lowered his pistol, whereupon the Texan raised his own weapon and fired at point-blank range. The Confederate was apparently aiming at Logan's chest, but the Coloradan spun just as the shot was fired and the bullet smashed through his left arm. Logan again raised his pistol and shot the Texan between the eyes.

Just then, several more Confederates came out of the woods and seized Private Logan. One of the Rebel soldiers was the brother of the man just shot by Logan. The fatally wounded Texan lived long enough to tell his brother that Logan had shot after promising to merely take the Texan prisoner. The other Confederates, furious at the alleged deception, prepared to lynch Logan, who told them his story. Possibly because he told it so earnestly, or because it was backed by the nature of the wounds he had received, the Texans not only believed him but eventually turned him loose so that he could get medical help from his fellow Coloradans.

As Logan talked with his captors the battle around him raged on at close range, frequently involving hand-to-hand combat. Another Union soldier, whose diary later became an official part of the government records of the battle, described the afternoon this way; "We got within 300 yards of the enemy, who had already got good positions for two pieces of artillery which they were unlimbering as we came in sight. The rapid, clear and cool orders of the Major (Chivington) had scarce left his lips when their cannon boomed, sending forth death messages among the stunted trees. . . . A few seconds sufficed to give us a position where we could see the enemy, when we returned a defiant cheer from each side of the canyon in reply to their grape shot, which was rattling thick and fast over our heads, accompanied by an incessant fire of musketry. Each one selected his man, as per order, and with deadly aim tried his best to fire and waste as little powder and lead as possible. [Eventually] they made another stand when their infantry attempted to outflank us. Their movement in this direction was perceived and prevented, they paying a severe penalty for their rashness, in this bold manner; most of those who attempted this dangerous experiment were either killed, wounded, or taken prisoner." [*The War of Rebellion*, Ser. 1, IX, 530–32]

It had now been about three and a half hours since the fighting started, and darkness was beginning to close in on the canyon. Both sides were weary and bloodied, and both seemed eager to break off the engagement. Complete darkness can come on in a matter of seconds in those deep mountain canyons, and so it did on this occasion. All at once it was too dark to see, and both sides began pulling back.

The battle had lasted from about 2:00 P.M. to about 5:30 or so, and both sides had taken a beating. The number of casualties actually inflicted in the contest are difficult to judge. No reliable records exist of Confederate losses, although they are thought to have been heavy. It appears the Texans may have suffered as many as 50 or more killed, and perhaps twice that number wounded. A high percentage of those wounded would die within 24 hours of the battle. As usual, estimates of casualties varied widely. Some Confederate officers would later claim as few as six dead and 14 wounded in the battle, although other Texas sources reported as many as 70 dead and 125 wounded.

Among the known Confederate dead were several commissioned and veteran officers. The only Union officer who fell victim to the combat was Captain Samuel Cook, who would eventually recover from his injuries.

In addition to the dead and wounded, records of the First Colorado Volunteers show that seventy-five Texans were taken prisoner, including seven commissioned officers. If all of those figures are accurate, and they probably are close, the Rebels suffered casualties (dead, wounded and captured) amounting to nearly fifty percent of their vanguard force.

The Coloradans fared far better; five dead, thirteen wounded (of whom four would later die), and three missing. The official records do not say whether the missing men were ever accounted for. The figures indicate Colorado's casualties amounted to only about five percent of their force.

The huge disparity in casualties is difficult to explain, especially given the fact that the Texans were already battle-tested and the Coloradans were not. A partial explanation may simply have been geography. The Coloradans, being always on higher ground than the Confederates, were at an advantage over the Texans. Still, one would suppose that the slope of the battlefield would not account for such huge differences in casualties. Another partial explanation is that when Major Chivington led the mounted troops across the arroyo and into the middle of the Rebels, they may have had a lopsided advantage for several minutes. It may also be true that as gold miners, the Coloradans were accustomed to living by their guns, hunting their food or defending their stakes. As such, they may have been more cool under fire or better shots.

All of these factors considered together may explain the differences in the number of dead and wounded, but they do not explain the relatively huge number of Texans who were captured in the battle. The extreme differences in the total number of dead, wounded and captured was as puzzling then as it is now, and commanders on both sides later commented that they had no logical explanation for the disparities.

Historian Dr. William Whitford gave this account of the battle in his book, *The Battle of Glorieta Pass*:

> At the opportune moment, Captain Cook's men tore down the road in a body and with a hair-raising yell compelled all of their 103 horses but one, which fell back upon its rider into the arroyo and injured him for life, to leap across the chasm at the bridge. Then they immediately, in the midst of the missiles that rained upon them from the high ridges, charged three times forward and back through the fleeing and crowded ranks of the Texans, running over them, trampling them down, and scattering them in every direc-

tion—as gallant an outset in war as ever was made. . . . By the time the Confederates were, in terror and disorder, rushing along the canyon at and beyond the bold curve in it . . . Captain Downing and his men had raced across the mountain to the right and were pouring into them a most galling and destructive fire . . . where [Union forces] took about fifty of them prisoner.

Evening coming on, further pursuit was abandoned. While the number of men on each side was comparatively small and the engagement occupied but two or three hours, the fight was furious while it lasted. The Texans were badly used up, and, beside their heavy losses in killed and wounded, some seventy or eighty of them were prisoners. Seven of their commanding officers were among the slain.

One of the ironies of the battle that while no Colorado officer was killed in combat, one was accidentally killed later that evening, long after the hostilities had ceased. Second Lieutenant William F. Marshall was examining a hand gun he had taken from one of the Texas prisoners. The weapon accidentally discharged and shot Marshall in the face; he died a few hours later.

Day one of the Battle of Glorieta Pass was over. It had been a good one for the First Colorado Volunteers.

But of course, no battle is really good, at least not for everyone. There were dead and wounded on both sides. After the Rebels withdrew back down the canyon, the Coloradans began searching the battlefield and tending to the wounded from both sides. An hour later, a number of Confederate soldiers came riding back up the trail under a flag of truce; they asked permission to also treat the wounded and bury the dead.

For the next several hours, men from the two opposing armies worked side by side, giving aid and comfort where possible and burying those who were dead. It was well past midnight when the last of the dead had been buried and the last of the wounded given some sort of help. Then the two sides parted, each going toward his own camp.

The ferocity of the battle and the aggressiveness of the Coloradans had apparently taken the Texans by surprise. One of the captured Confederate soldiers, not identified by name or rank, was taken back to the Pigeon Ranch shortly after the fighting ended. Later he wrote a letter to his wife, which gave some indication of the surprise felt by the Texans regarding the battle:

We felt like heroes, having had a fight at Fort Craig, scaring the Mexicans to flight and driving the regular soldiers into the fort, and getting past with our whole army, and cutting off all supplies and relief to the fort. We marched up the country with the fixed determination to wrench this country from the United States and we all thought it would soon be in our hands. But what a mistake! . . . All of us who were not killed or taken prisoner were obliged to destroy everything they had and flee for their lives.

We were [ordered] to march on and take Fort Union, which, we thought, was ours already; and then New Mexico would belong to the new government of the South and it would then be so easy to cut off all communication with California.

Six hundred of us were ordered to march to Apache Canyon and stand picket. On the 26th we got word that the enemy was coming down the canyon in the shape of 200 Mexicans and about 200 regulars. Out we marched with the two cannons, expecting an easy victory. What a mistake! Instead of Mexicans and regulars, they were *regular demons*, upon whom iron and lead had no effect, in the shape of Pike's Peakers from the Denver City gold mines. . . .

Up the canyon we went for about four miles where we met the enemy coming at double-quick, but our grape and shell soon stopped them, but before we could form in line of battle their infantry were upon the hills on both sides of us, shooting us down like sheep. . . . They had no sooner got within shooting distance of us than up came a company of cavalry at full charge, with swords and revolvers drawn, looking like to many flying devils. On they came to what I supposed was destruction; but nothing like lead or iron seemed to stop them, for we were pouring it into them from every side like hail in a storm. In a moment these devils had run the gauntlet for half a mile and were fighting hand-to-hand with our men in the road. The houses that I spoke of before were seven or eight hundred yards to the right of road, with a wide arroyo between it and them. Here we felt safe, but again we were mistaken, for no sooner did they see us than some of them turned their horses, jumped the ditch, and like demons came charging on it. It looked as if their horses' feet never touched the ground until they were among us.

It was a grand sight. We shot as fast as we could, and as that handful of men jumped the ditch and charged on us we expected to shoot the last one before they reached us. But luck was against us, and after fighting hand to hand with them and our comrades being shot and cut down every moment, we were obliged to surrender.

How any one of these men who charged us escaped death will ever be a wonder to me. Our men who were fighting them in the road were soon obliged to retreat and the fight was over. About eighty of us who were taken prisoners were soon marched off to Fort Union. How many were killed and wounded I don't know, but there must have been a large number. Such a sight I never want to see again. As I was marched off the field I saw some men with their heads nearly shot off, some with their arms or legs shot off, and one poor man that belonged to my company, I saw lying against a tree with his brains all shot out. Henry Asher had an arm shot off but made out to escape. He was standing by my side when he was shot. The [Coloradans] that charged us seemed to have charmed lives, for if they had not they could never as reached us alive.

The survival of the attackers apparently surprised some of the Coloradans as much as it did the Texans. Hollister wrote:

How we escaped so cheaply God only knows for we rode 500 yards through a perfect hailstorm of bullets. Many were the men lying behind rocks, almost near enough to knock us off our horses, taking dead rest and firing as we passed. Among the conflicting emotions of that evening, not the weakest was one of disappointment in the character of the foe we had met.

Hollister's opinion that the Texans had not fought well and were surprisingly easy to drive from the battlefield was apparently shared by virtually all the First Colorado Volunteers. Interestingly, General Sibley reported to San Antonio that his advance guard had encountered and defeated a sizeable enemy force in a brisk skirmish in Apache Canyon; he said the Texans "inflicted heavy casualties before the enemy fled the field." Many existing Southern histories still contain Sibley's erroneous report, presuming it to be factual.

Casualties among the Coloradans were not spread evenly through the ranks; Hollister's F Company had been particularly hard hit, reflecting their front-line position for most of the battle. George Thompson and Jude W. Johnson died on the battlefield; Martin Dutro, a close friend of Hollister's, was mortally wounded and died later that evening. Six men from Company F, Privates Bristol, Hall, Keel, Logan, Patterson and Pratt were all wounded.

Many of the Coloradans who fought the day's engagement returned during the night to Pigeon's Ranch, there to be joined by late-arriving infantry troops. There was a great deal of celebrating over the "licking" given the Confederates that day. The celebration was made somewhat sweeter by the fact that scouts had located a stash of Confederate supplies that day, so that the victors feasted that evening on flour, corn and other supplies intended for the enemy.

Hollister was not among those who celebrated. He spent the evening at the side of Martin Dutro, watching his friend's life slowly ebb away. It was quite a sad and sobering experience for the journalist-soldier, and the notations in his diary thereafter became a little less poetic and his views toward battle a little more realistic.

During the night of March 26, nearly four hundred Coloradans were dispatched down into the canyon to establish a front line of defense at the spot where the fighting had ended the evening before. These fresh troops were to prevent any surprise nighttime attack by the enemy. They would also be on the front lines when the battle was rejoined after sunrise.

Surprisingly, the battle was not rejoined, at least not that morning. March 27 passed in eerie silence down in the canyon, nervous Colorado soldiers constantly "certain" they heard the sounds of an approaching enemy which never appeared. When the sun sank in the west that evening, the troops prepared for simply another night of waiting and watching.

CHAPTER ELEVEN

THE BATTLE OF GLORIETA PASS, PART II

How our hearts beat! That tremendous event, the burden of history and song, a BATTLE, burst on our hitherto peaceful lives like an avalanche on a Swiss village. Were we worthy of the name we bore? A few minutes would tell.

Ovando J. Hollister, Company F
First Colorado Volunteers
(on the seconds before his first battle)

*T*he Texans spent March 27 making ready to wipe out this irritating enemy who had inflicted such pain, suffering and humiliation on the Western Expeditionary Force. However, General Sibley would not be hurried into another battle. He spent the morning of the following day mapping his strategy and the afternoon watching as his officers and men hastened to make ready for the showdown with the Coloradans.

Inaccurate Confederate intelligence reports indicated to Sibley that the Coloradans who had been encountered in Apache Canyon on March 26 was the entire First Colorado. None of the Texans had any idea that the men who fought in the canyon represented only a third of Coloradans. It also appears, however, that Confederate Major Charles Pyron may have greatly exaggerated the strength of the enemy that had whipped his five hundred-man vanguard. Pyron's report to General Sibley estimated he had been battling eight hundred to one thousand men. In that respect, the overestimation served his comrades well. As a result of the inflated figures, the Southern battle preparations antici-

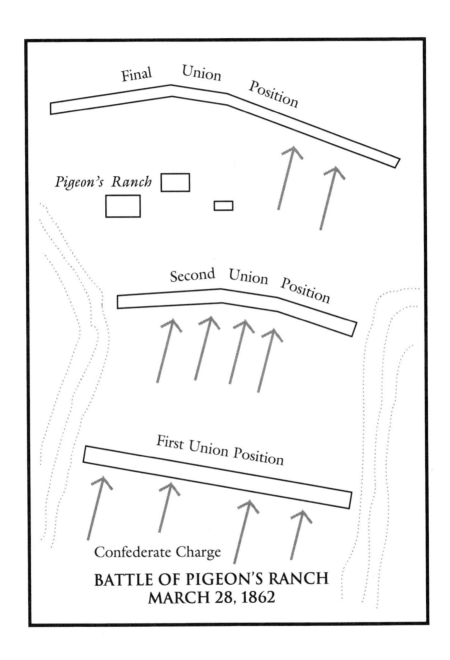

**BATTLE OF PIGEON'S RANCH
MARCH 28, 1862**

pated fighting a number nearly equal to the actual strength of the enemy.

On March 27, the Texans sent about fifty soldiers back to Santa Fe to obtain additional supplies; they would not return in time to participate in the upcoming battle. When the Rebels marched up the canyon to confront the Coloradans the following day Sibley left another two hundred and fifty men in camp as doctors, guards, teamsters and cooks, plus the sick and wounded. He sent still another detachment of approximately two hundred men down the main road some five miles to guard against any surprise attack from the rear. All remaining troops, the elite and most veteran soldiers of the Western Expeditionary Force, prepared to attack the enemy in Glorieta Pass.

Colonel Scurry took personal command of the attack force. Early on the morning of Friday, March 28, Scurry, Major Pyron and three Texas regiments, plus an independent company of volunteers called the Brigands, entered the western end of Apache Canyon and began moving upward, watching carefully for any sign of the Coloradans. They were accompanied by a battery of three large artillery pieces. Altogether, this vanguard unit of Texans numbered approximately eleven hundred men. Before the day was through the Confederates would have between eighteen hundred and two thousand men engaged in the battle; some estimates would say there were well over three thousand involved by nightfall.

The Texans were mildly surprised that they had not been attacked by the Pike's Peakers on the 27th, the day following the first battle. The lack of a follow-through by the Union forces led the Confederates to surmise that the Union forces were surprised to have found the Texans in the canyon and might have then withdrawn back to Fort Union. Even if the enemy had not withdrawn, however, their lack of follow-through seemed to indicate the mountain men had been badly mauled in the fighting or were fearful of another confrontation.

Having erroneously concluded, therefore, that the Pike's Peakers were badly hurt or seriously frightened, the Texans were now eager to chase down and engage whatever was left of the Coloradans. The Texans were supremely confident in their leadership, their experienced troops and their firepower. They were absolutely certain of victory and eager for the showdown.

On the evening of March 27, a high level meeting was held at Pigeon's Ranch. In attendance were General Canby, Colonels Paul and Slough and Major Chivington. Although elated at results of the first confrontation with the Rebels, none of the men had any allusions that a second encounter would be easy. There was considerable debate as to the best strategy for the next battle with the Texans.

Colonel Slough's plan was the orthodox one. He wanted to put all available Union troops into the canyon, to meet the Confederates head-on as they came uphill, or, if the Rebels failed to be in the canyon, to confront them somewhere between the foot of the pass and Santa Fe. Slough argued that only by massing all of the unit's strength could the Coloradans hope to meet the enemy on equal footing and have a chance at defeating him.

Major Chivington favored a different tactic altogether, one that was bold and unorthodox. Even though the Coloradans knew they were badly outnumbered by the Texans, Chivington proposed that the Union force be split. He suggested that all of the infantry units and whatever New Mexican volunteers were available, i.e., all those troops without horses, go down the pass and try to engage the Rebels at some narrow point in the canyon. He believed that even though this detachment would be outnumbered, the narrow confines of the canyon would force a narrow battle line and largely negate the enemy's advantage of superior numbers. And while that battle was taking place in the bowels of the canyon, Chivington proposed that he would lead the remaining four hundred men—those with horses—in a circling movement. He would try to drop down into the canyon behind the enemy, catching him in a pincers movement.

After lengthy debate, Colonel Paul and General Canby sided with Chivington. Canby agreed that the narrowness of the canyon meant that only limited numbers of men could be at the front at any given moment of time. That being the case, a smaller Union army might hold the Confederates at bay while the remaining Union soldiers got behind them and inflicted heavy casualties. And the very fact that splitting the small army was unorthodox made it more likely that it had a chance to succeed. It was unlikely, said the general, that Sibley would anticipate such a move. Getting support from Canby, of course, decided the issue on behalf of Chivington's plan.

At 4:30 A.M. on the morning of March 28, Major Chivington and all remaining mounted troops left Pigeon's Ranch and headed south along the ridge of mountains. At the same time, Lieutenant Falvia took two partial companies of men down the road toward Galisteo to make certain the Confederates did not plan an encircling movement of their own.

The remaining troops, consisting of about 250 to 300 New Mexico volunteers and somewhere between 600 and 700 men from First Colorado Companies C, D, F, G, I and K, reentered Glorieta Pass and began cautiously advancing down hill. They did not know the strength, disposition or intentions of the Texans, but fully anticipated meeting them somewhere in the canyon. The Union troops were accompanied by two light batteries of regular artillery directed by Captain John F. Ritter and Lieutenant Ira W. Claflin.

The Union commanders were highly concerned about the condition of their troops, however. Fully half of the men now marching down the pass and into certain combat had marched forty-five miles the previous day in order to reach Pigeon's Ranch. They had arrived well after midnight, and were, therefore, not well rested. In addition, the vast majority of the soldiers had never before been under fire, except for the small group of New Mexican volunteers, many of whom had broken and run from their first battle action at North Ford.

While the commanders worried about the men, the men worried about the commanders, or at least about Colonel Slough. By this time the men thoroughly distrusted and disliked Slough. He was never thought to be a strong commander and the men resented his arguing with more popular officers. To make matters worse, there were now many rumors that questioned the Colonel's loyalty to the Union. Some of the men openly declared that Slough could not be trusted, and one of the Union captains revealed many years later that, "I watched him closely during the fight, and if I had discovered that any movement or order of his intended to be favorable at the time to the enemy, I would have shot him on the spot!" (It should be noted that while Slough was thoroughly unlikeable, there is not a shred of evidence he was ever anything other than 100 percent for the Union.)

As usual, a number of scouts were sent ahead of the main body of soldiers to try to find the enemy. The advance elements of the Union infantry this time was a small mounted group of soldiers under the command of Captain Gurden Chapin. The pickets had barely entered the pass when they encountered the leading elements of the Confederate army. Surprised by the quick confrontation, the Union scouts went racing back to the top of the pass to warn the Coloradans that the battle was coming significantly sooner than they might have imagined.

The Confederates were encountered so quickly that the last of the Union soldiers had not even pulled out of the Pigeon Ranch when the first shots were fired. As Private Hollister put it, "The men were resting—some visiting the wounded in the hospital, others still filling their water canteens. Suddenly the bugles sounded assembly. We seized our arms, fell in and hastened forward perhaps 500 yards when their artillery commenced cutting the tree tops over our heads."

The front lines were quickly established in the canyon, barely a half mile below Pigeon's Ranch. This was a particularly wide place in the canyon, and the ground was comparatively level here, although a small, bush-covered ridge lay between the opposing armies. The terrain was not unlike that in which the first battle was fought, excepting only that it was considerably larger. There were tree-covered slopes on either side, rocky and uneven soil along the floor of the canyon, and scattered here and there along the flat ground were huge boulders. There were also two fairly sizeable hills at the edge on both sides of the canyon. Upon encountering the enemy, Confederate Colonel Scurry put a cannon atop each hill and established his infantry lines between the two. He sent three dismounted cavalry units under Major Pyron to his right, artillery supported by Major Raguet's Texans to the center, while his own command occupied the left.

For his part, Colonel Slough established his battle line just below the brow of the small ridge. He put his two batteries of four guns each at the center, with infantry units on either side. He sent two companies of foot soldiers into the hills on the right, in an effort to flank the enemy.

One of the Confederate artillery pieces was under the command of Lieutenant James Bradford. He had already established his reputation as fearless and as an excellent shot, having fought brilliantly and courageously at the North Ford. Bradford was among the first to open fire and sent the oncoming line of Coloradans scurrying for cover.

The first Union cannon into the fray was commanded by Captain Charles J. Walker. When the enemy artillery opened up, Walker ordered his gun hauled up into the heavy timber on the left side of the canyon, where he opened fire on the Rebels. He also found that he had more men than were immediately required to fire the weapon, so he ordered the extra troops to form a skirmish line and begin shooting at the Confederates.

Within a matter of seconds, fighting was furious all along the front. Heavy, thick clouds of smoke soon began to choke the canyon and in some places visibility became difficult. One of the soldiers described the scene this way; "The fighting was general and furious. The discharges of the artillery seemed incessant and the roar of them sounded at a distance in all directions like a heavy and continuous drumming of a military band."

With the artillery units locked in a thunderous duel, trees on the slope began to splinter, and several of them caught fire. The flames were never a serious problem, but the fire and more especially the smoke seemed to add greatly to the overall confusion of the battle.

Several companies of Coloradans formed a skirmish line on the right and soon went running toward the enemy, but they were halted by withering rifle fire and several cannon shots. As the Coloradans fell back, several Confederate companies under the command of Colonel Scurry counterattacked. Although the Coloradans seemed to escape with little damage, a company of New Mexican volunteers was overrun by the Rebels and suffered heavy casualties. Such thrusts and counterthrusts continued all along the front with neither side making any appreciable progress.

After several minutes, the Union cannons scored a lucky, direct hit on Lieutenant Bradford's cannon. The shot shattered the weapon and gravely wounded the Texas commander. The shot also killed several other Confederates, several horses, and wounded about a dozen men. Colorado sharpshooters poured a deadly volley into the confused and milling Confederate gunners, inflicting even more casualties. The Texans were in an untenable position; they turned and ran from the hill on which they had been shooting.

Colonel Scurry was standing a short distance away when the Union shot shattered the Confederate cannon, but was not injured. As he looked around to make certain his lines were still secure after the shot, he spotted a company of Union soldiers moving quickly down a streambed and about to pass his left flank. Scurry rallied the company of retreating Confederate soldiers and dashed back toward the enemy.

Holding a pistol in one hand and a machete in the other, the courageous Confederate Colonel ran directly into the midst of the line of Union soldiers. Now there was fierce hand-to-hand combat, with both sides using bayonets and pistols. Among the Confederate soldiers who fought in this bloody encounter was Private Joseph D. Sayers. Thirty-five years later Sayers would become governor of Texas. Later in the campaign, Sayers was promoted to the rank of sergeant and cited for bravery during the Glorieta Pass struggle.

The leader of the Colorado unit being engaged by Colonel Scurry was Lieutenant John Baker. Just before he and his troops were spotted by the Confederates, Baker had whispered to his men, "There is the enemy's artillery. Let's capture them all." At that instant, however, Colonel Scurry and two dozen Rebel soldiers leaped into the ditch. Baker was wounded twice early in the battle and fell to the ground. Eventually he tried to crawl back toward the Union lines but was spotted by a Rebel soldier who attacked Baker and clubbed him to death with the butt of his rifle. The beating death of the wounded and helpless Colorado officer was particularly repugnant to the men who witnessed it, and it solidified their determination to fight to the death if necessary.

But the fatal beating was not the only atrocity Lieutenant Baker would suffer, even in death. In his official report on the battle, Colorado Lieutenant-Colonel Samuel Tappan later wrote, "Lieutenant Baker was severely wounded during the early part of the engagement, and afterward beaten to death by the enemy with the butt of a musket or club, and his body stripped of clothing. He was found the next morning, his head scarcely recognizable, so horribly mangled. He fought gallantly, and the vengeance of the foe pursued him after death."

In actual fact, there is some question whether the final mutilation of Baker and the stripping of his body was the handiwork of the Confederates at all. The truth is that a roving band of transients who had nothing to do with either side of the conflict moved through the area in the hours following the battle. Many historians believe it far more likely that they and not the enemy stripped Baker of his clothing, ring and watch and mutilated his body during the night following the battle.

During the fight in the ditch, the Texans quickly got the upper hand over Baker's patrol. As the Coloradans were driven back, they left behind fifteen dead and seven wounded.

After securing the ditch, Colonel Scurry launched a number of new attacks against the Union lines, but each assault was thrown back. At the same time, Scurry sent Major Raguet and two companies of dismounted cavalry to scale a rocky ledge on the left (the Union right), and the Rebels soon had succeeded in flanking the Colorado lines at that point. As the Coloradans turned their attention to this new threat, Scurry ordered a full frontal attack all along the line, from one side of the valley to the other.

The Coloradans and several companies of New Mexican militiamen poured a deadly wall of rifle and cannon fire into this frontal assault, while another company of Colorado riflemen met and drove back the flanking movement. The Rebel attack faltered, then stopped, and finally was driven back to the original lines.

Now Major Pyron ordered his troops to charge the Union lines near the center of the valley. Ignoring the heavy gunfire from the Federals, the Texans climbed over a low embankment and raced at the Coloradans facing them from the small ridge. One of the Confederates carried the flag of Texas, and all of the charging soldiers whooped the famous Rebel yell as they poured across the narrow strip of land separating the lines. The Union force panicked, and many of them turned and ran from the onrushing foe until a Colorado captain rose to his feet and cut off the retreat. He soon rallied the soldiers to again turn and fire at the enemy, then counterattacked toward the top of the ridge from which they had just been driven.

The battle was fierce. Confederate Private Theophilus Noel wrote:

> . . . few of the men now stopped to reload their pieces after they had fired them. Here for the first time in the history of the present war, guns were used as clubs, and knives were used as weapons of warfare. For two long hours the battle raged with unceasing fury, with a desperation unequalled by any engagement of the war. The enemy fought with a desperate determination. With demoniac yells our little army drove them by inches at a time. . . .

Finally the weight of the numerically superior Confederate force was simply too much for the Union force to bear. As the Texans slowly advanced and occupied the original Union positions, Colonel Slough ordered the first pullback of the day, even though the Coloradans still held the high ground in the center of the valley. The Coloradans reluctantly gave up about four hundred yards of the valley floor as they retreated to new positions in obedience to the order. They were now at the top of the canyon, only a short distance below the buildings at Pigeon's Ranch. As was the case with everything he did, Slough's order to pull back was later seen as evidence of his cowardice, although the Colonel, himself, would say it was "the only way we could get the Confederates out of their entrenched positions."

As soon as the Coloradans vacated the ridge at the center of the valley, that position was seized by the Confederates. The Texans quickly planted their artillery on it and from this vantage point again opened fire on the Coloradans. Once again, however, the Coloradans got lucky when another of the Texas cannons was hit squarely in the muzzle by a cannon shot from the Union. The Texas gun was destroyed, and a number of its crewmen killed or injured. Moments later yet another Confederate cannon was disabled and its ammunition box blown to pieces by a chance hit from a second Colorado cannon. And with three of the four Confederate cannons now out of commission, the Texans lost much of their edge in firepower. The crews that survived the hits began to pull back, and many of the Coloradans stood up and began shooting at the retreating enemy soldiers.

With their three biggest guns disabled, the Texans were now reduced to fighting the battle with infantry and a couple of Sibley's mountain howitzers. As a result, the only way the Confederates could hope to gain ground was by repeatedly charging at various places along the Union line. For the first time in that day's battle, the Texans were at a distinct disadvantage. And since any attacking Confederates would have to run uphill into the face of the still active Colorado artillery, the Union lines seemed secure at last.

Amazingly, Colonel Slough now ordered a second withdrawal of forces. He would later say the latest retreat was to protect the men and keep as many alive as possible in the face of these full-scale enemy assaults against the Union line. Although the move infuriated most of the Union troops, they actually were able to get into much stronger defensive positions after the second pullback.

At this point about one hundred fifty additional Confederate troops reached the battlefield to reinforce Colonel Scurry. The new troops were accompanied by General Sibley, himself, who had decided to "come up and see what was going on at the front." Sibley, however, did not take charge of the fighting now or later; there is no evidence he gave a single order as the battle progressed through the day. This lack of command on the battlefield was again later attributed to "the general's drunken state," and several officers charged that Sibley seemed afraid to be near the front. Once again it is not clear whether those accusations were made shortly after the fighting or much later when the Confederates launched their effort to discredit the general.

In spite of Sibley's physical presence among the newly arrived and fresh Texas troops, the soldiers remained under the direct command of Major John S. Shropshire, assisted by Captain D. W. Shannon. Scurry positioned the late arrivals at the center of the valley and ordered them to make a new charge at the Union lines.

As the Confederates prepared for the latest attack, a Union officer, Lieutenant Luther Wilson, one of the original three Colorado officers, dashed from a nearby hiding place, shot and wounded Major John Shropshire, then captured both the major and Captain Shannon. (Shropshire would die of his wounds the next day.) With their leaders gone, the remainder of the Confederate unit fell back in disarray.

During all of this bitter fighting, Colorado Colonel Samuel Tappan sat astride his horse in plain sight of soldiers on both sides, issuing orders to various soldiers under his command. He had a pipe stuck in his mouth and occasionally took a drag from it. He also held a pearl handled pistol in each hand and constantly loaded and fired the weapons "as coolly as if he were rabbit hunting."

On the left, Confederates commanded by Majors Raguet and Pyron began a new advance on the Colorado lines. Union Lieutenants Peter McGrath and Clark Chambers were both mortally wounded early in this struggle, and the troops under their command now began to grudgingly give ground before the advancing Confederates. But the Coloradans were backing up much more slowly than the attacking Confederate forces were advancing, with the result that the opposing soldiers were soon so close together that they sometimes fired at one another from opposite sides of the same clump of cedar bushes. Several men on both sides later reported that on one occasion the muzzles of the rifles of men on opposing sides passed each other over the top of an embankment.

With the battle over three hours old, the Confederates appeared to be slowly gaining the upper hand. The Coloradans were already reluctantly retreating up the canyon little by little, when another two hundred or so Confederate troops arrived from the base camp and reinforced Colonel Scurry. Now the Rebels on the battlefield outnumbered the Federals at least two to one, and the number may actually have been closer to three or four to one. Colonel Scurry and Major Pyron calmly moved among their troops, calling out encouragement and orders in clear voices that could be heard all over the battlefield. Time after time, these two Confederate officers rallied their men or urged them forward to capture new ground; their bravery was noted by the Coloradans who after the battle talked of "those two Rebel commanders who just wouldn't quit coming."

For private Hollister, it looked like the end might be near for the Coloradans. He later wrote in his diary, "If the Texans had known how weak we were, doubtless they would have ruined us—but the lesson of the day before made them cautious. They would creep along up from tree to tree and from rock to rock, but as sure as one rose in fair view a dozen balls gave his soul choice in the way of departure."

It was now midday and the situation was definately getting desperate for the First Colorado Volunteers and the New Mexican militiamen fighting at their sides. The Union troops were ordered to pull back for a third time, and this time retreated to a hilly area behind the buildings of Pigeon's Ranch. Colonels Slough and Tappan and several other officers of the First Colorado now did for the Union what Scurry and Pyron had been doing for the Rebels. With unbelievable calm they moved among their troops in full sight of the enemy, encouraging, assisting, ordering, and generally restoring calm. That Slough was involved in such bravery astounded the Coloradans, some of whom later admitted a grudging admiration for the hated Colonel.

Now, as the Confederates tried to follow the Coloradans to this latest position, it was the Rebels who were out in the open with no cover. In order to reach the Union lines, the Texans had to cross a wide expanse of rocky, barren soil. So it was the Coloradans who were hidden in trees, behind rocks, and in gullies, protected from enemy view. If the Rebels were going to complete the conquest and win a victory, they would have to charge across the open valley and face the full fury of Union gunfire, including two cannons that were well entrenched atop a knoll.

Nonetheless, Confederate officers did not hesitate to give the attack order, and to their credit the brave Texans did not hesitate to obey the command. They charged, were met by withering gunfire, and finally retreated, leaving many dead and wounded behind. The Rebels regrouped and charged again, only to falter and be driven back again. And again. And again. And again.

Five separate times, Texans poured over the embankments and raced up the hill, across the open, rocky ground toward Union lines, sometimes literally running across the bodies of their fallen comrades. Five times they charged and five times they were repulsed. On at least two occasions, the attacking Confederates got within twenty yards of the Union cannons before the Rebel charge was halted and the survivors retreated to the ridge from which they had begun.

Lieutenant Ira Claflin, commander of one Union cannon, saw that the Confederates appeared dazed and confused when the fifth attack was repulsed. He ordered his men to cease firing the cannon and to charge as a skirmish line against the retreating Rebels. Then it was the Coloradans racing across the bloody, rocky ground, firing their rifles at the Confederates. The Rebels were completely disorganized at this point and were unable to ward off the attack. The Texans fell back again, suffering heavy losses. Confederate Captain Charles Buckholts and Lieutenant Charles H. Mills were among those fatally wounded in this Colorado counterattack.

Through all of the fighting, Colonel Scurry remained in the open, dashing back and forth and rallying the Confederate forces time and time again, often personally participating in the fighting. His courage drew the admiration of the Coloradans, who thereafter spoke of Scurry as "that brave Rebel Colonel." Twice during the afternoon he was slightly wounded, as rifle bullets on each occasion grazed his cheek and drew blood. His jacket was also pierced by a rifle ball during the fighting. Once, Colonel Scurry paused to talk with Major Pyron, and Pyron's horse was shot from beneath him. The men paused only momentarily and then continued their conversation "as coolly as if they had been chatting over drinks at the officer's club." Two years later Colorado survivors of this battle experienced genuine sorrow upon learning of Scurry's death in another battle.

There was a sad sidelight to this portion of the battle. The previous night, a nervous Colorado soldier, a boy about seventeen, told Captain Josiah Downing, "I dreamed last night that I was shot through my heart in the battle tomorrow, and I believe it will come true."

Downing tried to calm the boy, telling him "You just had a bad dream. Pay no attention to it."

But Downing had a soft place in his heart for the youthful private and sought to keep him out of trouble. Early in the conflict, he told the private to escort a group of Texas prisoners back to the Kozlowski Ranch and then to remain at the ranch and guard the prisoners. Downing was amazed when several hours later he found the boy back on the front lines at the top of Glorieta Pass.

"If you want to fight so bad," said the captain, "see if you can shoot that Rebel officer over there." Downing pointed to Confederate Major Henry Raguet, who was sitting on his horse about two hundred yards away.

The private steadied his rifle on a rock, took careful aim, and fired, killing Major Raguet. But a Confederate sharpshooter immediately returned the fire, the bullet piercing the boy's breast. Before he fell dead, the boy looked wide-eyed at Downing and said, "See? I told you this would happen!"

While all of this fighting was underway in the center of the battlefield, Colonel Scurry had disappeared from the front. He slipped to the rear, organized several companies into a circling movement and, undetected by the Coloradans, soon gained the high ground on the Union left. From this vantage point, the Rebels began pouring heavy fire onto the Union cannons and eventually forced the Union to abandon the ridge which they had controlled for several hours.

As the Colorado cannons withdrew, Scurry ordered the Texans to charge and try to capture the guns. For the sixth time,

Rebel soldiers raced across the open ground toward the Union guns. And once again, as they had five times earlier, the Coloradans reacted by pouring a wall of deadly rifle fire into the face of the enemy. The Texans faltered, staggered backward and finally fled back to their own lines.

Later, Confederate Captain Charles Buckholts was found dead on this battlefield, surrounded by the bodies of three Union soldiers. All of the latter had been stabbed to death with Buckholts's Bowie knife; he had been killed by the thrust of a saber from one of the men he had fatally wounded.

It was now past 4:00 P.M. at a time of the year when the days are still short. The sun was about to disappear behind the ridges to the west. The front-line Coloradans believed the tide of battle had turned in their favor since the enemy cannons were silenced. They began to worry because they had only a short time left to battle the Confederates before it got too dark to see. They tried to speed up the pace of the furious battle, feeling that the enemy was near collapse. Ironically, the Confederates also felt the Coloradans were near collapse, at least according to General Sibley's later report to San Antonio. Colorado Captain John Ritter spotted Captain Jacob Downing, and suggested the two of them launch a frontal assault on the Texans "and beat 'em completely before dark sets in." He was astounded and dismayed at Downing's reply; "I have come to tell you that Colonel Slough has ordered us to pull back to the Kozlowski Ranch."

Ritter spit and said, "To hell with Slough. Let's get the Rebs."

But as Ritter was speaking, an ambulance bearing a white flag came down the road from the direction of the Kowlozski ranch. In the wagon was Confederate Major Alexander M. Jackson, the assistant adjutant-general of General Sibley's Western Expeditionary Force. Jackson was the former secretary of the New Mexico Territory, an outspoken secessionist, and a personal friend of Confederate President Jefferson Davis.

Approaching Colonel Slough, Jackson formally requested a suspension of hostilities "for the next 18 hours," to permit the treatment of the wounded and burial of the dead. The Coloradans, convinced that the Confederates had taken an awful beating, believed that the request was made to cover the Rebels and permit them to retreat, rest and regroup without further fighting. Nonetheless, Colonel Slough agreed to the temporary cease-fire, and ordered the Coloradans to lay down their arms until noon the following day. After the battle, General Sibley insisted it was the Coloradans who wanted the cease-fire "because they were so badly beaten." However, since Jackson later confirmed in his book that it was he who requested the cessation on behalf of Sibley, the accuracy of this report seems certain.

The diary of Private Alonzo Ickis, quoted in *Bloody Trails Along the Rio Grande*, claims that the Confederates also asked to borrow wagons and horses or mules from the Union army in order to transport their dead and wounded. Ickis says the request was granted by Colonel Paul.

While the Rebel motive for requesting the cease-fire may never be known with certainty, the Confederates really were at something of a disadvantage at this point in the struggle. Even though they had fought well during the six-hour battle and had driven the Union forces back, their situation was not good. The Rebels had lost their artillery. They were miles from their supplies and most of the men were beginning to run desperately low on ammunition. In addition, the soldiers had not eaten since the battle started early that morning. Indeed, many had not even had a drink of water. The only way to replenish ammunition and food was to stop the fighting and either return to their base camp, or have someone bring food and water to them. The Rebels apparently chose the former, and were eager to start back down the pass. They may also have been encouraged to find a way to stop the battle by using the huge number of wounded who littered the battlefield and constantly called for help. Providing help was obviously not possible until the shooting stopped.

Both sides would always claim to have won the day's fighting. The Confederates clearly had continued to move forward during the day, actually driving the Yankees about six hundred yards back up the canyon and across Pigeon's Ranch. But on the basis of known casualties, the victory clearly belonged once again to the Union. The Northern casualties that day were 49 dead, 64 wounded and 21 captured; 130 out of 850 to 1000, or about 13 to 15 percent of the men on the battlefield. Some historians believe that this casualty count included only regular Union soldiers and men from the First Colorado Volunteers. There is some evidence that New Mexico militia losses were not included in the number. Canby had earlier set a precedent for ignoring the New Mexicans. After the battle of North Ford he had reported his casualties and added that ". . . the number does not include New Mexicans; their loss adds to, rather than diminishes, our strength!"

By all reliable counts, however, the Confederates fared far worse than the Union, despite General Sibley's insistence that his casualties were light. According to records later captured from the surgeons accompanying General Sibley, the Texans that day lost 281 dead, 203 wounded and 117 taken prisoner, a total of 601 men. It was never clear how many Texans were actually on the battlefield that day; estimates ranged from 1200 to 2500. At the most conservative figure, casualties reached 50 percent; at the most liberal, 25 percent.

In truth, there also is no way of knowing the number of Confederates who died in the fighting on the 26th or the 28th. No reliable records exist that enumerate casualties. Several days after the battle, Colonel Slough estimated that Confederate losses were at least 350 killed in the two confrontations. On March 30, the Governor of New Mexico reported the Confederates had suffered "fully double" the number of those who died or were wounded on the Union side. Six days later, New Mexico's Governor Connelly wrote to Secretary of War Seward that "the latest count of the loss of the enemy does not fall short of 400 men killed . . . with about 200 of their wounded abandoned on the battlefield and still being cared for by us."

In return for that terrible toll, the Texans had little on which to base their claims of victory. They had, in fact, gained nothing as a result of the two bloody days of fighting. Although they had driven the Coloradans back up the canyon about a half mile during the second battle, they had really secured nothing of a permanent nature. They did not hold the land conquered during the fight, they did not open a route from Santa Fe to Fort Union, and they did not destroy the Union army which faced them, nor even force it to leave the area. The Texans also had apparently suffered far more grievous casualties than the enemy.

Afer the Texans left the battlefield, exhausted Union troops began to cope with the "footnotes" to battle. Around scores of campfires at Pigeon's Ranch, soldiers were reliving the day's events and telling one another their eyewitness accounts to the fighting.

One soldier, Benjamin Baker, was carried into camp about 9:30 P.M., his leg shattered by an enemy cannon ball. Doctors told him they would have to amputate the leg, but "he declined being buried in pieces" and refused the amputation. He died a few days later.

CHAPTER TWELVE

CHIVINGTON CRUSHES THE CONFEDERATES

Let us have faith that right makes might; and in that faith, let us to the end, dare to do our duty as we understand it.

President Abraham Lincoln

Well before the sun had left the eastern horizon on the morning of March 28, Major Chivington and 450 cavalrymen pulled out from Pigeon's Ranch and began moving southward along the ridge on the left side of Glorieta Pass. His troops consisted of about 400 Coloradans and 50 New Mexican volunteers. In keeping with the battle plan devised the night before, their goal was to find a way to get behind the Texans during the fighting that was certain to come that day and try to hammer them in a pincers movement.

As any fur trapper could have told Major Chivington, those fingers of land that form the ridges and valleys of the mountains do not run parallel to one another. It is a simple matter for even the most experienced hunters and trappers to quickly stray off course in the mountains. John Chivington was not a true mountain man; he had been in Colorado only eighteen months after moving westward from Missouri, but he had ridden the circuit to preach at mountain mining camps. He should have been aware that even the most careful rider would have trouble staying on an unmarked mountain trail. One of his New Mexican volunteers was familiar with the area, however, and offered to guide the troops.

Hospital
Tent

Wagons

Chivington's
Attack

Union
Prisoners

Wagons

Wagons

Horses

ATTACK ON CONFEDERATE SUPPLY TRAIN
MARCH 28, 1862

In spite of the assistance of the guide, it was clear that the strike force was hopelessly lost well before 10:00 A.M. They had ridden up and down hillsides, through wooded areas and tree-less plateaus, but simply could not find the bottom of Glorieta Pass; the men had no idea where they really were, nor where the Confederates were. The soldiers were getting tired as well as frustrated, and Chivington was livid. Not only was he unable to attack the enemy from behind, he could not even lend a hand to the rest of the Colorado soldiers engaged in the savage fight-ing already underway. And the worst part of it all was that he did not even know how to find his way back to camp. His column was completely lost. They had been riding for five hours and had found no trace of either the Confederates or Glorieta Pass.

Chivington halted the troops and told the men to take a break. Then the major and two of his officers, Captains W. H. Lewis and A. B. Carey, began studying the few old maps in their possession. They were soon joined by Lieutenant Colonel Manuel Chavez of the First New Mexico Volunteers. Chavez was a personal friend of Governor Gilpin, having served with him in the Mexican-American War. Chavez had also fought bravely at the Battle of North Ford. Although he was not familiar with this particular part of New Mexico, he was a skilled mountain man.

As the Coloradans pored over their maps, Chavez studied the surrounding terrain. Finally, he told Chivington that from the position of the sun and one tall peak he could see in the dis-tance, he believed the Union troops were about five miles east of Glorieta Pass. In fact, he was willing to stake his life on it. If they would head due west, he said, they would eventually come to the canyon they were seeking. [This account is based on Boyd, "Thunder on the Rio Grande."]

"I hope you're right, Colonel," said Chivington, folding the map he had been studying. And having no better idea, Chiving-ton ordered his troops to "mount up," and led them due west.

For a little more than an hour the men rode, up hill, down hill, across streams and treeless valleys, through heavy forests and along high, narrow ridges. At about 11:00 A.M., Chivington raised his arm to halt the troops, and stood up in his stirrups. In the distance, somewhere ahead of them, Chivington could hear the faint, rolling echo of cannon fire! The men were at least heading in the right general direction, and hopefully would soon reach Glorieta Pass. Chivington spurred his horse forward in eager anticipation, and the men followed close behind.

They rode for another twenty minutes before one of the scouts riding in advance of the cavalry came racing back to Chivington in the cloud of dust. "You aren't going to believe this," said the scout, breathlessly. "Major, you've just gotta see what's below this next ridge" [Whitford, *The Battle of Glorieta Pass*, p. 19].

Chivington ordered the troops to stay put and trotted a quarter mile ahead with the scout. It was clear that they were coming to the rim of a deep canyon, and Chivington assumed that the battlefield would lay in the depths below them. Instead, when he looked over the ridge Chivington could hardly believe his eyes. His heart raced and he emitted a long, low whistle through clenched teeth.

Below him was not the enemy army, but its base camp. There were the wagons, the horses, the tents, the supplies to take care of General Sibley's army for its campaign. Below him in its largely unprotected glamor lay the key to defeating the Texans!

Climbing down to the Confederate base camp would not be a simple matter, however, because Chivington was atop a towering cliff. Between him and the Rebel camp was a thousand feet of steep slope, and sometimes sheer rock walls. The major lay face down on the edge of the cliff and studied both the terrain and the enemy camp through binoculars.

There were three items of particular interest to Chivington. Of foremost importance were the dozens of wagons filled with Rebel supplies. Chivington estimated there were "at least 75, perhaps a hundred" wagons lined up side-by-side and wheel-to-wheel along a trail at the foot of the cliff.

Next, the major noticed that hundreds of Confederate horses were being kept in a box canyon on the opposite side of the valley floor. Those horses represented the transportation required by the Confederates to get their supplies and artillery from here to Colorado and beyond. If he could do something about the horses, the Rebels might not be able to continue the campaign even if they received fresh supplies.

The final item to draw special attention from Chivington was a large six-pound cannon. It was at the lower end of the camp, facing down hill, apparently placed there to halt any possible encircling movement by the Union army. A dozen Confederate soldiers attended the cannon, and scores of other men could be seen wandering about the enemy camp.

Chivington summoned his soldiers and ordered them to dismount. Leaving a dozen men behind to care for the horses, while the major and the remainder of his troops started down the steep slopes toward the Rebel camp. He warned the men to be careful not to dislodge stones and to avoid open areas as much as possible. Chivington wanted to avoid or delay detection by the Confederates, especially the six-pounder, for as long as possible.

The first part of the descent was extremely difficult, even for men accustomed to working in rugged mountainous terrain. On several occasions, the soldiers had to use ropes to lower themselves, one by one, down the face of cliffs. They were dropping down the last of these rock walls, about a quarter of the way down the mountainside, when Chivington's worst fears were realized. One of the men accidentally sent a boulder crashing down the slope, and the noise of the rock, bouncing and crashing through the underbrush, alerted the Texans below that company was coming.

The Texans manning the cannon began scanning the hillside through binoculars and soon made out a dozen or so of the Union soldiers, dangling from ropes on the face of a rock wall. The Rebels turned the cannon toward the Coloradans and opened fire. Fortunately for the Union, the Confederate aim was bad. The cannon balls smashed harmlessly into rocks a considerable distance above and to the right of the Union troops.

Now the element of surprise was gone, but so was the worst part of the descent. Chivington pulled his pistols and began running down the mountainside toward the enemy, followed by more than four hundred mountain men, "whooping and hollering like Indians."

The Confederates in the camp were not, for the most part, combatants. Except for the crew manning the cannon, most of those left behind by General Sibley were the sick and wounded, the camp cooks, the doctors and the teamsters. They were quickly overwhelmed. Those soldiers manning the cannon were the first to face the Coloradans. Three of the Confederates were killed and several others wounded before the remainder surrendered to Captain Wynkoop and his men. The gun could not be taken with the Coloradans, so they spiked the weapon and rendered it harmless for all future battles.

Many of the Rebel teamsters, most of them in fact, managed to jump onto horses and race down the road toward Santa Fe. These men, numbering perhaps 120, were allowed to escape unhindered by Chivington, who felt he had more important things to do than chase the unarmed teamsters.

The Coloradans moved quickly through General Sibley's camp, taking about fifteen prisoners, including a number of officers. Most of the prisoners were teamsters and cooks, although a few were wounded soldiers recuperating from the earlier battles. Chivington ordered that the Confederate doctors should be allowed to remain in camp to tend the wounded who would eventually return from the battlefront.

To their great joy and the relief of those "Pike's Peakers" rescued, Chivington's soldiers also found five men from the First Colorado, who had been captured two days earlier and were being held prisoner. The five were uninjured and quickly armed themselves with captured Confederate rifles.

Now, Major Chivington gave what he described as "possibly the hardest order I ever had to give"; telling his soldiers to kill every one of the Confederate horses and mules. To men who lived in the thinly populated mountains of Colorado, six hundred miles from the nearest big city, a horse was an absolute necessity. In fact, horses and mules were such a precious commodity in the West that rustlers were hanged, no questions asked, and stealing or hurting a horse was tantamount to cold-blooded murder. Yet, the troops obeyed Chivington without hesitation. They recognized that the death of the animals might well spell the death of the Confederate army. In a manner of minutes, five hundred or more of Sibley's badly needed horses and mules lay dead in the box canyon.

Historians disagree on the method used to dispatch the animals. "Thunder on the Rio Grande" says the horses and mules were shot, and one would presume that to have been the most logical method. However, *The Battle of Glorieta Pass* says that because the Coloradans did not want to use up their ammunition in case they were attacked, all of the animals were bayoneted; Alvin Josephy agrees with the latter version. Official War Department records are silent on this issue.

Then the Coloradans turned their attention to the dozens of supply wagons lined up beside the trail. The wagons were jammed with ammunition, black powder, kerosene, food, forage, baggage, clothing, medical and surgical stores, and all the other miscellaneous supplies required to fight a war. Several of the men noted what a shame it was that these supplies could not be taken back to the Colorado camp, but there was simply no way to get the goods back up the steep canyon walls.

The most flammable material was taken from the wagons and poured into a huge pile in the middle of the camp. Then, overturned wagons were piled atop the flammable material, and other wagons were shoved into and against those already described. Then someone struck a match, and in a flash all the wagons were consumed in flames.

The men took great pleasure in looting the command tent of General Sibley and making certain all of his personal belongings were added to the fire. One such item was a trunk containing all of the general's spare clothing, including his spare uniforms. When it was hurled onto the pile of debris that was about to be burned, the Union soldiers cheered. The general would later complain frequently that he was unable to dress "as fitting a general" because of the loss of this trunk.

As stores of Confederate ammunition began exploding, Colorado suffered its only casualty of the day. Private David Ritter was severely wounded by one of the explosions. His fellow Coloradans would manage to get him back to the Kozlowski Ranch, but Ritter would never fight again.

With the Confederate animals all dead, the enemy (except for doctors) having either been captured, killed or put to flight, and the Texan's supplies being consumed by fire, it was time for the raiders to get out. Some of the captured Confederates claimed that a huge relief column of Texans was due at Sibley's camp at any moment, a story that had no basis in fact.

However, based on the information that another enemy column was due to come up the trail at any moment and not wanting to be caught between two Confederate armies, Chivington ordered the men to return the way they had come. It was nearly dark before the Coloradans and their prisoners had scaled the steep walls and finally reached the top of the canyon. Then they stopped to look back, almost in awe, at the destruction they had wrought. Where only moments before, hundreds of enemy tents, horses, mules, and scores of wagons were neatly arranged, there was now only smoke and debris, punctuated by occasional explosions.

Then came what the weary soldiers felt was the biggest stroke of luck that day. Atop the ridge, the Coloradans began to debate the best way to get back to Pigeon's Ranch. Colonel Chavez was unwilling to act as guide if the soldiers took any route other than the one they had followed that morning, even though their inbound trail had clearly gone far out of the way. There is no way of knowing how far the men had ridden that morning. The most direct route from Pigeon's Ranch to the Johnson Ranch where the Confederates were camped is a distance of sixteen miles.

Chivington wanted to head straight up the ridge to which they had climbed, hoping it would stay close to Glorieta Pass and make their homeward trip much shorter. He knew, of course, that such a route risked meeting superior numbers of Confederates returning from the battle, but did not want to travel the many extra miles required to return the way he had come.

Then came that stroke of luck. A Roman Catholic Priest, Padre Ortiz, came riding along the ridge on a snow-white horse. Ortiz saluted and began speaking to Colonel Chavez in Spanish. Chavez told Chivington that Father Ortiz was a staunch Union supporter and was volunteering to lead them by way of the shortest and most direct route back to their lines. Chavez added that he was acquainted with the Padre, and that he could personally vouch for him. Chavez advised Chivington to accept the offer. Chivington did so, and Ortiz headed off into a small valley running toward the northeast.

The trip home went surprisingly quickly and without incident. Shortly after 10:00 P.M., the weary Colorado cavalrymen and their prisoners came riding into Pigeon's Ranch. They were greeted with shouts of glee, because the men were safe and because those already in camp were eager to tell their story of battling the Confederates to a standstill. Then they learned of the great victory scored by Chivington and his men!

In his official report on the day's battle, Colonel Slough said, "Major Chivington's command fell upon the enemy's train of wagons, capturing and destroying one six-pounder gun and taking [several] prisoners. The loss of this train was a most serious disaster to the enemy, destroying his baggage and ammunition, and depriving him of provisions. . . ."

Historian William C. Whitford says the impact of Chivington's raid can hardly be overstated:

> It was, indeed, a stunning, fatal blow that Chivington's force inflicted—not only upon the rear, but upon the advance of [General Sibley's] army, and also upon the entire campaign of the Confederates in the Southwest. This rear was utterly scattered and ruined, and further advance was made hopeless. The Texans [found themselves] without shelter or blankets and practically without food.

Whitford notes that the Confederates were so desperate they soon abandoned more than two hundred of their wounded. They also, he notes, soon abandoned their hopes of capturing the West because of the shortages imposed by Chivington's raid.

Historian Josephy says "Chivington's astonishing exploit made it clear that Glorieta Pass, far from being a Union defeat, had been a debacle for Sibley's Texans, ending at a stroke, Confederate aspirations of conquering the Southwest."

Yet the Confederates themselves at first had trouble comprehending the full significance of their loss of the base camp. They also had trouble coming to grips with the fact that they had not, in fact, accomplished anything in the bitter fighting at and around Pigeon's Ranch.

In fact, twenty-four hours after the fact and after Confederate troops had withdrawn to Santa Fe, Colonel Scurry issued a victory statement to his troops. (See page 193.)

Several nights later Colonel Scurry apparently had second thoughts about who really triumphed at Glorieta. In a letter to a friend at the San Antonio headquarters, Scurry wrote, "Our train was burned by a party who succeeded in passing undiscovered around the mountains to our rear. The loss of supplies [has] so crippled me that after burying my dead I was unable to follow-up the victory. My men for two days went unfed and blanketless, unmurmuringly. I was compelled to come [to Santa Fe] for something to eat."

Even after the Confederates had abandoned their wounded and raced back to Santa Fe to make certain they were not overwhelmed by pursuing Coloradans, and even after Scurry and others confessed the losses inflicted upon them, some of the Texas officers were still claiming victory. One Confederate officer was quoted in the Santa Fe *Gazette* a week later as saying that the Battle of Glorieta "added one more to a long list of overwhelming victories achieved by the Confederates." The officer went on to say that the Union lost "perhaps 800 to a thousand men, dead and wounded," and added that the Coloradans are apparently "now in retreat—perhaps rout is a better word—back to Colorado."

CHAPTER THIRTEEN

INDECISION IN BOTH CAMPS

Victory in the battle was claimed by each side [at Glorieta Pass, March 28, 1862]; it is probably fairly described as a draw. Its vigor, however, is attested to in all the accounts of it. Confederate Colonel W. R. Scurry declared in his report of March 31 that "the conflict was terrible," and claimed that the fighting was at such close quarters that the muzzles of the guns of opposing forces passed each other. Major Chivington's destruction of the Confederate's train of supplies was more important than the battle; it broke the Texans' advance into New Mexico.

The War of the Rebellion, Ser. 1, IX, 533-45.

*H*onoring the Confederate request for an eighteen-hour cease-fire, Colorado's weary soldiers now turned to other challenges. Rescue parties went back into the canyon and began scouring the battlefield, looking for those poor mutilated victims of war who were not yet beyond help. With a combined casualty total of 324 wounded survivors and 384 dead, the rescuers had plenty to do. They worked through the night and well into the following day, patching up the wounded and burying the dead from both sides. The injured were carried first to a field hospital at Pigeon's Ranch and later were moved to a more permanent hospital established in a tavern at the Kozlowski Ranch. As the medics labored through the night and well into the following day, they were surprised not to have been joined by anyone from the Confederate side. The Rebels sent no one back to the battlefield to tend the victims of the conflict.

And while the medical and burial parties toiled on the battle-field, a sort of command paralysis seemed to descend on the Colorado headquarters. Soldiers awakened early on the morning of the 29th and prepared their weapons for what they anticipated would be yet another clash with the Rebels. There was talk that the enemy may be in retreat, since Chivington's force had destroyed the enemy's stores of ammunition and other supplies. Most of the soldiers were preparing for a long march as they tried to catch up with what they presumed would be the retreating Texans. Yet, breakfast was served at the normal time and nothing more happened whatsoever. The troops stood around, waiting for the arrival of senior officers and the order to move out, but the officers did not appear and the order was not given. An eerie sort of quiet expectation descended on Pigeon's Ranch.

Unbeknownst to the men, Colonel Slough had received orders from General Canby just after sunrise, ordering the Coloradans to pull back to Fort Union. They were to take up defensive positions and "protect it [Fort Union] at all hazards, leaving nothing to chance." The note said nothing more but the messenger explained that there were rumors that another detachment of Confederates were about to attack the fort. This new group of Texans were reported to be heavily armed and bent on seizing the fort and cutting off any possible retreat by the First Colorado. This mysterious Confederate force was said to be following a circular route in an effort to beat the Coloradans to the fort and possibly to capture it without a fight. Slough was disappointed at the order and felt it destroyed a golden opportunity to crush the Confederate's Western Expeditionary Force "once and for all."

In actual fact, this order and a lot of other confusion over the several days surrounding the battle of Glorieta Pass can be attributed to severe communications problems. It appears that Canby had no idea that the Union army had already engaged the Confederates, or that Colonel Chivington's destruction of the Rebel base camp had ended the enemy's offensive capability. Even if he did know of the fighting, his note was clearly written before the word reached his command. This possibility never seemed to have entered the minds of Colonel Slough or most of the other men at the Pigeon's and Kozlowski ranches. The reaction of all concerned made it clear that they assumed the order to pull back was given in spite of their victory. It is now known on the basis of official records that Canby's reported Confederate main unit about to attack Fort Union was really the main invasion force under General Sibley. In anticipation of such an attack Canby now organized all the troop strength he could muster at Fort Craig—1210 men, almost all of whom were New Mexico militiamen—and left Craig to join Slough in the anticipated defense of Fort Union.

When the soldiers saw the messenger enter Slough's tent rumors circulated that Colonel Slough had ordered the men to prepare to sweep down Glorieta Pass in pursuit of the enemy. The soldiers stepped-up their preparations for battle, and those who were already prepared stood around expectantly.

Then came word that for some reason the order had been rescinded and the soldiers were to "stand down." About 9:00 A.M., the men were actually put on alert, but fifteen minutes later were told they were not to leave the ranch until all the dead were buried and the wounded cared for. From the number of bodies still visible it was clear that the burial parties were going to take at least all morning and possibly the remainder of the day. Disappointed soldiers went back to waiting nervously, or volunteered to join the burial parties in an effort to hasten completion of the task.

Shortly before the eighteen-hour cease-fire expired at noon, a lone Confederate soldier rode up the canyon under a flag of truce and handed a message to Colonel Slough. The note was from General Sibley requesting an extension of the armistice until 8:00 A.M. the following morning. Sibley said the Confederates simply could not properly care for their wounded in any less time. Slough, who was still wrestling with Canby's orders that he pull back to Fort Union, readily agreed to the extension of the cease-fire. He ordered that the wounded men who could be moved should be taken either to the Kozlowski Ranch or, if able, be moved all the way back to Fort Union.

The report that the truce was to be extended through the day angered many of the Colorado soldiers. Some of those in camp began debating whether the armistice should be honored at all, or whether the First Colorado should be pursuing the Rebs. And faced with a lack of any real information, many blamed Slough for the apparent indecision and lack of action. One of the few exceptions was Ovando Hollister, now breveted to the rank of sergeant in recognition of his battlefield action a day earlier. Several days after the fact Hollister wrote in his diary that he believed Slough was not responsible, but could not account for the decision to pull back.

Possibly because of his new rank, Hollister seems to have gotten wind of some of the problems with which Colonel Slough was wrestling. His diary entry on March 29 said that "Canby, for some inexplicable reason, was determined on no more fighting then, and Canby was the commanding officer. Slough was dismayed at the order."

So were a lot of other people. The governor of New Mexico was infuriated at the decision to pull the troops back to Fort Union instead of aggressively chasing the Confederates. When Connelly learned of the pullback order several days after the fact, he sent off a series of angry telegrams to the War Department demanding to know why the Texans were not being pursued. Six days later he was still fuming. Unable to contact General Canby, the governor wrote President Lincoln that had pursuit began at once, "the Confederates could have been wiped out within twenty-four hours" [Beck, *New Mexico*, p. 314].

But there was no pursuit. Slough agonized over whether he should be doing what he thought was right or obeying the orders from his commanding general. Eventually, Slough simply waffled; he ordered about half of the men, including Company F, to return to Fort Union in compliance with General Canby's directive. But he ordered five hundred others to remain at Pigeon's Ranch camp, wait for the expiration of the extended truce, then "ride down the canyon at all possible speed, locate and engage the enemy if he is still there."

About five hundred troops began the unhappy march eastward toward Fort Union. Another two hundred soldiers were detailed to guard duty, or to assist the doctors at one of the two field hospitals. The remainder checked and re-checked their weapons and impatiently awaited the expiration of the ceasefire. And they waited.

On the morning of March 30, two days after the battle, five hundred Coloradans under the command of Major Chivington headed down Glorieta Pass, torn between expectations of fighting another bloody battle and the disappointment of finding no one at all. The latter proved to be the case. When the Coloradans arrived at the old Texas base camp they found it deserted except for a large medical tent, two doctors and a handful of Texas wounded. The injured Texans and their doctors were escorted back to Fort Union where better medical facilities were available.

As for the five-hundred-man Colorado fighting force, they were in another bind. Their orders had empowered them only to go to the Texas base camp, locate and fight the enemy. Since the enemy was not at the camp, the troops were in a quandary. Should they continue the chase without specific orders to do so? Should they return to the Pigeon's Ranch and await new orders? Chivington would later admit that he was "greatly tempted" to continue the pursuit, knowing full well that to do so might place "my little band of soldiers against overwhelming numbers of enemy." Eventually Chivington decided he had no choice but to march back up the canyon to Pigeon's Ranch.

History differs sharply on what transpired over the next twenty-four hours. Some accounts say that Colonel Slough, angered by the pullback to Fort Union and distressed over the awfulness of the Glorieta Pass fighting, had suddenly grown homesick for the calmer life of a Denver lawyer. He no doubt really was tired of war, tired of fighting, and tired of being away from his family and friends in Denver. It is one thing to be appointed to a high ranking military position, wear a carefully tailored uniform and enjoy automatic prestige among the local social circle; it is entirely another to face the rigors of the trail and endure the pain and suffering of battle. That night Slough is rumored to have told Major Chivington that "I have carried out my orders; I have located, engaged and harassed the enemy. Those were my orders. I have executed them to the best of my ability. It is time to go home." There is no reliable attribution of that report, however.

Another report said that Slough was thoroughly disgusted with General Canby, whom he blamed for not permitting immediate pursuit of the Confederates. This version says that Canby agreed with Chivington that immediate pursuit could have crushed General Sibley's army and was the only logical consequence of the two earlier battles in Glorieta Canyon.

Regardless of what the Colonel felt, it is a matter of record that many New Mexicans openly blamed General Canby for the lack of follow-up to the destruction of Sibley's base camp. Many of these angry citizens wrote scathing letters to the War Department or to President Lincoln, charging that Canby's timidity was due to the fact that the Rebels were led by his brother-in-law. Several high-ranking New Mexico politicians wrote to the War Department, demanding that Canby be charged with a crime for his failure to immediately and aggressively pursue the enemy. As it was—some people would say "as it still is"—wont to do, Washington ignored all of the letters from the West and apparently never raised the issue with General Canby.

Whether Colonel Slough was aware of this civilian outrage is uncertain, but it is known that the commander, himself, was in agony over the state of affairs. On Sunday, March 31, Slough spent the morning alone in his quarters. Shortly before noon, he strode to the old farmhouse that served as headquarters for the First Colorado. There he told the newly-arrived General Canby he was resigning his commission and would return at once to Colorado. Canby tried to talk him into changing his mind, saying there was great work yet to be done and possibly great battles to be fought, but Slough was determined. Although the resignation did not formally take effect until April 9, Slough left camp at once. Moments after departing Canby's quarters he was on his horse, riding north toward Denver.

Sergeant Hollister, who had earlier recorded in his diary the growing resentment for Slough (and his own softening attitude toward him) was among the few who appeared genuinely sorry to see Slough leave. He wrote, "Colonel Slough was a man of undoubted ability and bravery, but his personal contact with his men was never of a kind to make him beloved. He wanted tact and policy. Feelings will undoubtedly change regarding him, for his resignation was a necessary consequence of an order which, under the circumstances, both he and the regiment felt it was a disgrace to obey. He obeyed it as became a subordinate officer; he resigned as became a gentleman and a man."

The United States government apparently thought that Colonel Slough had acted bravely and properly throughout his association with the army. A year later, Colonel Slough was called to Washington and was commissioned a brigadier general by President Lincoln. Slough was placed in command of the Military District of Alexandria, Virginia. Following the war Slough returned to the West, and was appointed by President Andrew Johnson as chief justice of the Territory of New Mexico, an office which he held for many years.

There was no communications link of any kind between the First Colorado Volunteers and Denver. On the day that Slough's resignation took effect, Colorado was still unaware of the fierce battle that had taken place at Glorieta Pass nearly two weeks earlier. Denver newspapers that day carried only lengthy reports of the great Union victory (and stories of the awful casualties) in the Battle of Shiloh, two thousand miles to the east.

At the time of Slough's resignation, the Coloradans at Pigeon's Ranch viewed his departure with mixed emotions. While he was not well liked, they at least knew what they had to deal with when he was in charge. Now they were uncertain who would replace him. There was open distrust among the Coloradans for the officers of the "regular" Union army, and appointment of a career officer as their new commander might have brought serious repercussions.

Within hours of Slough's departure the men had begun to circulate a petition. It asked that Major Chivington be appointed to command them "for the duration." It also pointed out that the six-month enlistment period for the troops had already expired and warned that unless their request was honored the men might simply follow Slough back to Denver.

The petitions were intercepted by officers of the First Colorado, who warned that such petitions might be viewed as insubordination. On the other hand, the officers agreed with the sentiments, and promised to do whatever they could to see to it that Chivington was promoted. Thus a few days later, a letter signed by every single officer was presented by Colonel Tappan to General Canby. The letter formally requested that Chivington be made commander of the Colorado troops. Tappan also suggested that since he and Paul were both colonels, it would be fitting if the commander of Colorado troops were also a colonel. General Canby got the message and breveted Chivington to the rank of full colonel, and put him in command of "all the Colorado troops in New Mexico."

In addressing the troops after his appointment was announced, Colonel Chivington told the cheering soldiers, "in accepting this command, my sole and only rule will be to do my duty without fear, favor or affection—and when the time for action arrives, I will venture to predict that I will be found ready at my post in the hour of danger!"

Later that night, the soldiers brought another petition to Colonels Tappan and Paul. This one, signed by nearly every man in camp, asked that the Colorado base camp at Pigeon's Ranch be hereafter known as "Camp Chivington." The petition stated that the name was "in honor of the Colonel of the Regiment, who had lately abandoned the peaceful privacy of the pulpit and accepted in its stead the privations, fatigues and dangers incident to the profession of arms, having entered into the new profession with his whole heart and soul, he bids to become as distinguished an officer as he is justly celebrated as a preacher of the Gospel. He is much beloved by the officers and men under his command." The officers agreed with the troops, and the temporary camp was thereafter referred to (even in formal military reports to Washington) as Camp Chivington.

General Canby then left the Kozlowski Ranch to travel, by circuitous route, back to Fort Craig on the southern Rio Grande. Accompanied by several companies of now battle-scarred and veteran New Mexico militia and expecting to recruit more troops along the way (recruitment becomes much easier in the wake of a glorious victory!) Canby intended to leapfrog ahead of the retreating Texans and block any possible passage by the Confederates back to Texas or southward to Mexico. Canby's force took the southern route from Fort Union toward Santa Fe, and from there southward to Fort Craig. (Somehow, the Union army by-passed the Confederates and got all the way to Craig without finding the enemy.)

Colonel Chivington wasted no time in getting things moving again for the Coloradans. Either he convinced General Canby of the need for vigorous pursuit of the Texans or, as many like to believe, he simply agreed with what had been Canby's desire over Slough's objections all along. Whichever was true, and the truth will forever be buried in history, Chivington now took the First Colorado and all other available troops back to Pigeon's Ranch at the top of Glorieta Pass. There he was to await word from Canby before launching his search for the Confederates, wherever they might be. The brief delay would permit Canby to check out the southern route and make certain the Rebels had not doubled back toward Fort Union. Chivington's pursuit of the enemy would begin with a sweep down Glorieta Pass as soon as Canby gave the word.

That order suited the vast majority of the men just fine, and a cheer went up when the word spread that the long wait to chase the enemy was finally over. Most of the soldiers had been aching to go after the Rebels since March 28. Most, but not all.

When word came that the men would be chasing and most likely again battling the Rebels, Privates Dixon, Penn, Shay, Walling and Wells went AWOL. Perhaps by coincidence, all five of the deserters were from Company F, the company that had suffered the heaviest casualties in Glorieta Pass.

Sergeant Ovando Hollister found their desertion particularly distasteful:

> That five men could be found in the company who would thus disgrace their birth and belie their blood was discouraging. Cowardice is their only ground. They ought never to call themselves men again. After proving insensible to all the dictates of pride, honor or interest that usually influence men, they should sneak off to some region where manhood forms no necessary ingredient of character and forget the proud race from whence they sprung, but with which they have nothing in common but the form. But no! They cannot be descended from the men of '76. Other than American blood must stagnate in their degenerate veins, or they would call on the mountains to fall and cover them from the gaze of their fellows. All that men prize or hold sacred, cries out against them. Surely they could not have realized the step or they never would have taken it. Wells, especially, I would like to think better of. He was young, 19, and much under the influence of Penn with whom he enlisted. He was a fine fellow, well thought of by all, and his fall occasions much regret. But his case is that of Tray in the fable; found in bad company he must take his share of the beating. The others were what are emphatically termed "guts" and no one is sorry they are gone, but as the manner of their going disgraces us all!

The desertions were not the only negatives with which the men had to cope. There was yet another distasteful event just before Colonel Chivington assumed power. Sergeant Philbrook, while drunk, had shot and wounded Lieutenant Gray two weeks earlier and was now convicted by court-martial of "assault with a deadly weapon, attempted murder, assault against a superior officer, drunkenness" and assorted other crimes. He was ordered executed by firing squad "without delay," and the order was carried out at Fort Union. Although most of the men agreed with the sentence, it was, nonetheless, a most distressing circumstance.

On April 1, Private George Jefts of the Second Colorado collapsed and died of unknown causes while marching south to confront the Texans.

New Mexico citizens who earlier had hidden forage and provisions from the Texans now brought all such supplies to the advancing Union army of General Canby. Canby quickly agreed to purchase all such material.

On April 3, the Second Colorado reached Socorro and found 130 wounded Texans still hospizalized there as a result of the battle of Valverde. Eighty of the Rebels had died in the hospital since the battle, and many others were in grave condition because of the lack of medical supplies.

On April 5, General Canby's command was closing on Albuquerque. As the troops marched, Private John Tanzy of K Company, 3rd Cavalry, began lagging behind. Sergeant Edward Culana approached Tanzy and scolded him for being so slow. Tanzy whipped out his Colt Navy revolver and shot Culana in the face. Culana fell, pulled his own pistol and fired back, but missed. Tanzy then fired a second time, killing Culana outright. Private Ickis noted, "They were firm friends when sober, but rot makes men fools!" Twenty-four hours later, Tanzy was shot to death by a firing squad. "He was very cool and when marched out to the stool, kept step with the guard—as cool as any man ever was."

When the totality of the Confederate loss at Glorieta Pass finally began to sink in, General Sibley wasted little time. Only hours after the bloody fighting and returning to the remains of his base camp on March 28 despite his formal report to the contrary, Sibley reluctantly concluded that his army was defeated, his dreams shattered, and the Confederate hopes of capturing the West dashed, possibly forever.

Worse than that, those Pike's Peakers who had surprisingly fought so savagely in two previous encounters, would soon be in pursuit. Sibley was not eager to renew the confrontation, especially under these circumstances. His troops faced extreme problems. Sickness was rampant. They were virtually out of ammunition, most of their artillery pieces had been captured or shattered by enemy gunfire, and they were out of food and clothing. Sibley was almost completely helpless deep inside enemy territory, far away from any possible reinforcements or supply lines. It was a hopeless situation, and Sibley knew it.

The Confederate commander also knew several other things. First, travel for his troops was going to be difficult with so many of his wagons burned and the majority of his horses and mules dead—either killed by the enemy, or dead of starvation. Secondly, any effort to evacuate his wounded would slow down what was already likely to be an unacceptably slow pace of retreat. That meant some agonizing decisions that could not be postponed. Fortunately for Sibley, he felt the Coloradans and native New Mexicans were not likely to leave Confederate wounded unattended, regardless of any personal animosity they might feel toward the enemy.

Given the reality of the situation, therefore, Sibley evidenced no apparent remorse about the orders he issued shortly before midnight. All able-bodied men were to begin an immediate and hasty retreat toward Santa Fe and, ultimately, Albuquerque. They were to bring with them only their weapons and whatever ammunition they could carry, plus any horses still able to travel. Everything else of value was to be destroyed or abandoned. The order to "abandon" included all of the wounded in the base camp and all of the wounded still lying on the battlefield up in Glorieta Pass. History does not record the reaction of the Confederate soldiers, but they obeyed the command.

The Confederates, weary from the day-long battle and saddened by their heavy losses, set out toward Santa Fe at about 1:00 A.M. some five hours after discovering the destruction of their base camp. They expected at any time to be overtaken by the Coloradans and to be cut to shreds by enemy gunfire. But as each hour passed and the distance between them and their old base camp widened, it appeared more and more likely that the shattered Confederate army would get away.By dawn the next morning, they had reoccupied Santa Fe, at least temporarily. Scrounging around the village for horses, wagons, side arms, ammunition, food, blankets and clothing, the Rebels soon had taken everything of value. Amazingly, the latest ransacking of Santa Fe was unhindered. There still was no sign of the pursuing enemy.

General Sibley went to the local telegraph office and composed a wire to his headquarters in San Antonio. The message was apparently to be an appeal for reinforcements. However, the wire was never sent and its contents are lost to history. It seems that the telegraph operator was a Union sympathizer who simply tore up Sibley's message as soon as the general left the office. Sibley may have anticipated that his telegram would not reach San Antonio, because that same morning he wrote a letter to both his headquarters and the governor's office in Texas. The identical letters made an urgent appeal for help, saying "we have been severely crippled, and for this reason, ask your assistance." The letters would not arrive in Texas for many weeks, far too late to do the beleaguered Western Expeditionary Force the least bit of good.

As the day lengthened without sign of the Coloradans, the Confederates grew braver. Slowly, they began to relax and the signs of panic vanished. That night, they camped in the village with only a few guards on the lookout for the Coloradans. On March 30, the men began to conclude that they were not going to be attacked, after all.

In the absence of Union pursuit, the Confederates seemed to regain their previous demeanor as conquerors, walking and talking as if they had won a great victory in Glorieta Pass. Men who had stumbled into town ready to collapse from exhaustion in their haste to run away from the First Colorado now told villagers that the Coloradans had been soundly whipped in the fighting. Some of the soldiers wrote letters home telling of the great victory.

The Assistant Adjutant General of the Confederate invasion force, Tom P. Ochiltree, soon sent a fanciful claim of victory to rebel headquarters:

His Excellency President Davis:

I have the honor to inform your Excellency of another glorious victory achieved by the Confederate Army of New Mexico.

On the 27th March, Lieutenant Colonel Scurry, with 1,000 men from the 2nd, 4th, 5th, and 7th Texas volunteers, met, attacked, whipped and routed 2,000 Federals, 23 miles east of Santa Fe. Our loss was 33 killed and 35 wounded—among the killed was Major Raguet and Captain Buckholts of the 4th, and Major Shropshire of the 5th Texas mounted volunteers. Lieutenant Colonel Scurry, commanding, was twice slightly wounded, and Major Pyron, commanding battalion TMR, had his horse blown from under him by a shell.

The enemy's loss was over 700 killed and wounded, 500 being left on the field. Their rout was complete and they were scattered from the battlefield to Fort Union.

The Confederate flag flies over Santa Fe and Albuquerque. At the latter place, the flag was made of a captured United States flag, raised upon a United States flagstaff—the salute fired by a captured United States battery, and Dixie played by a captured United States band.

The Federal force defeated at Glorietta Pass consisted of 1600 Pike's Peak volunteers and another 600 regulars, under command of Col. Slough. I have the honor to inform your excellence that I will wait upon you with important dispatches in a few days.

Colonel Scurry seemed just as self-deluded in his formal address to the retreating Confederate army; his written commendation to the troops—posted throughout the city of Santa Fe—said:

Head-quarters, Advance Division, Army of New Mexico
Canon Glorietta, March 29, 1862.

GENERAL ORDER NUMBER 4

Soldiers

You have added another glorius victory to the long list of triumphs won by the Confederate armies. By your conduct you have given another evidence of the daring courage and heroic endurance which actuate you in this great struggle for the independence of your country. You have proven your right to stand by the side of those who fought and conquered on the red field of San Jacinto. The battle of Glorietta—where for 6 long hours you steadily drove before you a foe of twice your numbers, over a field chosen by themselves and deemed impregnable, will take its place upon the rolls of your country's triumphs and serve to excite your children to imitate the brave deeds of their fathers, in every hour of that country's peril.

Soldiers—I am proud of you. Go on as you have commenced and it will not be long until not a single soldier of the United States will be left upon the soil of New Mexico. The Territory, relieved of the burden imposed on it by its late oppressors, will once more, throughout its beautiful valleys, "blossom as the rose," beneath the plastic hand of peaceful industry.

Lt. Col. Wm. R. Scurry, Commanding
Ellsberry R. Lane, Adjutant

Even Sibley grew bolder as time elapsed. Apparently forgetting his letters and the telegram that was never transmitted, Sibley now wrote his official report on the battle. These documents, mailed to his headquarters at San Antonio, said the enemy had been "crushed" by his great victory. Possibly as a result of this "official" document, the myth of a lopsided Confederate victory in Glorieta Pass remains in some Civil War literature.

On April 5 and 6, seven and eight days after the battle, the now rejuvenated Rebels marched leisurely from Santa Fe to Albuquerque and reoccupied that town. They again scrounged for anything that would be of use to them. Although they grew bolder each day, many were still amazed at the lack of pursuit by the Coloradans. By the end of the first week following the battle Sibley concluded that his troops must have inflicted far more serious damage on the Union force than he had earlier believed. The absence of pursuit indicated that the First Colorado Volunteers were physically unable to pursue the Confederates! General Sibley began to believe his troops when they talked of having whipped the Coloradans, and he now felt less pressure to move quickly.

The Confederates occupied one side of the town but controlled the entire city. Sibley stationed his remaining artillery at different points around the community and prepared to stay indefinitely for rest and recuperation. Perhaps, he thought, all is not lost after all. He talked with his officers about recruiting friendly locals and continuing the Western campaign. He also remained hopeful about a possible relief column from Texas.

Sibley's troops were soon firmly entrenched at Albuquerque. They were especially strong in the vicinity of Armijo's Mill at the eastern end of the city, where Sibley had taken over a villa to serve as his headquarters. The Armijo brothers were strong supporters of the Confederacy, and had earlier donated considerable money and goods to support Sibley's Brigade.

Over the past several days the Confederates had been able to locate sizeable amounts of gunpowder. While there was not enough to fight a prolonged engagement, there certainly was enough to put up a spirited defense should that become necessary. Partially because of the increased availability of gunpowder and partly because they were camped in a civilian area that the enemy would be reluctant to attack, Sibley felt his battered army was sufficiently prepared to deal with any possible attack from a Union force.

By the morning of April 8, General Canby finally learned that Sibley's army was not racing southward, but was stopped somewhere between Glorieta Pass and Fort Craig. The news came from a Union scouting party, which during the previous night had raided a Confederate outpost between Santa Fe and Albuquerque, capturing ninety-four of the enemy's mules.

Canby and about one thousand militiamen left the fort and began marching northward again, half expecting to meet the Confederates along the way. Eventually, new reports reached Canby, indicating the enemy might be camped in Albuquerque. Canby headed for the city, hoping that no battle would have to be fought in a civilian area.

That same morning, Colonel Chivington finally received a message indicating that General Canby wanted him to leave Camp Chivington at Pigeon's Ranch and begin the pursuit of Sibley. Simultaneously, Colonels Tappan and Paul left Fort Union for Santa Fe. That meant that the Coloradans were converging on Albuquerque from the north and the northeast, while General Canby and the New Mexico volunteers closed in from the south. Sibley, who now believed his own claims of victory in the earlier fighting, apparently remained unaware of the approach of the Union forces.

Before leaving Fort Union, Tappan and Paul had to decide how to deal with a substantial number of Confederate prisoners. If the Rebels were held at the Fort, they would have to be fed and guarded, both of which seemed like an undue waste of money and manpower with another battle in the offing. It was not uncommon during the Civil War for prisoners to be released on "personal recognizance" after they swore to never again bear arms against the other side (or until they were formally exchanged for prisoners held by the other side). Faced with that practice and the alternative of committing men and resources to keeping the prisoners, the colonels decided to free one hundred Confederate prisoners who had been held since the battle in Glorieta Pass. Unfortunately, the "promise system" rarely worked; released prisoners were commonly back on the front lines within days.

As the former Confederate soldiers were preparing to leave Fort Union, Sergeant Hollister engaged them in a debate as to the real reasons for the war. The Southerners insisted the war was caused by the North's intention to impose its will on the South. Hollister argued that the war was caused by Southern secession and military attacks on the North. Hollister was dismayed at what he considered the misinformation which the prisoners apparently ardently believed to be true. It was as if none of them had the slightest knowledge of what Hollister thought were evident truths.

The experience hardened Hollister's personal feelings toward the enemy soldiers. Later, he wrote in his diary:

> I think that a war of extermination is all that will ever restore American unity. They hate us intensely. Kindness is accepted only as their due and as food for their haughtiness. Nothing can cure their insane prejudice against Northern men, whom they habitually stigmatize with every base epithet known to the vocabulary of abuse. All they want is the power to inflict a worse servitude on us than that which the unfortunate Negro suffers.

Then warming to the task, Hollister for the first time began to show open personal hostility toward the Texans.

> It is because of gratitude to the Ruler of all that in the attempt we have the strength and inclination to drive them to the wall. If they have ten millions of human lives to sacrifice to their pride and ambition, we have an equal number, and the eight millions left can then hold up their heads in a free country; neither insulted by the brutal haughtiness of the one race nor scandalized by the degradation and woes of the other, which together form the "style of civilization" upon which the new nation founds its civil policy. . . . Then let them hate and scorn us. We will teach them reason by killing them off as fast as possible. They have left us no alternative. We may as well submit to it gracefully. It is a sure cure. The patient is never taken with a relapse. Dead men never put on the airs of the "hereditary lords of the manor," nor seek paltry excuses for "venting the venom of their spleen" on their brethren. The history of Joseph and his brothers might teach them a successful lesson—or might have taught. It is now too late; there is nothing left them but death or submission!

On April 10, two Confederate colonels, Thomas Green and Charles McNeil, rode up the southern trail out of Santa Fe under a flag of truce to meet the Coloradans. They proposed a prisoner exchange, but said they were only willing to release New Mexico militia and not any captured Coloradan or Union regulars. Colonel Paul told the Rebels they had "better flee for their lives" as he was having trouble seeing their white flag. The Confederate colonels got the message; they put the spurs to their horses and raced back down the trail toward Santa Fe and Albuquerque.

Later that same day, General Canby's adjutant, Captain William J. Nicodemus, rode up the Glorieta trail to meet the Coloradans. Nicodemus told Colonel Chivington that the Confederates had all apparently once again abandoned Santa Fe in favor of Albuquerque. They are camped in the town, the captain said, and are "well protected from frontal assault." Nicodemus also reported that General Sibley still had about two thousand soldiers with him. The Rebel soldiers appeared to be about 80 percent Texans who began the campaign with Sibley, and 20 percent New Mexico citizens who joined up with the Rebel force along the way. The Union captain further reported that the Texans appeared, in a leisurely way, to be trying to get back to Texas.

The afternoon that the Coloradans tramped back down Glorieta Pass the weather turned cold, snowy, and windy. By late afternoon they had reached the bottom of the canyon without finding any sign of the enemy, except for the old, burned-out base camp. Chivington kept the troops marching until well after dark. Because Nicodemus had not been absolutely certain that the last of the enemy had departed Santa Fe, the Coloradans headed for that community.

At about 10:00 P.M. they had the lights of the village in sight, and were ordered to halt until daylight. As the tired soldiers began to make camp another Union scout appeared. This one confirmed to Chivington that all of the Confederates had pulled out of Santa Fe. He reported that the Rebels had again looted the city before fleeing, and now had taken almost everything of value, including money and artwork.

But it turned out that the Texans did not take everything out of the city. In fact, they left another gift for the Coloradans. The messenger said the Confederates had again abandoned all of their sick and wounded, a total of about 50 men. In addition, the messenger reported that a "substantial number" of Confederate soldiers had recently deserted the army and had lain down their weapons. They were waiting in the city to surrender to Colonel Chivington. The total number of former Rebel soldiers said to be in the city, "but neither wishing nor able to do battle," was reported to be possibly 250 men. No official records are available as to the number eventually captured by the Coloradans. Those who surrendered at Santa Fe were administered the oath and released.

Finding the sick and wounded enemy soldiers was not the only thing about Santa Fe that the Colorado soldiers didn't particularly care for; most of them were disappointed at the city itself. They were used to Denver, which was booming and was already significantly larger than the New Mexico capital city. Hollister wrote this description in his diary:

> Santa Fe, the Capital of New Mexico, is situated on a small creek of the same name, near the southwestern base of a spur of the Sierra Madre. It occupies an area of perhaps ten acres and is surrounded by bluffs. There are one brick and about four two-story buildings; the balance are adobe structures, squat, dingy and poverty-stricken. Burros may be seen packing corn, flour, wood, hay, etc., through the streets at all hours. At the Fonda, one can board for three dollars per day, or sixty per month.

Alonzo Ickis had a similar impression of the city; his diary entry said "Santa Fe streets are 10 to 15 feet wide, and there are about 10,000 Greasers in the city. The town supports one Presbyterian and two Catholic churches, but I do not think they exercise any good influence on the people. Santa Fe is one grande (excuse the expression) brothel—in fact, New Mexico could with propriety come under that head."

On the morning of April 13, General Canby's New Mexican militiamen arrived atop the hills just to the east of Albuquerque. From this vantage point they could clearly see the Confederate soldiers and the enemy's artillery in the city below. In spite of his reluctance to do battle in a civilian area, Canby gave the order to begin shelling the Rebels. At precisely 9:00 A.M., the New Mexicans opened fire with several cannons. However, as the soldiers were all natives of New Mexico, and in some cases, residents of Albuquerque, the men were even more reluctant than Canby to shell the city. As a result, the artillerymen were severely limited as to their possible targets, being under orders not to destroy any homes or businesses in the city.

The Union army began shelling a stockyards area and an abandoned warehouse near Sibley's headquarters. There were few enemy soldiers in the area, however, and those who were quickly scampered to safety. The Confederates returned the fire, but their shelling was also largely ineffective.

Twice during the day, Union patrols sent to probe the city's defenses encountered Confederate patrols at the perimeter of the city. There was a lot of gunfire and shouting during the brief fire-fights that followed the chance meetings, but neither side reported any serious injuries.

At mid-afternoon, General Canby sent a messenger into the city under a flag of truce. The messenger requested that General Sibley, "in the interest of decency" permit the civilian women and children to evacuate the city. Sibley refused. He knew that by staying among the civilians he ran little chance of any all-out Union attack.

When the messenger went back to General Canby with the Confederate rejection, Canby ordered his troops to "cease fire" and to pull back. The soldiers halted their shelling of Albuquerque and withdrew about fifteen miles west of the city, making camp at the quiet little town of Tijeras. Canby told his aides that he would not again assault the Rebels until Colonel Chivington arrived with the First Colorado Volunteers.

When Canby withdrew rather than shell a civilian area, the Confederates thought they had forced his retreat militarily. Sibley issued a statement commending his "heroic little garrison" for its great victory in driving away "1500 enemy with all the improvements that late inventions had made to arms." Texas Captain William Hardeman, who was commanding the Texans' cannons during the fight, was breveted to the rank of lieutenant colonel for "having forced the enemy into headlong retreat."

Although Canby didn't know it as he sat frustrated in the hills overlooking Albuquerque, the Coloradans were already only a few miles away. Earlier that morning, bugles awakened the Coloradans at 1:00 A.M., and by 2:00 A.M. they were again marching toward Albuquerque. They had gotten only three hours sleep, and had not been provided with breakfast before the march began. By dawn, the Coloradans had moved down Carnuel Pass and by 8:00 A.M. they linked up with Canby at Tijeras.

And now, for the first time in the fighting, the Union army had more troops than the Confederates. There were about one thousand men in the First Colorado Volunteers, while Canby had about eleven hundred New Mexican militiamen with him.

In addition, General Canby had brought along four pieces of artillery with plenty of ammunition. Both of the units were accompanied by several wagonloads of supplies. The Union was well prepared for a new confrontation with the enemy, if they could only draw the enemy out of the city of Albuquerque!

The joyful link-up of these two Federal forces was somewhat muted by other factors. The Coloradans had marched eighteen of the last twenty-three hours without eating. Along the way a number of their horses simply collapsed and died, unable to keep up the grueling pace. There were also a number of soldiers who became ill or who were physically exhausted, making an immediate advance on the enemy virtually impossible.

General Sibley learned the next morning that a "huge" Union force was gathered a few miles from Albuquerque, apparently preparing to eject him from the city. In the language of military rationalization, Sibley told junior officers it was time to continue what he called the "retrograde movement" out of New Mexico. Sibley knew that there was little likelihood of a Union attack so long as he remained in Albuquerque, but he also did not want to stay in the city and risk being surrounded and cut off by the Union army. At least by moving he still had a chance to escape to Texas.

By this time, the Confederates had remaining provisions for only about two weeks, and about thirty-five rounds of ammunition per man. Sibley thought he had enough ammunition to fight either General Canby or the Coloradans, but not both. He was also desperate for more food. In ordering the retreat from Albuquerque, Sibley told his troops that the enemy had forty-eight hundred to five thousand men and was preparing to attack the city; the general said he was outnumbered "five to one." Actually, the combined Union force at this point was twenty-four hundred men, while Sibley had seventeen hundred who were "fit for battle." The remainder of the four thousand or so Confederates who began the fight were either ill with smallpox, wounded, captured, or had deserted.

Now the Confederates faced a new problem; the troops had gathered so much loot in Santa Fe and Albuquerque that they had neither the wagons nor the horses to carry it all. Sibley ordered the men to abandon much of the goods. He also ordered that several brass cannons be unbolted from their two-wheeled carts and buried in the garden of the house that he had been occupying. He reasoned that the wagons were needed to haul supplies more than they were needed for the cannons, especially since he had so little remaining ammunition for the weapons.

It would later be determined that Sibley had also earlier buried a number of cannons in Santa Fe for the same reason. Ironically, the weapons he buried were the ones with which he had left Texas for the conquest of the West. The six cannons he retained to cover his "retrograde movement" out of New Mexico were the six guns he had captured from General Canby in the battle of North Ford.

On the night of the April 12 and 13, the Confederates slipped out of Albuquerque. The 1st Regiment and a battalion of the 3rd crossed the Rio Grande River by ferryboat at 1:00 A.M. and proceeded down the west bank to the town of Los Lunas. The other half of his command, the 2nd Regiment and those troops under Major Pyron and Colonel Green, left town just before sunrise and hurried down the east bank for about twenty miles.

Colonel Green attempted to cross the river about ten miles south of Albuquerque but encountered thick mud and quicksand. A number of his wagons sank to their axles and he finally had to abandon them. He ordered a unit of teamsters to come back for the wagons as soon as his unit rejoined the remainder of the retreating Confederates. Eventually, the two columns joined up on the east bank where the Confederates seized a ranch belonging to Territorial Governor Connelly. The ranch lay on the outskirts of the community of Peralta.

However, the teamsters unit delayed for more than twelve hours returning for the supplies packed aboard the mired wagons. That delay would soon have disastrous results for the Texans.

The main Connelly ranch house was constructed of thick adobe. The house was surrounded by courtyards, which, in turn, were surrounded by adobe walls. Although the walls would not withstand a heavy artillery barrage, Sibley supposed the Union troops would be reluctant to shell the home of the governor.

Once again, Sibley felt safe from an immediate Union assault. He ordered the 5th Texas to take up defensive positions between the building and the walls and to open fire at the slightest hint of an enemy approach. Then the general told his troops to "take it easy"—apparently hoping that those anticipated reinforcements from Texas would catch up with the Western Expeditionary Force at this point. The Confederates stayed at the ranch for two full days, helping themselves to chickens, cows and sheep as well as to the governor's private stock of wine.

The decision by the rebels to stop at the ranch and spend two days there instead of hightailing it on down the trail toward Texas baffled the pursuing Union army. Having no knowledge of Sibley's never-sent telegram, or the letter he had written, they could think of no reason for the Confederates to have halted their retreat. Chivington and Canby agreed that whatever Sibley's reasoning, the stopover was an error on the part of the enemy. The error would prove to be a costly one.

PART FOUR

Final Victory

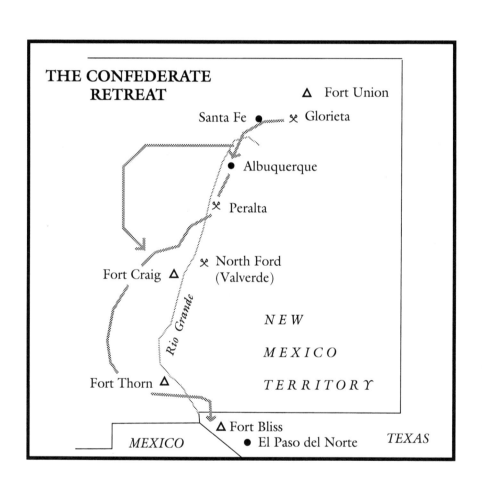

THE CONFEDERATE RETREAT

△ Fort Union

Santa Fe ● ⚔ Glorieta

● Albuquerque

⚔ Peralta

⚔ North Ford
(Valverde)

Fort Craig △

Rio Grande

N E W

M E X I C O

T E R R I T O R Y

Fort Thorn △

△ Fort Bliss

MEXICO ● El Paso del Norte *TEXAS*

CHAPTER FOURTEEN

THE BATTLE OF PERALTA

April 7, 1862. Supper tonight consists of bread that is not too stale, boiled eggs and salt, coffee and sugar. Our horses are well fed.

Ovando J. Hollister, Company F
First Colorado Volunteers

On the morning of April 14, the combined Union army was rested, fed, and ready for action. The troops pulled out of Tijeras shortly after sunrise and marched thirty-six miles southward along the east banks of the Rio Grande. Union scouts had already located the main body of Confederate troops, and the Federals headed straight toward the Connelly ranch. On the way, the officers debated whether to attack Sibley if it meant destroying the ranch buildings or buildings of the nearby city. That evening the Union soldiers made camp about a mile from Governor Connelly's ranch, apparently unbeknownst to the enemy.

When the scouts told Colonel Chivington how near he was to the Texans and then reported further that the Confederates "were enjoying music, dancing and lots of wine," he proposed to attack them at once, and thus put an end to the campaign.

General Canby refused permission for any attack on Sibley. This time Canby said his denial was because a night attack was generally disastrous and "not worth the risk to good men." Then, apparently in response to the obvious dismay of his troops, the Union commander shared his strategy for the first time with junior officers, a strategy that would come under heavy criticism from both inside and outside the military.

General Canby suggested that he might never attack the Confederates at all, providing they continued their retreat. He reasoned that it would be better if the enemy would simply and quickly leave New Mexico rather than to engage in a new battle. Such new fighting would run the risk of incurring more Union casualties, said Canby, and if they could be avoided, why pay the price? Besides, he said, if Sibley surrendered it would become both difficult and expensive to care for so many Rebel prisoners.

Chivington was absolutely incensed at Canby's reasoning and said so, but he agreed to obey the order. The Colorado soldiers were also furious, as were most of the New Mexican militiamen. The unhappy troops soon spread word around the countryside that "we would have wiped out the Rebs had it not been for Canby, who wants them to escape to Mexico or safely back home to Texas." The bitter rumor implying that Canby deliberately chose to let the invaders escape set off another spate of irate letters from New Mexico residents to President Lincoln. Once again, the letter writers presumed that Canby was disposed to injure his own cause rather than embarrass or injure his brother-in-law.

For the time being, however, Canby's orders left the Union troops with nothing to do that night but to make camp and wait for another dawn. It was nearly 11:00 P.M. before the soldiers were fed and ready for bed, and midnight before the camp was really quiet.

It did not remain that way long. A few minutes after 12 midnight, the soldiers were awakened by the arrival of a horseman who came racing into camp calling for Colonel Chivington.

The rider was one of the pickets assigned to guard the perimeter of the Union camp. He had spotted a Confederate supply train of seven wagons and a mountain howitzer, coming down the trail from the north of the Union encampment. The supply train was bringing to the Texans those supplies belatedly unpacked from the mired wagons back up the trail. Had they been retrieved a few hours earlier, they would have reached the Rebels safely.

In seconds, Chivington organized and dispatched two companies of men to intercept the Rebels. Nearly two hundred of the Coloradans raced out of camp and headed for the main trail.

When the Confederates saw the approaching Union troops they seemed uncertain as to what to do. They milled about in confusion for several seconds before finally unlimbering their rifles and beginning to shoot. By that time, the Coloradans had raced their horses to within two hundred yards of the enemy. At that point, the attackers leaped from their horses, deployed as skirmishers, and advanced on the Rebels.

Despite heavy return fire from the Texans, the Coloradans continued to rapidly close on the enemy. At fifty yards, the Union troops rushed forward. About a dozen of the Confederates threw down their weapons and surrendered, while the remainder began running. Some were shot, some were captured and a few escaped. During the brief fire fight, six Confederates were killed and three more seriously wounded; about two-dozen were taken prisoner. The Union troops had suffered only one casualty: Private J. H. Hawley of Company F was shot in the head and killed instantly.

As a result of the brief battle, the Coloradans seized seven heavily loaded supply wagons, a cannon, twelve horses and seventy mules. The prisoners, cannon, animals and wagons were taken back to the Union camp. There the victors were elated to learn that one of the captured wagons was filled with ammunition for the captured cannon. The other wagons were loaded with food, forage, and other supplies.

By now, the sun was beginning to soften the darkness of the night. The Coloradans took their five cannons, including the artillery piece seized during the night, and slipped closer to the Connelly Ranch. At 8:00 A.M., Union gunners opened fire on the Rebels. These Union positions, however, were exposed and exceedingly dangerous, while the Confederates were relatively safe and secure behind the adobe walls of the ranch. The enemy returned the fire in earnest and soon inflicted a number of casualties among the Union forces.

The situation very nearly proved fatal to Colonel Chivington. At the height of the cannon duel, he and one of his captains were standing in a little valley, protected from the gunfire by a hill that rose between them and the Rebels. The two officers were discussing strategy and paying little attention to the cannon duel. A Rebel cannon ball ricochetted off the top of the hill and came bounding down the slope heading directly for the two officers. Neither man was aware of the danger and the cannon ball skipped a few inches over their heads and plowed into a group of soldiers standing directly behind them. Two Colorado privates, Joseph Long of C Company and George Thompson of Ford's Independent Company, were hit by the cannon ball and killed outright. Several other soldiers were injured. Seconds later, as troops tried to aid the stricken men, another cannon ball fell into the same area, killing Private Richard Yates of C Company. The Union casualty toll from the capture of the wagon train and the morning shelling now stood at four dead and seven wounded.

The Confederates continued to pound the Union position from their places of concealment within the ranch, and the cannonading continued for several hours. At the height of the battle, Confederate gunners began stuffing glass bottles into the barrels of their cannon so that glass shrapnel sprayed the Union lines. Some of the bottles were filled with an unidentified liquid, leading many to believe that the Rebels were firing some kind of poison at the Union troops.

Alonzo Ickis said that Colonel Chivington quickly sent a man under a flag of truce with a note, telling the enemy that if they fired another bottle "or any other poisonuous substance" at us, we would kill and scalp "every S of a B" of them.

The Confederates stopped shelling for several minutes, then resumed, but without the glass and liquid. The shelling continued for several hours. Then, surprisingly, the Rebels stopped shooting. In the eerie silence, Union scouts could see that the enemy had begun withdrawing from the ranch back toward the river. It was about the middle of the afternoon and far too early to assume the battle would stop for the night. And, since the Union fire had not appeared to be particularly effective, the Confederate withdrawal was all the more surprising, especially since it appeared the Confederates could have held out at the ranch indefinitely. The Union officers were not sure what to do next and while they huddled or milled about in confusion, the Texans moved quickly to the west.

Actually, the Texans' retreat across the river looked much easier than it really was; in fact, it was a desperate and panicked flight. While some of them were able to use a ferry boat, most of the men were forced to swim or wade across the river, which was several hundred feet wide at that point. The water was filled with large chunks of ice and was, obviously, bitterly cold.

As the Colorado troops waited for further orders they watched in disbelief as the Confederates continued crossing to the west bank of the river under heavy covering fire. The evacuation took more than two hours to complete. When they were all safely on the far bank the Texans blew up and sank the ferryboat commandeered for the crossing and began moving down the trail toward the south.

By now it was once again getting dark. When informed of the strange chain of events General Canby said it was too late to continue the pursuit that night. He ordered the men back to their own camp until the following day. Once again the Coloradans were furious that they were not allowed to pursue, and believed they could have caught and wiped out the enemy that night had they simply been allowed to do so.

A small Colorado patrol was sent to search the Connelly ranch and reported back that they found it to be "totally defensible." The information led Canby, Chivington and the other officers to conclude that the Rebels fled Peralta and the Connelly ranch because they no longer had the resources to resist. There was considerable speculation about the exact nature of the shortages with which the Rebels were having to cope.

While the discussion was still underway, Assistant Union Surgeon Lewis C. Tolles walked into the Colorado camp. Tolles had been taken prisoner by the Confederates several days earlier when he went to aid a man wounded during one of Canby's skirmishes with the Rebels on the outskirts of Albuquerque. The doctor had been released by the Confederates just before they crossed the river.

Tolles said that while he was with the Rebels at Connelly's ranch he had overheard a group of about 250 Texans tell Colonel Scurry they would fight the Yankees no longer. The physician said he was told that the enemy was nearly out of ammunition and food, had few blankets, and was completely exhausted by the continuing Union pursuit. He said the slow pace of the Rebel retreat was because both men and animals were exhausted. Further, Dr. Tolles said General Sibley was battling a severe morale problem. Most of the Texans were frustrated and depressed over their lack of gunpowder and ammunition and by the humiliating retreat. The doctor said dozens, possibly hundreds, of Confederate soldiers had deserted and said the "totality of their defeat" was finally being realized by the enemy soldiers and "even by their officers who have had trouble coming to grips with reality."

Dr. Tolles' assessment of the Confederates could not have been more accurate. Before the Rebels pulled out of Peralta that day they had fired their last cannon ball at the Union soldiers. The only ammunition remaining in their camp was bullets for their rifles and pistols, and there were precious few of them. They were virtually out of food, medical supplies were completely exhausted, and their remaining horses were "dying like flies" because of starvation.

As a result of all these shortages, General Sibley faced a number of related problems. His troops were deserting not just by the dozens but in droves, many of them heading out cross-country, apparently hoping to reach California. Altogether an estimated twelve hundred Confederates eventully deserted over a period of several days. A number of the Texans' horses had been killed by cannon fire at Peralta and a majority of the remaining animals were simply too sick to continue. Sibley was so short of horses and mules that even his limited number of remaining wagons could no longer be utilized. He set fire to most of his remaining wagons to make certain they could not be put to use by the pursuing Union army. The general's only hope now apparently lay in making for the Texas border as fast as he and his troops could go.

Despite knowing that these conditions existed among the enemy, the Coloradans and their New Mexican militia companions were again denied permission by General Canby to immediately pursue the Rebel column. Instead, Canby ordered the Union army to stay in camp once again and wait for daylight.

Colonel Chivington did not sleep well that night, believing that he now had total victory within his grasp. If the Texans were hurting as much as the doctor had reported, he could likely catch up with them within a few hours. Then, he would either take them prisoner or wipe them out in battle. Chivington later said he "anticipated greatly" the opportunity to personally capture General Sibley.

Well before dawn on the morning of April 16, Colonel Chivington had his troops awake and ready to move out once again. The Colonel planned to lead his troops across the river and send his cavalry in hot pursuit of the enemy. He felt that this time there was no possible circumstance that would prevent him from catching up with Sibley and wiping out what was left of the hated Western Expeditionary Force.

Once again, however, it was not to be! This time it was the elements that came to the rescue of the beleaguered Texans. A cloudburst during the night, augmented by rapidly melting snow, had greatly swollen the Rio Grande River. Water was dangerously high and filled with trees and other debris. The only ferryboat in the area had been sunk by the Confederates and there appeared to be no way to get across the water.

It would later be charged by some of the soldiers and a great many civilians that the stream was not so flooded as to make a crossing impossible at one of several nearby fords. Those making these accusations would again say that Canby refused to cross the river in order to avoid a final and possibly fatal showdown with his brother-in-law.

Yet not everyone was certain that Canby had any ulterior motives. While many of the Coloradan soldiers believed they probably could cross the stream that day, many admitted the water was unusually high and dangerous. And none of the Colorado officers apparently felt that Canby's decision was based on anything other than considerations of safety for the troops. Even Colonel Chivington felt that the river was not fordable. As a result, the Union soldiers had no choice but to remain on their own side of the Rio Grande and work their way southward, hoping the Confederates would stick to the trail that paralleled the water on the west side of the river.

When the Union army pulled out of camp that morning, they finally got some good news. Union pickets told them the enemy had not been able to move very far during the darkness and had, indeed, remained on the trail. Despite his lengthy head start in terms of time, the Texans were only two to three hours ahead of the Coloradans on the opposite side of the river. As Chivington's troops moved out, they could see piles of burning debris on the Confederate side of the river. The fires marked places where the enemy were burning their luggage, personal papers, wagons, and everything else too heavy to carry.

At sunup that day a stiff wind was blowing from the south. By mid-morning the wind and blowing sand were beginning to make travel difficult. By early afternoon, swirling dust had reduced visibility to a few hundred feet, and the wind seemed to be blowing harder than ever. It continued to blow fiercely all during the day, cutting forward progress to almost nothing.

The Coloradans were able to travel only about ten miles before sunset that night, causing Hollister to write this angry and sarcastic entry in his diary: "Sixty miles per day to catch the traitors and ten to let them go! Of course, it is all right; we do not want to take any unfair advantage of them. We would be chivalrous, like them. God grant they may never get the same advantage of us!"

As if the day was simply destined to be a bad one for the First Colorado, a cold rain began falling at sunset and the strong wind and muddy ground made it difficult for the men to pitch their tents. One of the wagons belonging to the commissary caught fire, presumably from a candle inside by which a sergeant had been reading. The sergeant had been drinking and may have been asleep; in any case, he died in the fire.

On the morning of the April 17, Chivington once again had his troops moving by sunrise. The weather was not quite as difficult as it had been one day earlier, but there was still a cold wind and blowing sand and forward progress was slow. About midmorning, however, the Union caught sight of General Sibley's retreating Rebel army only three or four miles ahead of them on the opposite bank. Union scouts working ahead of the main body of troops estimated the enemy force at that time to be approximately twenty-five hundred men, or about the same size as that of the pursuing Union army. There were considerable differences between the two armies, however. The Coloradans were tired and their animals hungry, but compared to the Texans, the Union army was in great physical shape. The Union soldiers also had plenty of ammunition with them, a striking contrast to the retreating Texans who had almost none, even for their side arms.

Shortly after noon, the Confederates halted for lunch and the First Colorado caught up with and actually passed them. The Union soldiers entered the little village of Joya de Ceboleta before stopping for lunch. During the break, the Coloradans used binoculars to watch the Texans on the far side of the Rio Grande. Several of the Colorado officers said it appeared to them as if the Texans were preparing to make a break for it. They were seen burning luggage and unnecessary supplies. The officers again requested permission from General Canby to cross the river and attack. Canby again refused, this time without giving a reason.

The two armies moved out almost simultaneously after a lengthy lunch break and stayed exactly opposite one another for the remainder of the day. From time to time, soldiers would shout derisive remarks across the water at the enemy, who always responded with comments of their own.

It was painfully slow going. The Coloradans had to keep pausing to let the slower moving Confederate army keep pace. That night, the enemies made camp as they had marched: directly across the water from one another.

CHAPTER FIFTEEN

FINAL VICTORY

April 24. The idea of pursuit has been abandoned. Our animals are worn out, we have no forage and little grub; there is but one course left—to lay up and recruit. All around us are the debris left by the retreating Texans—dead animals, broken and burned wagons, half-buried arms and supplies.

Ovando J. Hollister, Company F
First Colorado Volunteers

*W*hen the sun rose on the morning of April 18, the Coloradans were surprised and angered to see that the Rebel camp on the other side of the Rio Grande was empty. During the night, the Texans had quietly pulled up stakes and headed into the hills behind them. From their side of the water the Coloradans could see the hoof prints left by the enemy's few remaining horses.

The Confederates had chosen to take a circular and harder route through the mountains well to the west, rather than follow the main path paralleling the river. The choice was made because the latter eventually passed directly in front of Fort Craig, which the Confederates had learned was defended by at least some sort of a Union force.

A week earlier, General Sibley had intended to seize Fort Craig, which he felt could be defended almost indefinitely. Since the army chasing him seemed to be the total Union force in the territory, capturing the fort would amount to nothing more than walking inside and changing flags. Sibley apparently had a vague notion of being able to regain physical and troop strength there, somehow replenish his meager supplies, and then once again possibly attacking New Mexico. However, he abandoned the plan when his scouts told him on April 17 that the fort was not empty after all. Colonel Kit Carson and four hundred New Mexican militiamen were still defending the fort. The news caused Sibley not only to abandon the idea of seizing it, but also forced him to take a lengthy, circular route well away from the fort on his way back to Texas.

In place of the Confederate camp on the opposite bank the morning of April 18, there were only a handful of tents and a few wagons. Captain Graydon, commander of the independent spy unit, crossed the river to check out the wagons and found them to be filled with sick and wounded Confederate soldiers. Once again, those Texans unable to continue had been abandoned by their comrades who were trying to escape. General Canby ordered three Union surgeons and an escort of twelve men to attend to the sick and injured Confederates and to accompany them to the nearest hospital.

Chivington sent soldiers in every direction to question residents about the fleeing Rebels. Several persons living near the mountains said the Texans had taken an old trail that passed twenty miles west of Fort Craig and would return to the banks of the river about thirty miles south of the fort.

As usual, Colonel Chivington was eager to plan for battle. He asked General Canby for permission to take the First Colorado straight to the point downstream at which the trail will reappear. He could reach the spot well ahead of the retreating enemy ". . . and put him out of his misery, once and for all." To no one's great surprise, General Canby again refused permission and ordered all of the Union troops to go to Fort Craig. Again, many people would argue that Canby had let his brother-in-law off the hook.

Yet there were compelling reasons for Canby to abandon the idea of pursuit and take his troops to the fort. The men had been in the field for nearly two months. The Coloradans had survived a forced march of more than a thousand miles, some of it through a terrible blizzard, in order to reach New Mexico in the first place. Then they had marched nearly a hundred miles further, fought two bloody battles, existed on inadequate food, and finally marched another 150 miles in pursuit of the Rebels. During the last portion of the march, they had fought another duel with the Confederates, coming out on the short end, and had fought the skirmish to capture the enemy wagon train. The men were exhausted, and the animals in even worse condition. The army was terribly short of supplies and had no access to needed quantities of food for themselves or forage for the horses and mules.

Colonels Chivington, Tappan, Paul and Chavez reluctantly agreed with Canby that it was time to abandon the chase. They also agreed that it was highly unlikely the battered remnants of the Western Expeditionary Force would even try to regroup and remain in the area. Accordingly, the following morning, the weary Coloradans and their New Mexico companions finally reached Fort Craig.

Hollister said that the men ". . . rested all day because the horses were hungry, sick and weary. Sandy land makes grass and forage scarce." During the day, local civilians brought thirty captured Texans to camp, and "they looked even worse than us!" The Texans were fed and administered an oath of allegiance to the United States, and then were released. The Coloradans wondered aloud whether they would see those same soldiers in the "next battle," but in this case it seemed highly unlikely. In fact, none of the Texans was eager to try to rejoin Sibley. Many hung around Valverde or Socorro, and a few were known to have struck out for California to try their luck at gold mining.

On the morning of April 20 a long Union supply train pulled into Fort Craig. Hollister said "this was exceptionally good news because we were tired of rotten bacon and bread without soda, coffee or sugar."

That same morning Captain Graydon led a sizeable Union scouting party down the trail taken by Sibley. The patrol found a place where the Texans had buried all of their remaining cannons. (Some Southern writers say Sibley still had four small cannons with him when he reached Texas days later.)

They also discovered the burned-out hulks of all but perhaps twelve wagons in which the Confederates had left their last camp. Along the trail were also the ashes of a number of small fires where the Rebels had burned personal possessions, including papers identifying them as Confederate soldiers. There were also a considerable number of dead horses, animals that apparently simply collapsed and died from overwork and starvation.

At the same time, a second Union scouting party rode into the town of Socorro and found a hospital where the Texans wounded in the battle of North Ford were still being treated. The Confederates at the hospital were well aware of what had been going on, and none seemed eager to leave the hospital or the town.

That afternoon another seventy-five Texans were captured as they sat apparently aimlessly in a grassy valley ten miles west of Fort Craig. The Texans were disarmed by two farmers, taken back to the fort and fed. Then they were administered the oath and sent on their way.

Almost as soon as they left their final campsite across the river from the Union army, the Texans were hit by a vicious sand storm "such as does not often visit New Mexico." The soldiers quickly began discarding everything: guns, any remaining ammunition, back packs, tents, blankets, and spare clothing. Within hours they would regret being without food or extra clothing, especially when the temperature at night plunged to the low 30s.

But their agony was just beginning. It would be ten terrible days before any of them reached the Texas border. During those ten days, the wind storm never abated. Usually it was accompanied by cold rain, and on occasion the rain turned to sleet or snow. Horses collapsed and died, as did a substantial number of the retreating Rebels. A number of the Texans starved to death on the grueling march, others died of thirst, and still others of exposure. The retreat soon degenerated from an orderly military procession to a sort of military free-for-all in which every man had to watch out for himself.

The few remaining Confederate horses were noticeably ill, most of whom collapsed and died within the first forty-eight hours on the trail. Every horse that was still healthy carried a sick or wounded Confederate soldier. When there were no longer enough horses to carry the ill Confederates, the other soldiers carried them "rather than abandon them to the animals or the Indians." Most of those who were ill were sick with smallpox, and as a result of such close contact with their brothers, they passed the disease on to dozens of other men during the retreat.

By the fourth day, survivors were turning over rocks trying to find snakes, scorpions, large bugs, or other animal life that they could eat. One soldier later reported watching twenty-three men die before noon on the fifth day of the march. On the tenth day, having covered no more than ten miles, the soldiers once again reached the Rio Grande. They were amazed that the Union army was not there waiting for them.

On the twelfth day, the one thousand remaining Confederates (out of at least seventeen hundred who began the march), passed through the town of Alamosa. They camped that night in a small valley near the town. During the night, someone cut a gaping hole in the side of a nearby canal, and a small wall of water rolled through the camp of the sleeping Confederates.

By the fourteenth day, most of the sick were simply left lying where they dropped; no one had the strength to pick them up and carry them onward.

The Texans were desperate for water, and water holes were increasingly scarce. One day, the sick and weakened men pushed forward thirty-six miles trying to reach a water hole called the Van Horn well in west Texas. When they finally got to the well, they found that hostile Indians had stuffed it with the carcases of dead animals, then covered it with dirt. The next well was thirty-eight miles further.

The soldiers had a small amount of water remaining in their canteens, but after ten more miles on the trail this, too, was gone. With twenty-eight miles still to go, Theophilus Noel wrote in his diary:

Hot! Hot! And no shade, vine or cloud to hide the sun or break its parching rays from us. Here it was that we were again made to suffer, such sufferings, too, that many of us—myself for one—never before had to experience, and God grant that we may never again. Many there were who gave completely out and threw themselves down by the side of the road to die. Many kept on forward with their tongues so swollen that they could not articulate a word; more crazed than rational, they looked like frantic mad men. I remember seeing one man shoot a beef steer that had been left by the herdsmen in their frantic flight for the water. . . . Cutting his throat with his pocket knife, [he] drank of the animal's blood to quench his thirst. This, I was afterwards told, increased rather than dimished his thirst for water. The sun was nearly down and fairly in view was the hill at the foot of which the springs were situated—called the Del Muerto (Dead Man's Hole), yet it was [still] 14 miles off. "Great God have mercy upon us!" I heard exclaimed by one of my companions as he lay down to die or be killed by Indians, as he told me more in sighs than in words. I myself laid down resolved upon meeting the same fate, but life, oh! how pleasant! prompted me to try, try again.

Noel says the men forced themselves to march another six miles and finally saw a Confederate water wagon rumbling up the road toward them. In ecstacy, the men ran toward the wagon. Private Burrewell C. Allen, who had suffered terribly from thirst, raced to the side of the wagon, collapsed and died. He was buried on the spot.

Historian Josephy said that the seven-hundred-mile trek across southeastern New Mexico and west Texas, soldiers struggling from waterhole to waterhole, was the "ultimate ordeal." Josephy quotes the diary of Sergeant Alfred B. Peticolas, one of the Confederate soldiers who endured the forced march:

> In the burning heat of mid-summer, men abandoned their last possessions, even their weapons, in order to keep moving. No order was observed, no company stayed together; the wearied sank down upon the grass, regardless of the cold, to rest and sleep; the strong, with words of execration upon their lips, pressed feverishly and frantically on for water. [Josephy, *The Civil War in the American West*, p. 91.]

At one point in the retreat, the ragged column of Texans, dressed in tatters, their faces gaunt, straggled past a west Texas farmhouse. A woman stood on the porch watching the soldiers and later wrote, "The men were wretched, suffering terribly from the effects of heat; very many of them were afoot and scarcely able to travel from blistered feet. They were subsisting on bread and water, both officers and men; many of them were sick, many ragged, and all hungry."

Alvin Josephy says that during the final retreat, Sibley abandoned all of his sick and wounded, burned or simply walked away from all of his wagons and baggage, and dumped supplies unless they were absolutely essential. During that flight, Josephy says that "discipline dissolved, and according to one survivor, it was every man for himself. Famished and exhausted men collapsed and were simply left to die where they fell. Others too sick to be carried along were thrown out of the few remaining wagons and abandoned.

Later in his book, *The Civil War in the American West*, Josephy says that during this final, desperate retreat General Sibley rode in an ambulance, accompanied by the wives of several pro-Confederate New Mexico residents. He says Sibley virtually ignored his desperate and suffering troops during the retreat.

In commenting on Sibley's failed campaign, Josephy adds:

[Sibley] . . . should have known how difficult it would be for a large army to live off the land in the arid, sparsely-populated country between Fort Bliss and Albuquerque, where people could scarcely raise enough to support themselves; that while most of the Hispanic population of New Mexico was apathetic about the war, they hated and feared Texans and were not likely to flock to his army; and that officials and many of the prominent citizens in the northern part of the Territory were strongly pro-Union. . . . Although an experienced administrator, [Sibley] was a weak strategic planner and a poor leader of men, who was even accused of cowardice in time of crisis. Moreover, he was often in poor health and had become so addicted to drink that one of his men described him as a "walking whiskey keg."

In a letter written sometime later to Governor Connelly, Lieutenant George Nelson said:

Sibley's retreat was a most desperate one. . . . His command was entirely worn out and nearly finished. The distance from where he left the Rio Grande until he reached it again was over a hundred miles, and the Confederates were ten days accomplishing this distance, five of those days without rations of any kind. The route of travel was through the worst country in the territory, with no guides, trail or road. The undergrowth and brush were so dense that for several miles they were forced to cut their way through with axes and Bowie knives. Nearly all of the ammunition was abandoned on the way, as was nearly everything else except what the men carried on their persons. On passing over the route of these unfortunate men nearly a year later, I not infrequently found a piece of a gun carriage or part of a harness, or some piece of camp or garrison equipage, with occasionally the white, dry skeleton of a man. At some points it seemed impossible for men to have made their way. During this retreat the Confederates were unmolested by Union troops with the exception of the ubiquitous Captain Graydon, who with his independent spy company followed them alone for a long distance, picking up a large amount of serviceable articles which they had abandoned on the way.

General Canby sent a formal report to the War Department on the defeat of the Western Expeditionary Force and the rout of the invaders. In commenting on the last days of General Sibley's command Canby said:

Scouts and prisoners report this enemy force as greatly demoralized and that they have abandoned everything that could impede their flight. Sick and wounded have been left by the wayside, without care and often without food. Many of them have been collected and are properly cared for, and arrangements have been made to bring in the others and secure any valuable property that has been abandoned by the enemy [Whitford, *The Battle of Glorieta Pass*, p. 24].

From the warmth and security of Fort Craig, Sergeant Hollister thought about his unfortunate and desperate enemy struggling just to stay alive and softened his attitude toward them.

Poor fellows! Many, very many, "softly lie and sweetly sleep low in the ground." Let their faults be buried with them. They are our brothers, erring, it may be, still nature will exact a passing tear for the brave dead. And doubt not there are those who will both love and honor their memory if we cannot. Any cause that men sustain to death becomes sacred, at least, to them. Surely we can afford to pay tribute to the courage and nobleness that prefers death to even fancied enthrallment.

But even with the Texans gone, the effects of battle lingered. On June 5, Captain Wingate of the Second Colorado died of wounds suffered at Valverde, the final officer victim of that battle to succumb. And on August 4, a Private Shakspear died of wounds inflicted in the same fighting, the final recorded Union casualty of the New Mexico Campaign.

When the Texans left El Paso in late January to begin their ill-fated invasion of the West, they brought with them between three hundred and four hundred supply wagons, eighty cannons and an undetermined number of caissons and closed carriages. Sibley's Western Expeditionary Force had an estimated five thousand horses and mules and close to four thousand soldiers. In May, less than five months later, General Sibley stumbled back into Texas with seven wagons and thirty-six horses, and a total of only about six hundred to fifteen hundred men. Everything else was lost.

Although the estimates of men and equipment who were able to return to Texas vary widely, one of Sibley's own men confirms the general estimate given above. An unidentified Confederate sergeant, who was held prisoner by the Coloradans at Fort Craig for a brief time, told his captors that "We left Texas with 3800 men and 327 wagons of supplies, plus our artillery. When we began our forced retreat into the mountains west of [Fort Craig], we had only 1200 men and 27 wagons. The rest of the men were killed, captured, or deserted. . . . If it had not been for the devils from Pike's Peak, this country would have been ours!"

The losses suffered by the Western Expeditionary Force were staggering, even by Civil War standards. Although accurate records are impossible to find, it appears that the Texans suffered a total of over 1200 dead, 1100 wounded, 192 captured and 1100 desertions (mostly men who headed for California during the final days of the fighting). The dead and wounded amounted to nearly 60 percent of Sibley's Brigade. Total losses including the deserters and those captured amounted to over 85 percent. In striking contrast, the Union suffered about 800 total casualties, of which 300 were Coloradans. The First Colorado had 125 killed, 171 wounded and 7 desertions, or about 25 percent casualties.

Why such a lopsided toll? The Confederate desertions, of course, may be explained by the fact that the invading Rebel army was defeated; the famous Texas pride was badly wounded. It is not surprising that such a huge number would rather desert than go back home and have to explain the whipping they suffered.

As to the Confederate battlefield casualties, explanations are somewhat more difficult. At least a portion of the explanation may lie in the "role reversal" of the two opposing armies as opposed to their ordinary role in the Civil War. Throughout the conflict, the Confederates had a tremendous advantage in being the army that was fighting to defend its own home from invaders; men protecting their own homes always fight like tigers. The Confederates recognized this as a great advantage and frequently used that situation not only as a rallying point for their troops, but to elicit help from foreign nations.

Jefferson Davis and Abraham Lincoln were among those who felt that the war's overall casualty toll, favoring the Confederates by a margin of more than two to one, reflected the fact that men protecting their homes will fight fiercely. It is much more difficult to get the same level of commitment from men fighting for an esoteric cause ("save the Union"). But in the New Mexico campaign, it was the Confederates who were the invaders fighting for the esoteric cause (get new sea ports for the Confederacy); it was the Coloradans and New Mexico militiamen fighting to protect their homes and loved ones from an invading army.

Another explanation, although it goes against the image Texans have always liked to portray, is that the Texans may have gone a little "soft" by this time. Much of the state was highly civilized by 1860, and many of the men fighting for Sibley presumably were recruited in the city of San Antonio. Some may have chosen to join Sibley's Western Expeditionary Force because it was expected to see little action, and therefore, to suffer few casualties. The suggestion is that they might have been men reluctant or unable to exert themselves in battle. Many other Texas units fought bravely throughout the war, particularly those assigned to Hood. It is possible that by joining Sibley's army some men were deliberately avoiding what they thought would be the tough fighting in favor of the simple walk through the West.

The Coloradans, on the other hand, were recruited from the rough and tumble gold mining camps of the Rockies. These were men used to hardships, struggle, and living by their guns. They hunted in order to eat; they fought to protect their claims. And because they were the type of men who would leave their homes and go into the mountains, alone, to seek their fortune, the Pike's Peakers were not the sort to be easily cowed. Quite simply, they were accustomed to fighting to stay alive, and the fact they had lived this long indicated they were pretty good at it.

Historian Alvin Josephy said of the men of the First and Second Colorado:

> . . . its members, on the whole, were of a different cut. Coming largely from pioneer families and a demanding frontier environment, they were used to the rigors and hardships of the rugged western country. Although they were less disciplined and tended to be more independent minded and unruly than the Regulars, many of them possessed a notable spirit and fighting ability. Hardy, often daring and aggressive, they were usually more than eager to kill secessionists . . . on any excuse.

Simultaneous to the final retreat of Sibley's army, Colonel John Baylor pulled his "Baylor's Babes" out of southeastern New Mexico and hastened back to El Paso. His so-called "Territory of Arizona" collapsed without ceremony two weeks later. The soldiers who had seized the Gila River Trail and those who had set up camp in Tucson hurried south and crossed the border into Mexico, where they could avoid harassment by Union troops. From there, most of the men, over a period of six months or so, made their way back to Texas, some to fight in other battles for the Confederacy. Many others, however, showed up later in California, choosing to become citizens of the only part of the nation not touched by the combat. A few simply vanished.

A Denver newspaper reported that ex-governor William Gilpin's "pet lambs" had soundly whipped "Baylor's Babes" and "sent them crying all the way home!" There was rejoicing in New Mexico and Colorado, but the victory was largely ignored throughout the rest of the country and the world. Although later writers would begin calling the battle of Glorieta Pass "the Gettysburg of the West," most of the world would never learn of the fighting or its significance.

A part of the silence about the western campaign was deliberate, a choice made by Southern leaders who then sought to discredit General Sibley and keep the whole matter as quiet as possible. In this they were greatly aided by the lack of communication from Denver to the East, and Washington's tendency to ignore the frontier anyway, and by the absence of news reporters. Colorado had no historians, save only Sergeant Hollister, and whatever was written about the victory was soon forgotten. A few accounts managed to be filed with the historical societies of New Mexico and Colorado, but little was written of the fighting outside the two areas most directly involved.

For Jefferson Davis and the Confederacy, there were immediate serious implications of the collapse of the Western Expeditionary Force and its campaign in New Mexico. As historian William C. Whitford put it:

> Whatever indications existed among the Mormons in Utah and elsewhere, and among the Indian tribes of the Southwest, of favoring the Confederacy, were rudely checked and held in full restraint. The malignant element in Colorado was completely quieted; and only once thereafter during the great and long conflict for the Union was any portion of that territory alarmed or disturbed by hostile inroads from the Confederacy and that was in 1864 when a troop of Texan guerrillas, coming from the southeast, penetrated beyond Canyon City [Colorado] on their way to plunder in the South Park country. But they were soon hunted down and all were either killed or captured.

At the time Sibley's invasion collapsed, a Union army of five full regiments and two batteries had gathered at Fort Riley, Kansas, and were about to be sent to New Mexico to assist the First Colorado Volunteers. When the Confederates were put to rout, this army was sent instead to Tennessee to assist other Union forces there. Another army of about a thousand Union soldiers had been organized in California. They marched to Tucson only days after the last of the Confederate soldiers fled that town.

The First Colorado Volunteers remained at Fort Craig for six months to make certain the Confederates did not try a second time to capture the West. The Coloradans finally returned to Denver about Christmas, 1862.

Colonel John Chivington several times wrote to the War Department, asking that the First Colorado be kept intact and transferred to the Army of the Potomac, but Washington decided the trained soldiers were more badly needed at home to stop a growing Indian uprising that stretched from Minnesota to the Rockies. Chivington and his men were ordered to return to Denver.

The "independent companies" and the elements of the Second Colorado became a part of a continuing Union presence at Fort Craig. They remained in New Mexico more than a year to make certain the Confederates would not attempt a second invasion. They were finally returned to Denver in July, 1863. By that time, General Canby had recruited more than twelve thousand men, a substantial portion of them from New Mexico, to defend the Territory against any further Southern aggression.

The two leaders of the Second Colorado were both promoted and decorated. Captain Dodd was promoted to lieutenant-colonel, and Captain Ford to major. Eventually, Dodd was made a full colonel, at which rank he retired. Ford remained in the service longer, led several expeditions against warring Indians, and retired as a brigadier general.

Even when he finally reached the safety of San Antonio, as incredible as it seems, General Sibley seemingly failed to understand the tragedy that had befallen his army. Or perhaps his Texas pride simply refused to permit him to admit defeat! When the handful of survivors staggered into San Antonio, Sibley sent them a message which said:

Soldiers of the Army of New Mexico: It is with unfeigned pride and pleasure that I find myself occupying a position which devolves upon me the duty of congratulating the Army of New Mexico upon the successes which have crowned their arms in the many encounters with the enemy during the short but brilliant campaign which has just ended.

Called from your homes almost at a moment's warning, cheerfully leaving friends, families and private affairs, in many cases solely dependent upon your presence and personal attention, scarcely prepared for a month's campaign in the immediate defense of your own firesides, you have made a march, many of you over a thousand miles, before ever reaching the field of active operations.

The boasted valor of Texans has been fully vindicated. Val Verde, Glorieta, Albuquerque, Peralta, and last, though not least, your successful and almost unprecedented evacuation, through mountain passes and over a trackless waste of a hundred miles through a famishing country will be duly chronicled, and form one of the brightest pages in the history of the Second American Revoltuion.

That I should be proud of you—that every participant in the campaign should be proud of himself—who can doubt?

During the short period of inaction which you are now enjoying, your General indulges the hope that you will constantly bear in mind that at any moment you may be recalled into activity.

God and an indulgent Providence have guided us in our councils and watched our ways: let us be thankful to Him for our successes, and to Him let us not forget to offer a prayer for our noble dead.

H.H. Sibley, Brigadier General Commanding
[Whitford, *The Battle of Glorieta Pass*, p. 27]

The general may have ignored reality, but many others did not. When Sibley finally led the ragged remains of his shattered army back to Texas, there was some talk of a court martial. It was charged that he had badly bungled the expedition, wasted manpower and supplies and had spent "considerable of his time" away from the battle front or drinking, rather than tending to important military matters.

Sibley himself began to pass the buck. He started by indicating that the West was never worth capturing in the first place, as if it had not been he who had argued for the invasion. Writing in his official report to San Antonio, Sibley said that "having seen the land, the territories weren't worth the effort of holding them anyway."

Sibley also rationalized that much of his difficulty in New Mexico was due to poor planning on the part of his superiors in San Antonio. The general said he had been expected to stretch his supply lines beyond reason and therefore could not have been expected to be victorious in the Western campaign. His report suggested that it had never been a good idea to try to capture the West because of the long supply lines that would be necessary to sustain his army. He also charged that he had been given "second rate officers" who were incapable of carrying out his orders, accounting for the battle losses, ignoring the fact that he had insisted on appointing his own officers.

Sibley's popularity with the Confederates took a nose dive following his retreat from New Mexico. The suggestions of a court-martial lingered for some time before fading way; charges were never filed. Even so, Sibley was removed from command of his brigade and reassigned as the commander of a supply train accompanying Confederate troops fighting in Lousiana. When the Rebels were driven from Bisland, Sibley's wagon train failed to carry supplies to the troops, or to help them with the retreat, as ordered. For those failures, General Sibley was court-martialed on charges of disobedience of orders and "un-officerlike" conduct. Although eventually acquitted of the charges, Sibley was not returned to any command position. A short time after the court-martial, Sibley retired from the Confederate army.

Many Civil War writers believe that the Confederate government made a deliberate effort to cover up their intentions in the West. Virtually all official Confederate records pertaining to the campaign vanished from the archives. The only remaining entries indicate that Sibley's single assignment had been to secure the west Texas border from a Union flanking movement. To accomplish that purpose the records say Sibley was to drive Federal troops out of New Mexico and then assume a defensive position. Although virtually everyone associated with the campaign believed far more was at stake, the official Confederate line was that there never had been a plan to capture the West, a contention supported by few modern historians.

The indications are that the Confederates hoped to pass off Sibley's incursion into New Mexico as an isolated and insignificant part of the war. Presumably, the South hoped, thereby, to discourage any Union troop build-up that would prevent some future Confederate drive to capture the West.

His obituary in a home-town Louisiana newspaper said that in 1865 Henry Sibley went to Egypt and served in the military of the Khedive until 1870, apparently holding a responsible position in that army. He then returned to the United States and eventually died penniless on August 23, 1886.

Colonel William Scurry returned to San Antonio and served the Confederate military until near the end of the war. He was killed in the battle of Jenkin's Ferry, Arkansas, on April 1, 1864.

Colonel Thomas Green also died in battle. Promoted to general, he was killed at Blair's Landing on April 12, 1864.

Sibley's Brigade, the Western Expeditionary Force, survived. After a sixty-day furlough granted when they returned to San Antonio, the men were called back to active duty, along with hundreds of new recruits now under the command of General Green. They were sent east, fought gallantly in Lousiana and Arkansas, and were among the last troops to surrender when the war ended.

As already reported, Union Colonel John Slough returned to Denver and then was sent to Washington where, in the spring of 1863, he was commissioned as a brigadier general by President Lincoln. General Slough commanded the Military District of Alexandria, Virginia, until 1866. Then he was appointed chief justice of the New Mexico Territory. In November of 1867, a New Mexico state lawmaker, W. L. Ryerson, introduced a bill of censure against Slough, charging (among other things) that he had mishandled the New Mexico campaign. Slough and Ryerson met on a Santa Fe street a short time later and got into a heated argument. During the argument, Ryerson produced a pistol and shot Slough to death. Ryerson was arrested, but argued that he had fired in self-defense after Slough tried to kill him. There were no witnesses to the fight, and Ryerson was eventually acquitted of the charges.

General Edward Canby held various commands in the U.S. Army, mostly as an Indian fighter. In 1873, Canby and the Reverend Eleaser Thomas went to an Indian village at Tule Lake, California, in an effort to negotiate the end to hostilities between the Modoc Indians and local white settlers. Neither Canby nor Thomas was armed, and both were shot to death by the Indians. The trigger-man, a Modoc brave named "Captain Jack," was hanged, and three other Indians sentenced to life in prison.

John Chivington served nearly a year more in New Mexico as a part of the Union troops assigned to protect against any new

Confederate invasion and against Indian raids. He returned to Colorado in 1863 and petitioned President Lincoln and War Secretary Stanton to accept the First Colorado into the regular army for assignment fighting Confederates. Stanton rejected the request, saying the First Colorado was more badly needed in Denver to protect against increasing Indian raids. Chivington retained immense popularity and was being groomed by the Colorado Republican Party to run for congress whenever the territory was granted statehood.

In 1864, Chivington was placed in charge of a new group of Colorado volunteers, the Third Colorado, assembled to battle Indians who now controlled all of the Great Plains from Kansas City to Denver. The Indian war was preventing Colorado from getting the statehood that John Chivington coveted so much. Chivington was a leading "anti-Indian" spokesman for the region. A number of soldiers from the First Colorado joined the new unit, although it consisted primarily of men who had never seen military duty before that time.

In November 1864, the Third Colorado attacked an Indian camp where they believed the leader of the renegade Indians, "Roman Nose," had his headquarters. In reality, the camp was a village of mostly peaceful Indians who had already surrendered to the U.S. Army at Fort Lyon and were on their way to a reservation in Oklahoma.

About 130 Indians, mostly women and children, were killed in the attack, which became known as the "Sand Creek Massacre." Many local residents applauded any attack against Indians, including this one, and Chivington was still regarded as a hero in Colorado by some. However, the U.S. Congress made it clear that the attack was a travesty and indicated that Colorado would never be granted statehood so long as it appeared possible that John Chivington might become its congressman.

Other Colorado leaders, including Governor John Evans, convinced Chivington to leave the area. He went to Ohio for a short time and later to California where he returned to the pulpit, although he came back to Colorado many years later. Chivington never again was in a position of influence over the people of Colorado, however, and died in obscurity of old age.

Ovando Hollister returned to Colorado and resumed work as a mapmaker and journalist in Boulder. He eventually was appointed to several different government positions, eventually serving in Utah with the Internal Revenue Service. He retired near the turn of the century and eventually died a peaceful death.

Alonzo Ickis was assigned to work with Colonel Kit Carson in Kansas. Ickis served as Carson's official secretary, and also became a recognized leader of the scouts.

In his diary, Ickis reported several other scrapes with the enemy during the remainder of the war. On one occasion, Carson's scouts captured two men suspected of being Confederate spies. The men, who claimed to be father and son, protested their innocence. While they were being taken to a Union fort for questioning, the boy escaped by stealing a Union horse. Ickis and two other men gave chase.

When the boy reached the Red River, he stayed on his horse as the animal swam across the river. That slowed him down so much, however, that Ickis and the other pursuers caught up. As the boy emerged on the far side, the Union soldiers opened fire. Their bullets struck and killed the horse and the boy surrendered. While he was being questioned, Ickis was astonished to discover that the "boy" was really a young woman. She had maps and detailed information about Union troop movements sewn into the lining of a coat she carried with her.

On another occasion, Ickis and another Union scout were captured by Confederate troops while scouting in Texas. Ickis convinced his captors that he was just a farmer and they let him go, but continued to hold his companion. That night, Ickis crept back into the fort and broke his friend out of jail. Rebel troops gave chase and eventually shot the horse from beneath Ickis. However, he was able to reach a ranch and steal another horse, and make good his escape back to Union territory.

Ickis recorded in his diary that he was shot by a pistol, suffering a flesh wound in the thigh, on October 22, 1862. However, he gave no details of the incident, and it is presumed he was shot in a barroom brawl or some similar incident, and was never wounded in any conflict with Confederates.

Ickis was finally mustered out of the service on December 28, 1864. He returned to his hometown of Creston, Iowa, married and fathered six sons. However, he began to suffer from asthma and was advised to "go out West." The Ickis clan moved to Wray, Colorado, where they lived for the next eleven years. Finally,

Ickis moved to Denver where he died peacefully in his sleep on June 5, 1917.

So when all is said and done, how important was the New Mexico campaign? Was it, as Gene Amole wrote, merely a "savage little fire-fight in the backwaters of the frontier"? Or was it, as historian LeRoy Boyd wrote, "the turning point of the war"?

History records that because of the effectiveness of the Union blockade of Atlantic and Gulf Coast harbors, the South slowly died of malnutrition, a starvation for arms, ammunition, clothing and food that could not be obtained because trade with Europe was not possible.

Would the capture of those deep-sea ports in California and Oregon have been sufficient to change the outcome of the war? And would the infusion of gold from the capture of those rich lodes in Colorado and California have been adequate to permit the South to buy a victory?

Knowledgeable historians struggle over the answer to the questions, but it seems clear the Confederates, themselves, believed that capturing the West would have solved their most critical problems. After the Western Expeditionary Force was crushed in New Mexico and Henry Sibley humiliated by the Confederacy he served, the South was overwhelmed by the tide of Northern victories across the major battlefields of the East. Never again was Jefferson Davis in a position to try to capture the West, no matter how much he might have felt a Southern victory hinged on success in that theater.

Two prominent Southern historians—Martin Hall of McNeese State College and Edwin A. Davis of Lousiana State University— believe a Southern victory in the West might have altered the course of the war. Writing in the Foreword to *A Campaign From Santa Fe to the Mississippi*, they say:

> The advantages of securing California were enormous. The immense gold supply would be diverted from Washington to Richmond. The prestige of conquering the West would influence the chief western European nations in the recognition of the Confederacy. The excellent Pacific ports would be opened to trade, and being so far distant, it would be extremely difficult for the Union navy to blockade them. There is little doubt but that a successful Western campaign would have altered the entire course of the war, and it is not inconceivable that it might even have determined the war's final outcome.

In *War on the Frontier*, Alvin Josephy wrote that:

The collapse of Sibley's campaign ended the Confederacy's grand dream of expansion to the Pacific. . . . Preoccupied as it was with fighting the main Confederate armies east of the Mississippi, the Federal government often made a terrible botch of the war on the frontier. [Yet,] despite misdirection and tragic bungling, the struggle on the frontier formed an important and dramatic part of the Civil War. In contrast to the fighting in Virginia—most of which took place in a cramped corridor only 100 miles long 'between Washington and Richmond, the conflict in the West spread from Minnesota to Oregon, from southern California to the Lousiana bayous. Armies trudged hundreds of miles to engage the enemy; if defeated, they fell back in harrowing retreats half the breadth of Texas. Ill-trained troops found themselves crossing trackless deserts and unexplored reaches of the Rocky Mountains. They fought furious engagements in an untamed land still inhabited by people the troops thought of as savages. It was warfare in its rawest state and often so implacable that it would have appalled even veterans of Gettysburg and Spotsylvania.

In his subsequent book, *The Civil War in the American West*, Josephy says:

One may speculate on what might have happened if the Texan train had not been destroyed at Glorieta and Sibley's troops had been able to take Fort Union's suplies and go on to Colorado and California. Through the years, there have been those who believed that the war would have lasted longer or even have ended differently. The European powers might have given speedy recognition to a Confederacy in control of the Pacific Coast, and western bullion, going to Ricmond rather than Washington, could have reversed the ability of each side to finance and sustain the conflict.

Historian Erna Ferguson said that "although little noted among the greater battles being fought far to the east, this skirmish was a decisive one [for the war]. If the Confederacy had held New Mexico, its way would have been open to California and sorely needed gold. Instead, Sibley left Santa Fe on April 8 and retreated down the valley, where he was given a final trouncing at Peralta near Albuquerque."

Warren A. Beck says that "had the Confederates won, the story might have been entirely different and far more significance might have been attached to the New Mexico campaign." Beck says General Sibley failed for four primary reasons. First, the Rebels failed because Sibley's army was too small for the task assigned to it. Second, the Texans lacked proper supplies and the poverty of New Mexico made it impossible for the invaders to live off the land. Third, the Confederate force suffered from a lack of discipline, due to Sibley's "alcoholism and his failings as a commander." Finally, he failed because the Northern commander, Canby, realized that "his basic task was to hound the Confederate army out of New Mexico and to never endanger his own army."

He might as well have added two more reasons: fifth, sickness and disease, which severely crippled the Texans throughout the campaign. Smallpox struck more than half of the troops at one time or another during the brigade's time in New Mexico. And sixth, he failed to rekon with the determination and physical strength of John Chivington and William Gilpin's "pet lambs."

One of General Sibley's own senior officers and Confederate historians, Major Trevanion T. Teel, wrote that if the Texans had been successful in New Mexico, they would ultimately have seized the entire west, they would have won the war. More than that, however, Teel says the Confederacy would also have expanded at once by annexing three northern states of Mexico. Teel wrote that once the Western territories and California had been won,

> ... negotiations to secure Chihuahua, Sonora and Lower California—either by purchase or by conquest—would be opened; the state of affairs in Mexico made it an easy thing to take those States, and the Mexican President would be glad to get rid of them and at the same time improve his exchequer. In addition to all this, General Sibley intimated that there was a secret understanding between the Mexican and the Confederate authorities, and that as soon as our occupation of the said States was assured, a transfer of those States would be made to the Confederacy. Juarez, the President of the Republic, was then in the City of Mexico with a small army under his command, hardly sufficient to keep him in his position. That date—1862—was the darkest hour in the annals of our sister republic, but it was the brightest of the Confederacy, and General Sibley thought that he would have little difficulty in consummating the ends so devoutly wished by the Confederate Government. [Whitford: *Battle of Glorieta Pass.*]

Dr. William C. Whitford, writing in *The Battle of Glorieta Pass,* says:

It is usually unprofitable to speculate about what "might have happened": yet there can be no reasonable doubt that if the Confederate army . . . had not been stopped and defeated at La Glorieta . . . our histories of the War for the Union would read differently. In their dreams of the future some Southern leaders saw their Confederacy extended to the Pacific Coast and embracing more than one-half of the territory of the United States. . . .

With the Pacific Coast in their possession by conquest . . . the world would have been open to the Confederates, since it would have been impossible for the Federal navy effectively to blockade that coast. Furthermore, the oceans could have been made to swarm with Confederate cruisers and privateers preying upon the commerce of the Union. [Had the Confederates succeeded] they probably would have secured recognition of the Southern Confederacy from the English and French governments at once, and perhaps from others in Europe. What, then, might the consequences have been?

But victory was not his. The "pet lambs" had whipped Baylor's Babes, and the war for the West was over.

On January 28, 1863, in sending home the last of the Colorado soldiers from New Mexico, U.S. General James H. Carleton wrote to Colorado Governor John Evans,

I have just returned from northwestern Texas and from what I could learn I do not believe any considerable force from that state will attempt to invade this country again—at least for the present. That the so-called "Southern Confederacy," looking to a permanent separation from the Union, *desires* to have a strip of territory extending across the continent to cover the silver and gold fields of Arizona and to have a port on the Pacific there cannot be a doubt; and that there will be a strong effort made to this end sooner or later unless we are more successful in the East than we have recently been, is more than probable. But the chances for such an attempt appear to be so remote at the present moment as to warrant my sending the remainder of the Colorado troops home. I have therefore issued an order to this end which please to find herewith inclosed [sic].

In 1865, the New Mexico legislature authorized erection of a monument in Santa Fe in order to honor the Union forces who fought at Glorieta Pass and "saved the Territory and the Union." In part, one of the plaques thereon reads: "To the Heroes of the Federal Army who fell at the Battle of Valverde, fought with the Rebels, February 21, 1862; To the Heroes of the Federal Army who fell at the Battles in Cañon del Apache and Pigeon's Ran-

cho (La Glorieta), fought with the Rebels, March 28, 1862, and
to those who fell at the Battle fought with the Rebels at Peralto,
April 15, 1862."

Yet, few people today know of the battle for the West, or the
implications of the victory won in New Mexico by the First Colorado Volunteers, the New Mexico militia, and a handful of
Union regulars. Dr. William Whitford is among the historians
baffled by this lack of historical attention to the New Mexico
campaign. He speculates that the battles, and the importance of
the fighting, got lost in history because ". . . the means of communication from the Southwest to news centers in the East were
slow and imperfect, the nearest telegraph line [to the East]—
one of a single wire—being at Denver City. Public attention was
intensely fixed upon gigantic preparations of the forces under
General McClellan for the Peninsular campaign in Virginia.
Three weeks before, the Monitor had disabled the Merrimac in
Hampton Roads; Fort Donelson had already been taken, and
the fierce struggle at Shiloh happened a week and a half later."
He also notes that the numbers of soldiers involved in the New
Mexico fighting was insignificant compared to the tens of thou-
sands of troops engaged on other battlefields.

Yet Dr. Whitford notes:

> . . . the immediate and permanent results of the victory gained here
> were among the most conspicuous and valuable to the Union that
> were won during the war. Here was utterly defeated, in a very brief
> time, the bold and comprehensive scheme of the Southern Confed-
> eracy to acquire, by invasion and force of arms, the possession and
> control of all this southwestern mountainous country, including its
> forts, passes and towns, [and thereby] to secure a pathway to the
> Pacific Coast, the harbors of which could not then be easily block-
> aded by the Federal navy.

The U.S. Army history of the era said that the West was a key
element in Confederate strategy to win the war. (It should be
noted that the book concentrates only on regular army troops,
and did not consider either the First Colorado Volunteers or the
New Mexico militia as part of the "official" military action in
New Mexico.) The book quotes an unnamed Confederate military commander as saying, "The vast mineral resources of Arizona, in addition to affording an outlet to the Pacific, makes its
acquisition a matter of some importance to our government."

But, says the book, after General Sibley's troops reached Santa Fe en route to capturing the unprotected West, ". . . Sibley was dangerously overextended, and Federal troops—reinforced by Colorado volunteers—surprised the advancing Confederates in Apache Canyon on March 26 and 28. . . . Unable to capture Union posts, unable to resupply his forces, . . . Sibley began a determined retreat down the Rio Grande valley and the Confederate invasion of New Mexico was ended."

Hall and Davis concur:

> Though victorious on the major battlefields in New Mexico, Sibley's attempt to wrest the southwest from the Union was destined to end in failure. Confident of easy victories and the consequent seizure of vast amounts of supplies and matériel of war, he had not counted upon an energetic Union commander seriously opposing his advance. . . . In a short time, the Confederates found themselves deep in the heart of an inhospitable land without adequate provisions [because] the expected cooperation of the Mexican population in most instances did not materialize. William Gilpin, the governor of Colorado, not only overawed the Southern elements of that state but also sent a regiment of volunteers to New Mexico where a detachment of this unit managed to destroy the brigade's main wagon train, thus making the Confederate situation untenable. Lack of supplies compelled Sibley to hastily withdraw from the territory lest the Union forces unite and capture his entire army.

Contributing to the lack of attention to the battle were two additional factors. First, the Confederates tried to disguise and downplay the campaign, and the Union, apparently ignorant of its significance, ignored it. Second, New Mexico and Colorado were poorly organized, sparsely populated territories which had no one to write any official history of the campaign. As a result, much of what happened there simply faded away.

And as Gene Amole wrote in the *Rocky Mountain News*, "President Lincoln didn't come out here to make a speech. Mathew Brady didn't photograph the battle. Walt Whitman didn't write about it. Colorado didn't even have a state so that we could either secede from or remain with the Union; we were just an outpost in the vast Kansas Territory." Amole's geography was wrong. Colorado was its own territory by that time—but the region and the battle were ignored by the rest of the world. The "Gettysburg of the West" may have saved the Union, but it is destined to remain mostly hidden in the annals of history.

EPILOGUE

I turned my gaze from the twinkling stars in which men have so long sought to read the mysteries of human life, to the shining river below; threading its silvery track through cottonwood groves and tuffy meadows, reflecting from its glassy bosom the pallid light of the cold moon now ascending the eastern sky, shorn of half her glory. The sight recalled the scenes of other and happier days. And as borne on the weird night wind the soft sad wail of the departed time stole into my heart, visions of disappointed hopes and blasted faith passed as a reality before me and I thought death could hardly be bitter.

Oh happy days of youth, trust and innocence—only prized when gone forever! Is it then impossible for man to learn but by experience? Must he burn his hands to test the nature of fire, or plunge to the depths of vice to know that its fruits are ruin? Must he trust in humanity but to be betrayed? The purest, noblest aspirations for truth and virtue wither and die in the stricken heart—a new world opens before you. Do loved and trusted friends fail you? Learn to be selfish and do without them. Does the divinity who won your heart's virgin adoration prove faithless, weak, degraded even? Wipe off the tear though it burn into they soul. She and you and all are alike.

Pass on to other and similar lessons. Thou art studying human nature. To conquer its baseness cost Divinity, tears and sweat of blood. Why should we look for nobleness in it? Who ever saw it divorced from weakness and frailty, or ere will? Echo answers, never will. Launch your bark, you can sail without ballast or rudder as well as others, and will doubtless go to pieces on the same breakers. No efforts can avert or alter your destiny. Live fast and pray for death to end the farce and usher another on the stage which may be better, but cannot be worse.

But hark! There go the horns, and now the drum, taking up the strain, rattles and rolls till the camp is thoroughly aroused. Soon I had buried my melancholy and found around our campfire the boys who know no fear nor sorrow!

Sgt. Ovando J. Hollister, Company F
First Colorado Volunteers

BIBLIOGRAPHY

Beck, Warren. *New Mexico: A History of Four Centuries.* Norman: University of Oklahoma Press, 1961.

Boatner, Mark M. III. *The Civil War Dictionary.* New York: David McKay Company, 1959.

Boyd, LeRoy. "Thunder on the Rio Grande." *Colorado Magazine,* July 1947.

Catton, Bruce. *The Centennial History of the Civil War: The Coming Fury.* Garden City: Doubleday & Company, 1936.

Colton, Ray Charles. *The Civil War in the Western Territories.* Norman: University of Oklahoma Press, 1959.

Fergusson, Erna. *New Mexico: A Pageant of Three Peoples.* New York: Alfred A. Knopf, 1964.

Historical Society of New Mexico. "Causes of the Confederate Invasion." Santa Fe, April 1933.

Hollister, Ovando J. Ed. Richard Harwell. *Colorado Volunteers in New Mexico, 1862.* Chicago: R. R. Donnelley & Sons, 1962.

Hollister, Ovando J. *The Mines of Colorado.* Springfield, Mass.: S. Bowles & Company, 1867. Reprinted New York: Promontory Press, 1974.

Ickis, Alonzo Ferdinand. Ed. Nolie Mumey. *Bloody Trails Along the Rio Grande.* Denver: Old West Publishing Company, 1958.

Josephy, Alvin. *The Civil War in the American West.* New York: Alfred A. Knopf, 1991.

Josephy, Alvin. *War on the Frontier: The Trans-Mississippi West.* New York: Time-Life, Inc., 1986.

Ketchum, Richard M., ed. *The American Heritage Picture History of the Civil War.* New York: American Heritage Publishing Company, 1960.

Noel, Theophilus. Ed. Martin Hall and Edwin Davis. *A Campaign from Santa Fe to the Mississippi.* Houston: Stagecoach Press, 1961.

Rocky Mountain News. Denver, Colorado. September 18, 1861; October 24, 1861.

Sandburg, Carl. *Abraham Lincoln: The War Years.* New York: Harcourt, Brace & Company, 1936.

United States War Department. *The War of the Rebellion,* Series 1, Washington, D.C., GPO, 1893.

Whitford, William C. *The Battle of Glorieta Pass.* Glorieta, New Mexico: The Rio Grande Press, 1971.

INDEX